100
HIKES in™

YOSEMITE
NATIONAL PARK

100 Hikes in™

YOSEMITE
NATIONAL PARK

Marc J. Soares

THE MOUNTAINEERS BOOKS

Published by
The Mountaineers Books
1001 SW Klickitat Way, Suite 201
Seattle, WA 98134

First printing 2003, second printing 2004, third printing 2005, fourth printing 2007,
fifth printing 2008, sixth printing 2010, seventh printing 2012, eighth printing 2016

Project Editor: Laura Slavik
Copy Editor: Paula Thurman
Acquisitions Editor: Christine U. Hosler
Cover and Book Design: The Mountaineers Books
Layout: Mayumi Thompson
Mapmaker: Marge Mueller, Gray Mouse Graphics
Photographer: All photographs by the author unless otherwise noted

Cover photograph: *Oak tree, Sentinel Rock* © Pat O'Hara
Frontispiece: *North Peak and Shell Lake*

Library of Congress Cataloging-in-Publication Data

Soares, Marc J.
    100 hikes in Yosemite National Park / Marc J. Soares.—1st ed.
        p.   cm.
Includes index.
    ISBN 0-89886-867-X (pbk.)
    1. Hiking—California—Yosemite National Park—Guidebooks. 2.
Trails—California—Yosemite National Park—Guidebooks. 3. Yosemite
National Park (Calif.)—Guidebooks. I. Title: One hundred hikes in
Yosemite National Park. II. Title.
    GV199.42.C22 Y6776 2003
    917.94'470454—dc21

                                             2002153763

ISBN (paperback): 978-0-89886-867-8
ISBN (ebook): 978-1-59485-174-2

CONTENTS

EMIGRANT AND HOOVER WILDERNESS AREAS

TIOGA ROAD: SADDLEBAG LAKE WEST TO TUOLUMNE MEADOWS

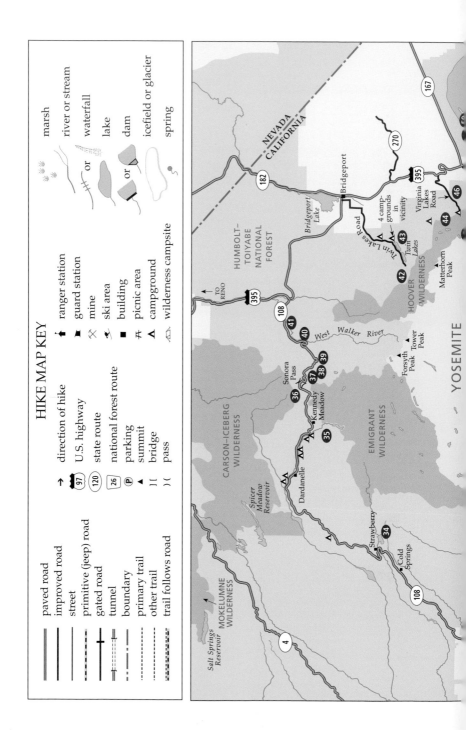

HIKE MAP KEY

	paved road
	improved road
	street
	primitive (jeep) road
	gated road
	tunnel
	boundary
	primary trail
	other trail
	trail follows road

→ direction of hike
🛡️97 U.S. highway
120 state route
26 national forest route
Ⓟ parking
▲ summit
)(bridge
)(pass

✝ ranger station
✝ guard station
✕ mine
⛷ ski area
■ building
⊼ picnic area
⛺ campground
⬦ wilderness campsite

marsh
river or stream
waterfall
lake
dam
icefield or glacier
spring

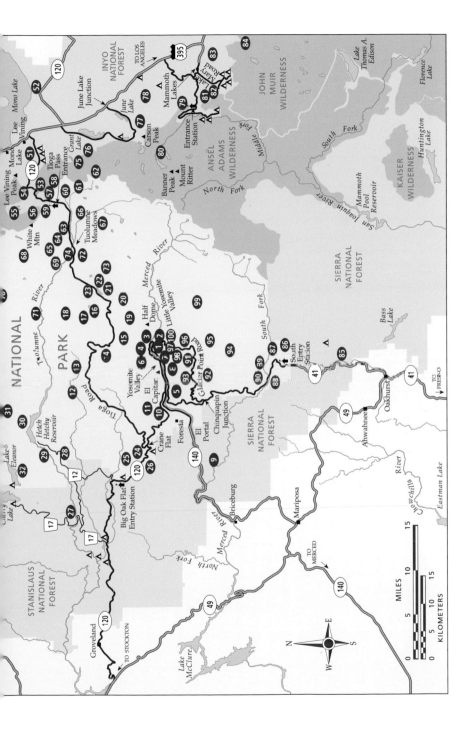

ACKNOWLEDGMENTS

Heavy praise and thanks for the following hiking folks, friends, and family who gave love, kindness, and inspiration to me:

Wife Patricia Soares, daughter Dionne Soares, son Jake Soares, brother John Soares, brother Eric Soares, sister Camille Soares, Nancy Soares, mother Mozelle Berta, Les Berta, Rick Ramos, Derek Moss, Eric Pace, Peter Pace, William F. Nicol the 2nd, Anne Nicol, William F. Nicol the 4th, Jayme Nicol, and Johanna Schroeder.

Special thanks goes to Yosemite National Park Wilderness Ranger Mark Fincher for pouring over every bit of this book with a fine-toothed comb to help make it even more accurate.

INTRODUCTION

Yosemite National Park is truly nature's ultimate masterpiece—no wonder artists and poets migrate to it for inspiration. Yosemite is a tremendous mosaic of leaping waterfalls, soaring granite cliffs, miles of magical meadows, noble groves of giant sequoias, and dramatic displays of wildflowers enhancing glacier-carved backcountry. In this land of ice-sculpted canyons and polished granite domes, photographs come easy. It's an amazingly diverse wonderland of rolling oak woodlands, stately forests, and tuneful streams.

The treasure trove of trails described in this book is in essence John Muir's stomping grounds. This book takes you deep into a land of major place-names known 'round the world, such as El Capitan, Half Dome, Yosemite Falls, Bridalveil Fall, Nevada Fall, Glacier Point, Merced River, Mount Dana, Tuolumne Meadows, and Tioga Pass.

Yosemite National Park is so vast, it takes all day to cruise its outskirts in a car. Tioga Road cuts through the middle of the park and U.S. Highway 395 skirts its constantly climactic eastern edge, both thoroughfares offering a plethora of trailheads above 8000 feet that quickly get you into the heart of the supremely gorgeous backcountry described in this hiking book. Most of the nearly countless peaks are above 10,000 feet in elevation, numerous

Aspens

mountains are more than 12,000 feet tall, and Mount Lyell and Mount Dana stand above 13,000 feet. It's like a city of Mount Whitneys, Mount Shastas, and Lassen Peaks.

Virtually all the hikes in this book are readily accessible from major highways, and in most hike descriptions, there are specific and helpful tips for escaping the hordes of humanity and achieving satisfying solitude. Explicit and accurate trailhead directions are detailed in each hike account. You'll learn about what plants, wildlife, and geological features are there, along with occasional tidbits of interesting local history in each hike summary.

Roughly a third of the hikes in this book are located just outside the park boundaries on U.S. Forest Service lands, and about half of them lead into the park. Most of these hikes are within a few miles of Yosemite National Park and are ideal excursions in the summer when there are peak crowds in the park. Peruse the handy trail guide index at the back of this book to help you select the right hike for your mood and situation. It indicates combined hikes to make epic backpack trips, peak-bagging trips, ideal wildflower excursions, top family outings, birdwatching trails, and more.

The intent of this book is for you to discover Yosemite National Park's numerous ultimate getaways and in doing so, have more fun, be more comfortable, more informed, more motivated, and above all, more touched. This guidebook features hikes to suit all abilities and moods, with a blend of "cakewalks" and "buttkickers," backpacking trips, and family walks. Keep this book in the glove compartment of your vehicle during the drive for easy access, then take it with you so you can read excerpts along the way.

YOSEMITE HISTORY

Indian people first inhabited the Yosemite area about 8000 years ago. The last tribe to live in Yosemite Valley was the Ahwahneehee, led by Chief Tenaya. Conflict with fortune-seeking miners reached a feverish pitch in 1851, when the Mariposa Battalion, a punitive expedition under the authority of the state of California, stormed the area to put an end to the "Mariposa Indian War." As a result, the tribe's settlements were burned and they were driven out. The chief and several of his braves later returned to the valley, only to be pursued and killed by Mono Indians as revenge for stealing some of the rival band's horses.

Tourism first came to Yosemite five years later, when two tourists built a toll trail up the South Fork Merced River and over to Yosemite Valley. They charged a hefty $2 per person. Stagecoach routes and later the railroad bought a steadily increasing stream of homesteaders, ranchers, loggers, and tourists to the valley. Several visionaries saw that commercialism was ruining the area, and coaxed Congress during Civil War times to pass a protective bill placing a part of the land under the control of the state of California. John Muir arrived in Yosemite a few years later, spearheading the call for federal protection. In 1890, Yosemite became the country's third national park.

EVOLUTION OF YOSEMITE VALLEY

Yosemite Valley's flat floor and mostly rock walls formed as alpine glaciers lumbered through the Merced River canyon. Under warmer, wetter climates some 65 million years ago, ice gradually scoured the weaker granite sections, but left virtually intact the essentially joint-free monoliths such as Half Dome, El Capitan, North Dome, and Sentinel Dome.

Glaciers substantially enlarged the canyon that the Merced River had chiseled via several uplifts of the Sierra. When the last glacier melted, its terminal moraine dammed up the melting ice water to form ancient Lake Yosemite. Through time sediment filled in the lake, forming the flat Yosemite Valley you see today.

At the time of the dinosaurs, all those rigid domes bordering Yosemite Valley would not have extended as much above the valley as they do presently. The primary falls of the Yosemite Valley—Yosemite Falls, Bridalveil Fall, Staircase Falls, and Sentinel Fall—probably attained their full heights by the time the climate drastically became cooler and drier some 33 million years ago.

THE OAKS OF YOSEMITE

Whether it's the photogenic black oak groves adorning Yosemite Valley's floor, or the majestic live oaks thriving virtually everywhere below 6000 feet in elevation, oak trees have amazed and delighted California native Indians and visitors alike for a long time. Frequently mentioned in many of the following hike chapters, native oaks are much more abundant in the west segment of Yosemite National Park, and spread westward into the Upper Sacramento and San Joaquin Valleys. If you drive towards the park after leaving I-5, deciduous valley oaks and blue oaks grace the scenery. Valley oaks are the fastest growing and largest of all the western oaks, while blue oaks are the most drought tolerant, slowest growing, and longest lived. By the time you near Yosemite country in the yellow pine belt, these oaks are gradually replaced by live oaks and black oaks, described below.

Live Oaks

Growing to 50 feet in height, canyon and interior live oaks feature several huge and crooked branches that spread out in all directions, often hiding the trunk and giving the illusion the leaves are arising in bulk from the ground. It hurts to walk barefoot over the sharp edges of fallen live oak leaves, but many birds seek cover and often nest in their dense canopies.

Continued

To fully appreciate a full grown live oak *(Quercus wislizenii)* in Yosemite country, lay beneath its massive trunk and gaze into the plethora of leaning limbs. Catch filtered rays of sunlight as the tree squirrels scurry and the woodpecker insistently nods.

Wildlife activity is frequently brisk beneath the interior live oak. The red-tailed hawk dives for gophers while western fence lizards and dragonflies feast on mosquitos and flies. King snakes slither in the dry grasses while sparrows frolic on the reddish brown twigs.

The newer the leaves, the more holly-like spines interior live oaks have. The mature leaves become smooth-edged, and usually fall after about two years. Oftentimes in winter, the tree appears to be semi-deciduous, but a flush of growth kicks in by March or April.

Although typically slow growing, long-lived interior live oak tolerates heavy shade. The leaves are smaller (one inch) in full sun, and much larger (up to four inches) in dense shade.

The two-inch-long flowering catkins are dull yellow—a mature tree tends to hold an astounding amount of pollen. It drifts willy nilly in the early spring winds, causing hay fever misery to some.

The long and slender, chestnut-brown acorns serve as decorative ornaments when viewed from close up, and mature in early autumn.

Although amazingly persistent against the forces of nature such as floods, fires, fungi, and lightning, changes wrought by humans can spell slow catastrophe for oaks.

Left uncut, interior live oaks can form orchard-like groves in the foothill grasslands and chaparral belts of Yosemite country. In many areas of Yosemite, interior live oak hybridizes with black oak to produce a smallish evergreen tree commonly called "evergreen black oak" or "oracle oak."

A close look at the leaves is the best way to tell the difference between interior live oak and its close cousin, canyon live oak. The underside of interior live oak leaves are a light yellow green, whereas canyon live oak leaves are pale gray green.

Canyon live oaks can form nearly pure groves in boulder piles beneath cliffs, near waterfalls, and in deep, shaded gorges.

The dark green small evergreen trees that seem to protrude through the sheer granite walls of Hetch Hetchy and nearby Tuolumne River canyons are canyon live oaks. John Muir called this tree species "a sturdy mountaineer of a tree . . . in tough unwedgeable, knotty strength, it is the oak of oaks, a magnificent tree."

The heavy, close-grained wood has long been used for wagon axles, wheels, tool handles, furniture, and floors. The crisp green foliage of canyon live oaks furnish a home for more than 50 species of gall-forming insects (look for the hacky sack–sized galls on all types of western oaks).

The acorn crops feed band-tailed pigeons, who can swallow the entire acorn.

Black Oaks

The largest mountain oak in Yosemite National Park, black oaks feature sturdy, forked trunks and giant limbs clad in blackish bark, hence their name. The trunks can get to a yard thick on a tree that can reach up to 80 feet high.

Tiny new red and velvety leaves emerge from their buds in early May. Come June, they transform into bright, yellow green foliage (each leaf has bristle tips) that appears translucent in the bright sun. By autumn, the leaves turn to yellow, dull orange, or golden brown.

In winter, look for the large bushy clusters of a parasite called mistletoe clinging to the bare limbs high above. The California native Indians worshipped black oaks, harvesting their acorns to cook a mush, first soaking the acorns in creek water to leach out their bitter tannic acids.

Deer often browse black oak leaves and western gray squirrels munch the acorns. The red-topped acorn woodpecker hammers acorn-sized craters into the trunks, then crams acorns into them, pointed ends first.

ACCOMMODATIONS

Other than sleeping deep in the gorgeous Yosemite National Park wilderness (permit required) there are two ways to spend the night in Yosemite: stay in one of many concession-operated lodging facilities or set up camp in a campground.

Yosemite Concession Services offers more than 1500 rooms within the park. These range from luxurious suites in the distinctive Ahwahnee Hotel to canvas tent cabins where showers and restroom facilities are dependent on water availability. Prices change from year to year and vary widely between lodgings. Reservations, available 366 days in advance, are strongly suggested, especially during the crowded summer months. To make reservations, call (209) 252-4848, fax (559) 456-0542, or book your stay online at *www.yosemitepark.com/html/accom_reservation.html*.

Several lodging options exist outside of Yosemite National Park. There are a few hotels along each of the highways leading into the park, each about 30 to 60 minutes from the park. There are also several campsites along these highways. On weekdays when it's not summertime, there's a good chance you can get a room or a campsite outside of the park on the day you arrive, especially if you sign up by late morning. Log onto *www.yosemite.com* for more information.

Within the park, there are thirteen campgrounds. Those that take advance reservations often fill up the first day they become available, so book as early as possible. As of press time, reservations were being taken up to five months in advance, on the 15th of the month. Call (800) 436-7275 or log onto the National Park Reservation System at *http://reservations.nps.gov* from 7 A.M. to 7 P.M. Pacific Time. For those campgrounds that operate on a first-come, first-served system, it's best to show up at the site by the 10 A.M. checkout time.

THINGS TO DO IN YOSEMITE BESIDES HIKING

1. Art classes are featured spring through fall in Yosemite Valley at the Arts Activity Center . . . or bring along your own supplies and start sketching or painting along the Merced River.
2. There are 12 miles of bicycle paths in Yosemite Valley. Bring your own 2-wheeler or rent one spring through fall at either the Curry Village or Yosemite Lodge Bike Stand. Call (209) 372-1208 for rental information.
3. Buy a tree, wildflower, or plant guide from the Yosemite Valley book store, then try to identify as many plants as possible along the many easy trails nearby.
4. Enjoy a summertime rafting trip down a couple of calm miles of the Merced River in Yosemite Valley on a rentable raft. Call (209) 372-8319 for rental information, or else bring your own non-motorized vessel.
5. Guided programs, including nature walks, are offered daily throughout the year.
6. Other activities include stargazing far from the city lights, fishing, swimming, horseback riding, and rock climbing.

HOW TO USE THIS BOOK

The hikes in this book are divided into eight geographical regions in and around Yosemite National Park to assist you in locating and choosing a hike. The regions approximate a clockwise loop, starting from the southeast and finishing in the southwest. Each hiking chapter is broken up in three basic parts. The information block, which helps you size up the hike while telling you how to get there and what to expect; the opening, which gives you a feel of what the hike is like; and the body, which describes the landmarks and trails, providing blow-by-blow accounts of the actual hike, preceded by trailhead directions. It's a good idea to read the entire hike chapter before choosing that hike, or prior to actually doing it. You'll find out about trail characteristics, where the tough climbs might be on the trail, how much shade is offered, important landmarks, and special scenes you won't want to miss. The body of the hiking chapters often identifies the most prominent native trees and shrubs at these described landmarks and special places, helping you to boost your native plant knowledge and awareness. Here's what each brief topic in the information block means:

Distance. This provides the trip's total mileage, indicating if the hike is one-way, round trip, a partial loop, or a loop. Note that many of the long hikes feature great scenes within a couple of miles, and therefore most people lacking time and/or energy can often turn back early.

Hiking time. This provides the approximate time frame it takes to do the hike and still enjoy it, hiking at a leisurely but proactive rate, accounting for stops to drink water, look at maps or this book, and adore views.

High point and elevation gain. The high point is the highest elevation reached on a hike, while elevation gain is an approximate measure of actual feet you'll climb from beginning to end. This is usually a better indicator of difficulty, because it factors in all ups and downs encountered.

Difficulty. The terms *easy, moderate,* and *strenuous* are subjective, factoring in distance, elevation gains and losses, and trail conditions. Many hikes use two of these terms *(moderate* to *strenuous)* to better describe the difficulty factor. Easy could seem moderate to a nonhiker while strenuous could seem moderate to a distance runner. Other factors can make hikes seem difficult, such as heavy winds, soreness, or being thirsty or hungry. Some hikes rated strenuous might be easy for the first couple of miles, and therefore might make an ideal short hike.

Season. Many hikes in this book are accessible year-round, while others are restricted to summer and early fall only. As a bonus, a handful of prime snowshoe or cross-country ski trips are described for winter and early spring.

Map. Each hike description is accompanied by a computer-generated map that includes all the major place-names contained in the hike description, the trails, and major bodies of water (sometimes more than one hike is on one map). Topo maps (recommended) are listed in this section because they usually include more details and information. This may come in handy if you're temporarily lost or simply enjoy studying maps. For getting to your destination, take along a state highway map or state atlas.

Nearest campground. This is the nearest car campground to the hike. Spending the night in the area also gives you the option of doing more than one hike. Most campgrounds are not open year-round (call ahead though), charge a fee, and at least have running water. You may have a national forest campground outside the park all to yourself during the off season, especially on weekdays. For more solitude, keep in mind many hikes offer backpacking camps along the trails (see trail index in Appendix B). From Memorial Day through Labor Day, many of the campgrounds in the park fill up, especially on weekends. Call the park in advance. You will receive the detailed and handy park map that shows trails and campgrounds when you pay your park fee at the entrance station. In many cases, the closest campground is located on the hiking map for that hike in this book. Outside the valley, only Hodgdon Meadow and Wawona are open year-round. In Yosemite Valley, only Camp 4 and Upper Pines are open year-round.

Agency Information. This section lists the governing agency for the area. Appendix A lists the phone numbers and websites, if applicable, at the back of the book. Call to determine weather, fees, camping, and trail conditions. You may have to leave a message on a machine (so call well in advance) or call a neighboring governing agency to get information.

WHAT TO BRING

The absolute essentials, which keep you much safer (some also heighten enjoyment and overall hike success), come in handy. They include the Mountaineers' Ten Essentials (shown in boldface): water (a lot), **extra food** (especially complex carbohydrates), **extra clothing** (in layers, plus a thin poncho or light raincoat), a **first-aid kit,** a Swiss army **knife, matches in a waterproof container, trail maps,** a **compass,** and a light **flashlight** or **headlamp** (with extra batteries).

It's a good idea to leave most of these items in the day pack at all times, updating the first-aid kit and matches annually. It's also best to include **firestarter** (for wet wood), a whistle, iodine, a water filter, toilet paper, a watch, and this book.

For long and strenuous hikes, a pair of broken-in (important), lightweight hiking boots (an ankle-high tennis shoe with Vibram-like soles) is recommended. The sun can easily drain your energy and cause sunburn. Wear a shirt, a wide-brimmed hat, **sunglasses,** and sunblock.

WILDERNESS ETHICS

Going to the wilderness is granted via special invitation from nature. We should show our appreciation by taking nothing but photographs and leaving only footprints.

Resist the temptation to shortcut up and down switchbacks. This destroys trailside plant life and accelerates trail erosion. And always try to minimize the impact of your feet on the land by stepping on rock or firm, dry ground when possible. Be especially careful in meadows, which contain a variety of sensitive plants. Your philosophy should be that of minimum impact, which means you strive to leave no trace of your visit.

Camping. Minimum-impact philosophy also applies to campsites. Select a site at least 100 feet away from lakes, streams, and rivers so that you won't disturb waterside plants or pollute the water. However, if the only site you find is an established site less than 100 feet from the water, then use it carefully. Whenever possible, use an existing site in the forest or on bare rock that's far from the water. Finally, put a plastic tarp under your tent to protect yourself from rain water. Never dig ditches.

Fires. The minimum-impact hiker doesn't need a fire. Burning wood removes organic material from the ecosystem, contributes to air pollution, and scares away animal life. Bring enough clothes to ensure night warmth. If you must have a hot meal, bring a gas stove; however, you can enjoy a wide variety of foods that don't require cooking. If you insist on having a fire, do

Pond lilies

so only in or near heavily wooded areas, make it a small fire, and use only dry and down deadwood in an established campfire ring. When finished, douse the fire thoroughly with water until you're sure it's completely out.

Washing. Detergents and food particles harm water life and can alter water chemistry, so wash yourself and your dishes far from lakes and streams. Carry water off to the woods or bare rock for washing, and use biodegradable soaps available at outdoor stores or no soap at all!

Sanitation. Defecate in a shallow hole 6 to 10 inches deep, preferably in forest duff where the covered feces will more quickly decompose. Be sure your spot is at least 200 feet from water and well away from trails and campsites. You needn't be so careful with urine because it's sterile. But do stay away from water sources if possible, and don't pee all over any single plant. Spread it around and let it provide the soil with valuable nitrogen.

Garbage. Pack it all out, including any you find that's not yours.

Hiker courtesy. Your goal is to be as unnoticeable and unobtrusive as possible. Choose subdued colors such as gray, green, and brown for your clothing and equipment. Travel only in small groups. Set up an inconspicuous camp. Talk in quiet tones.

Bears. Roam in Yosemite country long enough and you'll see black bears. They're called black bears, but sometimes their color ranges from gray to brown. Although nobody yet has been killed by a black bear in

Polly Dome and Cathedral Peak

Yosemite National Park, there have been a lot of injuries and property damage. Yosemite bears present little danger to visitors, but visitors present a great danger to the bears. Assume that the bears are everywhere, and no trail or region is exempt of bears. Hanging food no longer works in many areas of the backcountry. The bears have simply figured it out. Canisters are the best option. It's also important that all scented items (sunscreen, lip balm, deodorant, etc.) be stored correctly. Use the bear-proof food storage boxes installed at the trailheads, High Sierra Camps, parking lots, and campgrounds. Keep food and garbage out of your vehicle if possible, especially coolers, and keep your windows tightly rolled up before hiking away. Do not underestimate a bear's keen sense of smell. You can rent bear-proof canisters for a nominal fee at locations all over Yosemite. Do not feed the bears or any wildlife.

Pets and firearms. Pets are allowed on paved trails only and on a leash, and firearms are prohibited in Yosemite National Park.

STAYING SAFE

Rattlesnakes and mountain lions are not even close to the biggest dangers. More hikers by far are harmed or even killed from bee stings. Even deer injuries outnumber rattlesnake bites. Hypothermia, dehydration, getting lost, or falling are the main dangers hikers should guard against. Hiking can easily rate among the safest activities by following three guidelines:

1. Be prepared. Study maps beforehand. Keep your day pack full of the essentials (see "What to Bring," page 18). Make sure you can handle the mileage and climbing of a given hike. Get the weather report.
2. AA stands for "always alert." Sprained ankles, perhaps the most common hiking injury, are most often caused when a hiker lets his or her guard down, usually on the way down. Assume that each step could result in a fall. "Watch your eyes." This means to make sure branches don't poke your eye. Gather and break firewood carefully. Be extra attentive to slippery rocks and mud.
3. Make good decisions. If the watch indicates it'll be dark sooner than later, allow sufficient return time. If the creek is too swollen to cross, cross in a safer place or not at all. When you arrive at a trail junction, stop, study the map, and wait for the others. It's better to be a wuss than a stud.

Hiking alone. It's imperative to leave a hiking itinerary with someone, then stick to it. A solo hiker must maintain the mindset that there is absolutely no room for error.

Weather. Always get an accurate and recent report. If stormy weather hits, you'll be ready with raingear and waterproof tent. Keep clothes dry (use garbage bags). Hightail it down a mountain pronto if lightning is looming.

Poison oak. Poison oak causes skin discomfort. Learn to recognize and avoid contact with these plants, even in winter. Anyone can get it at anytime, even those who swear they never get it. Poison oak is common along partly to mostly shaded trailsides at elevations in and around the park below 3500 feet, especially near streams, creeks, and rivers.

Ticks. Ticks are more of a health risk than snakes and lions combined. They live in brushy and grassy areas that hikers tend to come into contact with. If hiking along an overgrown trail (more common in mid- to late spring), check for ticks often. If it just came aboard, it can be flicked off. If it's lodged, see a doctor, for some ticks carry Lyme disease, which makes people very sick.

Rattlesnakes and mountain lions. Keep in mind, most rattlesnake bites occur because people were trying to kill or handle them. They occur in and around the park at elevations mainly below 5000 feet. If you encounter a mountain lion (rare), don't run, as sheep do. Stand your ground, look it in the eye, look big, and talk loud. Chances are that cat is already gone.

Bears. See also "Wilderness Ethics." If a bear is in the process of raiding you, don't walk away. Make yourself big by holding up your arms. Yell, scream, and be obnoxious enough to cause the bear to leave. If a bear gets your food, don't try to get it back and don't get within 50 feet of any bear.

Black bear (photo from Yosemite Museum, National Park Service)

Never get between a mother and her cubs, but if you are a safe distance away, yell and scream.

Water. Assume that all water from streams, lakes, and ponds carries harmful microorganisms, including *Giardia,* which gives hikers stomach flu-like symptoms. Use a filter that eliminates *Giardia,* iodine tablets, or briskly boil the water for 10 minutes. Better yet, bring plenty of your own (about a quart for every 3 miles hiked), and refill water bottles at safe faucets. If a hike description involves a lot of climbing and/or dry regions, be sure to top off your water bottles with *filtered* water when you come to a safe stream.

PERMITS

Wilderness permits, free of charge, are required for all overnight trips into Yosemite backcountry. Permits are not necessary for day hikes. Keep in mind that permits are issued under a quota system geared to prevent overcrowding, and based on trailhead entry, not final destination. If your preferred trip is full, check this book for a nearby alternate trip that is still open. The wilderness centers at Yosemite Valley and Tuolumne Meadows, the visitor centers at Wawona and Big Oak Flat, and the Hetch Hetchy Entrance Station all issue wilderness permits. If your overnight trip begins outside the park, get your permit from the Forest Service designated in the Information section in the information block of each hike description. For Yosemite National Park permits, call 209-372-0200. The Wilderness Reservation line is 209-372-0740. For permits in Toiyabe National Forest, call 619-932-7070. For permits in Inyo National Forest, call 619-647-6525.

Entry Fees and Driving Directions

A $20 fee is charged to vehicles entering the park. This fee allows vehicles to enter and leave the park as many times as desired during a seven-day period. For adults (17 and older) entering the park via foot, horseback, motorcycle, or bus, a $10 fee is charged.

To reach the park, which is located east of Interstate 5, take either State Route 120 south of Stockton, SR 140 in Merced, or SR 41 in Fresno.

OTHER CONSIDERATIONS

Mosquitoes. Assume that mosquitoes are rampant in boggy meadows, moist forest floors, and lakes with muddy shorelines until they dry out. At lower elevations, this will be late spring. At higher elevations, things may not dry out until mid- to late summer, depending on snowpack. They are a particular nuisance in early morning after dawn and when the late afternoon shadows creep in. Add mosquito repellent to your first-aid kit.

Forest fires. They're becoming increasingly common in Yosemite country, and it could mean access roads are closed or your favorite views tainted with smoke and haze. It's best to call ahead.

Rockslides. They occur occasionally, especially east of Tioga Pass, and can close Tioga Road indefinitely. Call ahead.

Facilities. Stores, restaurants, and lodging are located throughout the park. Call 559-252-4848 for more information.

A NOTE ABOUT SAFETY

Safety is an important concern in all outdoor activities. No guidebook can alert you to every hazard or anticipate the limitations of every reader. Therefore, the descriptions of roads, trails, routes, and natural features in this book are not representations that a particular place or excursion will be safe for your party. When you follow any of the routes described in this book, you assume responsibility for your own safety. Under normal conditions, such excursions require the usual attention to traffic, road and trail conditions, weather, terrain, the capabilities of your party, and other factors. Because many of the lands in this book are subject to development and/or change of ownership, conditions may have changed since this book was written that make your use of some of these routes unwise. Always check for current conditions, obey posted private property signs, and avoid confrontations with property owners or managers. Keeping informed on current conditions and exercising common sense are the keys to a safe, enjoyable outing.

The Mountaineers Books

TAKING PHOTOS IN YOSEMITE

Yosemite National Park and its surroundings are so strikingly photogenic, great shots are just a click away. For that added edge, the keys are being patient, understanding your camera and what makes a good photo, and being in the right place at the right time.

Your camera. A camera that lends to taking improved photos includes manual focus, and has knobs and/or switches for manually changing F-stops and shutter speeds. Better yet, get one also with a telezoom that goes from wide angle all the way to telephoto with a simple turn of the lens dial. This lets you compose the best possible photo by zooming in or out while viewing the scene.

The art of taking superb shots in Yosemite backcountry. If you've come to a spot where there appears to be a great photo opportunity, then chances are you're at the right place at the right time. Then again, maybe the right time might be even better, later. My advice is to take photos right away, do some more hiking or picnicking, then check the spot again before heading back to see if light conditions have perhaps improved. The main thing is to capitalize big time when you sense you're at a good spot. Take time to shoot using a variety of light meter readings and framing angles.

Here are some other tips:

1. Bracket your shots. Take two to three photos of the same scene, altering the exposure by a half to a full stop (aperture click) or the shutter speed one full click, after metering with your light meter. Your light meter isn't always correct.
2. Be persistent, think clearly, be confident, and artful.
3. Allow your heart rate to slow down from the hiking exertion, drink some water, and don layers of warm clothes if it's cold out.
4. If the sun is about to dip behind major cloud cover, then proactively get a few shots beforehand. The sun shining on your subject as well as the background provides more even lighting, greater detail, more highlights, and more shadows, all desirable attributes in a good photo.
5. Walk around the area, sampling photo candidates through your view finder. Refuse to settle for the first thing you see, for there's likely to be a better shot in a spot perhaps a few feet away.
6. Squat down, lean over, stand on something—one of these acts is bound to reveal an improved composition through the view finder.
7. Before clicking off a shot, make sure your camera isn't tilted. In most cases, it should be level and straight, especially for photos including lakes and skylines.

Facing page: Two hikers gaze at Crystal Crag from Lake George

Mock orange, photographed as a close-up

8. Before clicking the shot, double check the four corners in the frame to make sure there's nothing obtrusive, distracting, or unexpected in the frame.
9. In most cases, the primary subject should be anywhere from slightly to considerably off center for artistic effect.
10. Avoid bright rocks or snags in the foreground; or pour lots of water from a nearby creek or lake over them to create a darkened effect and remove the glare.
11. Avoid clutter, especially in the foreground. This includes power lines, roads, litter, or other signs of civilization, as well as branches or indistinct objects such as bushes.
12. Always check to determine if a vertical shot might be better than a horizontal shot. This may especially be the case for subjects such as waterfalls, tall mountains, and standing humans.
13. To compose a good photograph, open your mind to what is around you. Look for graceful lines and shapes, unique boulders, moving water with white in it, totally still water with reflections, fall colors, cloudscapes (especially streaky cirrus and puffy cumulus clouds), trees casting shadows in the foreground, colorful rocks (maybe with lichens), branch patterns (such as willows in winter), and exposed ground next to snow. Also note that higher quality shots are often found above tree line because of the open and improved views.

GOOD TIMING

The days are short during winter, and the sun moves from east to west dipping toward the south, not directly overhead like in midsummer. This means there's a much shorter window of opportunity taking photos, for in the mountains during the short days, there's too much shadow in the early morning and late afternoon.

The best times for taking winter and early spring photos are usually from 9 A.M. to noon and 2 P.M. to 4:30 P.M. In the summer, it's 7 A.M. to 10 A.M. and 4 P.M. to 8 P.M. If the sun is, at least, mostly out, this will likely get you more intense highlights and more dramatic shadows. Plan ahead, so that your anticipated primary subjects are in full light.

PEOPLE IN THE BACKCOUNTRY

Taking outdoor photos with human models can result in a quality nature photo that doubles as a photo of your friend(s) or family member(s). The main key is for them to look comfortable, like they belong to the scene. Generally, you want them positioned at the side of the frame, or near the bottom or top, but not in the middle. In most cases, you want them looking into the scene, not away from the picture. Avoid taking photos of folks wearing bright white shirts or clothing that advertises a brand name.

CLOSE-UPS AND DEPTH OF FIELD

Sharply focus on the main subject, whether it is a mushroom, a flower, an icicle, a swollen willow branch, snow-covered log or boulder. If someone is with you, you can have them place an item with big, easy-to-read print in the exact spot where the main subject is to help set your focus. Be sure to do your meter reading and form your composition first. It also helps the subject look sharper and the frame matter in the background look more artistic when only the subject is in focus. To achieve this, open your f-stop to somewhere around f4 or f5.6. It's important to note that the lower the f-stop number, the less that is in focus, which is desirable most of the time in close-up nature photography. Lower f-stops mean faster shutter speeds. With any close-up photography featuring subject matter that may move in the wind, a fast shutter speed helps stop movement, leading to sharper photos. If you're shooting flowers or grass or any other subject matter that is blowing in the wind, keep aiming the camera steady until the wind abates, then click away.

When you want both the foreground and background to be in focus, you can try turning the focus dial about a quarter inch from the total infinity setting. And, turn the f-stop to a high number such as f11, f16, or f22. The higher number of f-stop on the aperture, the more is in focus. Most manual cameras have a focus chart on the camera that indicates in meters and feet, how far away items are that will be in focus, based on where the focus dial is and what f-stop it's switched to. For long distance shots from 30 feet to infinity, focus all the way to the far end of the focus dial on infinity.

Since depth of field is not crucial in this situation, shoot with a faster shutter speed and a lower f-stop number.

This helps make the shot sharper. If light and extra depth of field are not an issue, set the f-stop at f5.6 or f8, then use the meter to determine what the shutter speed is.

SHUTTER SPEED

Shooting at slower than 1/60 of a second generally means using a tripod. You can go tripodless down to 1/30 of a second or perhaps a bit slower by doing the following: slow your heart rate by resting first, then breathing deeply and slowly; brace your elbows; lean against something solid; wait until wind gusts cease. Of course these four steps should be followed all the time, and can improve sharpness in fast speed shots.

For creamy rapids and cascades, use a tripod at 1/8 of a second or slower. Or, find a level surface, rest the camera flat on piled or folded clothing, then shoot without holding the camera.

FILM SPEED

Even in snow, light conditions can vary. Unless you pack a tripod, which most people don't when they're snowshoeing or hiking, it's best to carry high-speed films such as ASA 400. This allows you more depth of field when you want it, or a faster shutter speed if you need it. The difference between and ASA 400 film speed and an ASA 64 film speed is as follows: with the same f-stop setting, you can shoot ASA 400 at 1/250 of a second shutter speeds, compared with being stuck with 1/30 of a second shutter speeds if using ASA 64.

SPECIAL LIGHT CONDITIONS

Use a polarizing filter in most situations where there is blue sky. This darkens the sky and reduces glare, but keeps the clouds bright. Keep in mind that using a polarizing filter reduces the light entering your camera by up to 2 full f-stops. All the more reason to use a higher speed film such as ASA 400, or a tripod. Be sure to take off your polarizing filter for anything but subject matter involving blue sky or blue lakes. Be sure to bracket your shots.

For bright, hazy, or overcast skies, use as little sky in your frame as possible. Take your light meter reading off everything but the sky. With a sun and cloud mix, compose your shot, then wait until the sun comes out fully from behind the clouds before shooting (meter first, then shoot). Avoid shooting directly into the sun, which causes glare and loss of detail.

When metering for snow, try metering on everything but the snow, then shoot. Or, meter on just the snow, then open up two to three f-stops, then shoot. Or, meter off the whole scene, open up one f-stop, then shoot.

Facing page: Yosemite Falls and Merced River

YOSEMITE VALLEY

1 HALF DOME AND THE JOHN MUIR TRAIL

Distance: 16–28 miles round trip
Hiking time: All day or 2–3 day backpack
High point: 8842 feet
Elevation gain: 3200 to 4800 feet
Difficulty: Strenuous
Season: Mid-May through early October
Maps: USGS Half Dome, USGS Yosemite Falls, USGS
    Tenaya Lake
Nearest campground: Sunnyside Walk-In Campground or
    Tuolumne Meadows Campground
Information: Yosemite National Park

Prominent and popular, the smooth and sheer, gray pure-rock monolith known throughout the world as Half Dome sticks out above Yosemite Valley like a sore thumb—a massive one at that. It can easily be seen from thousands of places in the park; fabulous views beckon from its flat pinnacle.

All you need to do to experience this awesome rock bulk is choose among

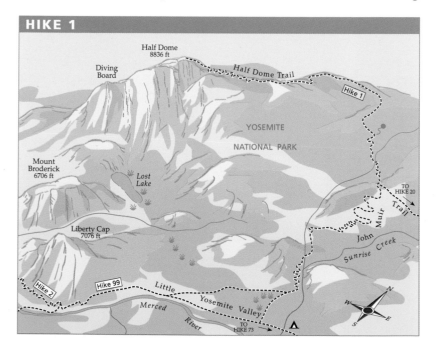

HIKE 1

Merced River and Half Dome

the four routes that lead to a classic trail junction along the famous John Muir Trail, a mere 2.5 miles from Half Dome. The most common way is via Happy Isles (see Hike 2), which is a 16-mile round trip encompassing 4800 feet of total climbing. The next easiest course starts from Glacier Point (see Hike 99) and winds up being about a 19-mile round trip with 4200 feet of climbing, some of it at the very end. Another option is to come in via Tenaya Lake (see Hike 20), which tallies 22 miles round trip and about 3000 feet of total elevation gain. The final route makes for a 28-mile backpack trip via a long span of the John

Muir Trail from Toulumne Meadows (see Hike 73). Whichever wonderfully scenic route you choose, the John Muir Trail will escort you at least 10 miles round trip and up to 24 miles round trip.

Camping is not allowed on the bald summit of Half Dome to protect the rare Mount Lyell salamanders that hide under the granite rocks. Most folks backpack to and then camp in Little Yosemite Valley, but the permits are hard to get, especially on summer weekends when everybody wants them. There are many other spots to camp along the John Muir Trail that are not in Little Yosemite Valley. Permits are required for these as well.

When you reach the trail junction signed for Half Dome for the final 2.5-mile climb, head northwest on this wide and dusty path. About 0.5 mile along this trail, look for a small spur trail to the right that leads a couple hundred yards to a spring, your last chance to get water (purify). The trail soon swings west past Jeffrey pines and red firs to reveal a clear view of Clouds Rest (Hike 20) to the right and Half Dome to the left. Basket Dome and North Dome guard Yosemite Valley across the way. The path soon faces the scantily conifer-clad shoulder of Half Dome. Heed the sign warning you to turn back if bad weather threatens. Beat the bad weather by being off the mountain by midafternoon. The trail snakes steeply up gravel over the shoulder crest to reach the set of steel cables attached to the slick and steep rock to assist you in negotiating the final 400 feet of climbing to the top.

The flat and spacious top is littered with oddly weathered granite slabs to picnic on while watching the begging golden-mantled ground squirrels. All of Yosemite Valley and Tenaya Canyon is spread out 4700 feet below, with El Capitan (Hike 11) looming to the west. The Cathedral Range takes center stage to the east while the Clark Range and Mount Florence dominate to the southeast.

2 HAPPY ISLES TO VERNAL FALL AND NEVADA FALL

Distance: 6-mile loop
Hiking time: 4–6 hours
High point: 6000 feet
Elevation gain: 2000 feet
Difficulty: Moderate to strenuous
Season: Year-round
Map: USGS Half Dome
Nearest campground: Lower Pines Campground
Information: Yosemite National Park

Vernal and Nevada Falls are neighboring twins that you can tell apart, although they're both narrow in shape, and they plummet and charge over

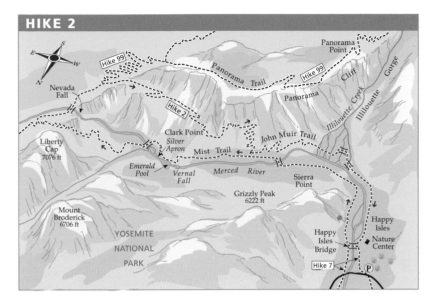

broad, vertical, sheer rock cliffs. The primary notable difference is that Vernal Fall is more of a free fall (320 feet) with much more mist, and Nevada Fall does some cascading for nearly 200 yards.

This steady climb to the falls is both extremely popular and memorable. The scenery is so superb that throngs of folks know about it by reputation, so go on weekdays before Memorial Day weekend or after Labor Day weekend to achieve some solitude. The experience will be forever etched in your mind because of the virtually constant mist sprayed in your face from Vernal Fall in spring and summer, and the sheer beauty and awesomeness of being so close to a pair of Yosemite National Park's most spectacular waterfalls. If snow is present during winter (check ahead), you can snowshoe this route at least part of the way and perhaps have the whole place to yourself—a rare occurrence. The best photos are taken after midmorning. Much of the trail passes over bedrock, slick from the mist, so wear shoes with good gripping soles and walk alertly.

To get there, take the Yosemite Valley shuttle bus from anywhere in the valley and depart at Stop 16, which is Happy Isles. Toilets and drinking water are available here.

The trail, which consists of rough asphalt for the first part, climbs gently at first through a forest of ponderosa pine and black oak. The trail steepens as more and more huge, lichen-coated boulders appear along the north bank of the Merced River. Just before the path plunges to a bridge crossing at 0.8 mile, there's a spot where you can peer up Illilouette Gorge and spy Illilouette Fall pouring 370 vertical feet into the Merced River. Gaze behind you from here and check out Upper Yosemite Fall.

Nevada Fall, Vernal Fall, and Liberty Cap

Bigleaf maples, Douglas firs, canyon live oaks, and some occasional incense cedars and bay trees accompany you on the Mist Trail. Soon a long set of solid rock stairs assist you up the mist-shrouded canyon. Sometimes when the sun shines just right amid the mist, unique rainbows arc across the slick rock and tumultuous water. Vernal Fall keeps appearing through tree cover to urge you on during the stiff ascent. If the day is sunny and warm, you won't need any raingear—just get refreshingly soaked. Then dry out quickly near a bench and some oaks in an open area at the top of the fall. Here the loudness of crashing Vernal Fall contrasts dramatically with the quiet serenity of aptly named Emerald Pool. Liberty Cap looms above. Continue upstream and adore a slanting rocky strip of the Merced River called Silver Apron (don't get in to slide down it—it's dangerous) that pours swiftly into Emerald Pool.

Cross the bridge at Silver Apron at 1.6 miles and resume steep climbing via switchbacks, where you are occasionally cooled by light mist from Nevada Fall. Bear right onto signed John Muir Trail and reach a plethora of viewpoints with railings for watching Nevada Fall charge over the rocky lip and drop 594 feet.

At 2.8 miles, stay to the right at a trail junction and follow a trail cut into the side of a cliff past a rock overhang featuring water drips and dainty ferns. Descend to Clark Point and then turn around to capture the view behind you of Nevada Fall, Mount Broderick, and Liberty Cap—a whole lot of rock in one scene. For variety and dryness, avoid the Mist Trail junction on the return and stay instead on the John Muir Trail. Pass the Vernal Fall Bridge at 5.2 miles and retrace the first 0.8 mile of your journey to Happy Isles.

3 | MIRROR LAKE AND TENAYA CREEK

Distance: Up to 6-mile loop
Hiking time: 3–5 hours
High point: 4100 feet
Elevation gain: 200 feet
Difficulty: Easy
Season: Year-round
Map: USGS Half Dome
Nearest campground: Lower Pines Campground
Information: Yosemite National Park

Explore an isolated corner of Yosemite Valley, the world's best-known example of a glacier-carved canyon, for fantastic views of stark granite peaks and domes. Hundreds of years ago, huge boulders tumbled down the steep mountain to partially dam Tenaya Creek, helping to form aptly named and very popular Mirror Lake. The lake has receded to become mostly a meadow, but it still reflects its mountainous surroundings in winter and early spring when rainwater and snowmelt transform it into a temporary large pond. This journey is often an ideal snowshoe or cross-country ski trip if snow is plentiful.

Rust-colored, boulder-strewn Tenaya Creek is a precious gem of a

Tenaya Creek and Mount Watkins

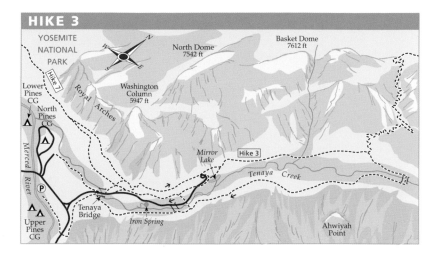

HIKE 3

stream that gets lovelier and more remote with each step east of Mirror Lake. Everyone assumes that since popular Half Dome looms triumphantly above the lake that its vertical face reflected in Mirror Lake takes center stage, but it's Mount Watkins to the east that is often photographed in the lake's shallow and usually calm waters.

To get there, drive to Lower Pines Campground or Upper Pines Campground in Yosemite Valley and park in one of the lots. The trailhead is the paved road (closed to vehicles) that heads east.

This trail starts along the Merced River, crosses the road, then crosses Tenaya Bridge. It's a pleasant 1.2-mile-long stroll in an open forest bordering meandering Tenaya Creek to willow- and alder-lined Mirror Lake. As you explore the shapely shoreline, gaze up to the rocky crevices in the cliffs looming over the lake to the south, knowing that up there are several prime nesting nooks for spotted bats and peregrine falcons, two of Yosemite Park's endangered species. Swifts, swallows, and ouzels also inhabit the steep, granitic flanks.

Getting around the lake and surrounding meadow, now a dirt trail, covers 0.4 mile. Listen for the chorus of croaking Pacific tree frogs in the mushy meadow. As you ascend gently up the canyon, look for patches of bracken fern, once used by the local Indians to make baskets.

Beyond the meadow, your route passes through a rockslide below stark granite cliffs, where the nicest views are behind to the left and across the canyon to Half Dome (Note: this area closed due to rockfall in 2009). Reenter light forest of ponderosa pine, incense cedar, and Douglas fir and follow Tenaya Creek a short while. Reach a junction at 2.8 miles, where you either turn around or bear right to make a loop trip, soon crossing a bridge over Tenaya Creek. While heading back, look for views westward of stark and steep Washington Column and its rocky neighbor, Royal Arches.

4 | BRIDALVEIL FALL AND LOWER YOSEMITE FALL

Distance: Up to 2.5 miles round trip
Hiking time: 2 hours
High point: 4065 feet
Elevation gain: 200 feet
Difficulty: Easy
Season: Year-round
Maps: USGS Half Dome, USGS Yosemite Falls
Nearest campground: Sunnyside Walk-In Campground
Information: Yosemite National Park

Call this more of a sightseeing stroll, an endeavor to study and compare two of the world's most popular and photographed waterfalls. Throngs of folks from around the world will be on hand to share the moments of delight with you. Parking will be much easier, and the crowds smaller, if you visit on a weekday, especially after Labor Day or before Memorial Day.

Like most mighty waterfalls, the flights of Bridalveil Fall and Lower Yosemite Fall in spring are loud, incessantly powerful, misty, and the white churning water hides much of the sheer rock cliffs. It's a different story come fall, when both waterfalls become partial screens of streaming water, more subtle, and with streaks of gray contrasting their free falls.

To get there, drive to the west end of Yosemite Valley, where the Bridalveil Fall parking lot is located on State Route 41 (Wawona Road) 100

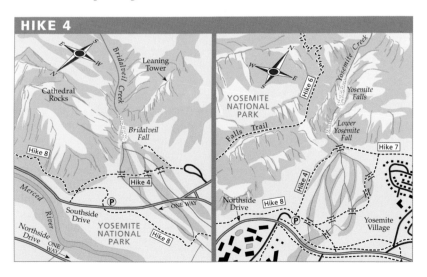

HIKE 4

Bridalveil Fall

feet south of the junction of SR 41 with Southside Drive. If you miss this lot, or if it's full, proceed northeast on Southside Drive and park on the side of the road where other cars are parked.

Paved trails lead from wherever you are parked to the base of the falls. Be sure to walk on all of them, for combined, they feature special views of Bridalveil Fall, an awesome open vista of El Capitan and its rugged and vertical rock face, and three bridges for admiring lovely Bridalveil Creek. The mixed forest features dappled and filtered sunlight, and consists of incense cedars, black oaks, canyon live oaks, California bay trees (fragrant evergreen leaves), white firs, and bigleaf maples.

Resembling a long, exotic veil, Bridalveil Fall nosedives over a shiny and slick, black vertical cliff, V-shaped at the top. When breezes kick up, mist blows into your face and wets your hair. It's especially refreshing on hot summer days. Bridalveil splits into three streams that flow over boulders, and a trio of stone bridges show off their wares.

Hop in your car and drive northeast a short distance on Southside Drive to an often crowded parking lot signed for Swinging Bridge. Park here and stroll over to the bridge for an incomparable view of the meandering Merced River, lined with cottonwoods, fronting Yosemite Falls. Your walk can be lengthened by wandering in the nearby meadow.

Back in your car, proceed through the valley, eventually looping around to Northside Drive and the large parking lot signed for Lower Yosemite Fall, 0.5 mile west of the Yosemite Valley Visitor Center.

The long and narrow Lower Yosemite Fall is framed by regal conifers, such as incense cedar and ponderosa pine, as the paved path winds toward your goal. After a bit over 0.25 mile, arrive at a bridge spanning Yosemite Creek and a viewing area to photograph the fall. A series of little pools and gentle cascades highlight Yosemite Creek. Because of the exhilarating mist in spring, the boulders are too slippery to safely scramble over to reach the very base of the fall, but by late summer, a lot of folks scurry over them to get a closer look.

5 INSPIRATION POINT, STANFORD POINT, AND DEWEY POINT

Distance: 10 miles round trip for Dewey Point; 2.6 miles round trip for Inspiration Point
Hiking time: 2–9 hours
High point: 6950 feet
Elevation gain: From 1000 to 3300 feet
Difficulty: Strenuous
Season: Year-round
Map: USGS El Capitan
Nearest campground: Sunnyside Walk-In Campground
Information: Yosemite National Park

Here's a fast way to escape the crowds by heading up a north-facing flank of Yosemite Valley canyon that leads to far-reaching and jaw-dropping views of major place-names normally seen by throngs of tourists below.

For inaugural views of Yosemite Valley seen in privacy, make your goal Inspiration Point, the original view of the valley for travelers along the old Wawona wagon road. For energetic and toned souls who want even more seclusion and better views, press on to Stanford Point (8 miles round trip) and Dewey Point (10 miles round trip). Simply follow the signed Pohono Trail in a light to medium forest via switchbacks. For ultimate solitude, do this on snowshoes when there's sufficient winter snow, even if you have to lug your snowshoes up to the snow line.

To get there, drive to the east end of Wawona Tunnel on Wawona Road, and park in the south lot across from Discovery View.

At first, climb steadily past shrubby canyon live oak, incense cedar, ponderosa pine, Douglas fir, black oak, and large specimens of white leaf manzanita. Sporadic gaps in the forest cover allow teasing glimpses of Bridalveil Fall, El Capitan, and Half Dome punctuating Yosemite Valley. Cross an abandoned road at 0.6 mile. Built in 1875, this was the original

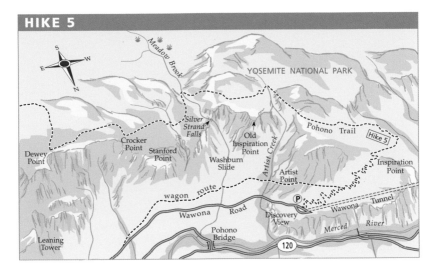

wagon route to Yosemite Valley. Continue switchbacking through forest as the live oak, black oak, and manzanita begin to disappear on the Pohono Trail, a Miwok Indian name for Bridalveil Fall, literally meaning "fall of the puffing winds."

Reach a pair of metal signs at 1.3 miles that indicate Inspiration Point. Cedars and pines interrupt your view here, but a brief scamper west followed by a short descent to the edge of some cliffs renders a spectacular view. Stretching north to south, check out El Capitan, Clouds Rest, Half Dome, Sentinel Dome, and Cathedral Rocks. The enormous weight and erosive power of moving ice spiked with rock fragments plowed wide the formerly V-shaped Yosemite Valley and steepened these stark granite walls.

Light forest soon takes over as the route bends and zigzags up the mountainside. Cross a small creek, continue ascending across the mountain face, and climb more steeply just before reaching Artist Creek (sometimes dry in summer) at 2.6 miles. You can scramble northeast 0.25 mile to Old Inspiration Point, gather your fantastic views, and call it a day if you like. To continue the route, veer eastward, and soon you're rewarded with opening views as you climb out of forest into more open country. Reach willow-choked Meadow Brook at 3.1 miles, a cute creek above a cliff where delicate Silver Strand Falls free-falls until June. Skirt around a rock promontory at 3.5 miles, then gradually descend northward toward tempting Stanford Point, which you reach 0.5 mile farther. All the previously mentioned views simply become more commanding, pronounced, and jaw-dropping here. Late spring and early summer wildflowers are strewn all around, including monkeyflower and lupine.

Make the short detour to Crocker Point at 4.5 miles to capture Bridalveil

Higher and Middle Cathedral Rocks

Fall shooting down into Yosemite Valley. When you get to Dewey Point 0.5 mile farther, scramble carefully to it and savor unrivaled views down into the steep valley and across much of the mountainous park.

6 | YOSEMITE FALLS AND EAGLE PEAK

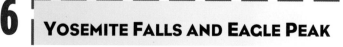

Distance: 12.6 miles round trip for Eagle Peak; 6.8 miles round trip for Yosemite Falls
Hiking time: 10 hours or overnight
High point: 7300 feet
Elevation gain: 3500 feet
Difficulty: Strenuous
Season: May through October; often year-round for Yosemite Falls
Maps: USGS Half Dome, USGS Yosemite Falls
Nearest campground: Sunnyside Walk-In Campground
Information: Yosemite National Park

Climb close to two of the most photographed and memorable waterfalls in the world, then continue to Eagle Peak for top-of-the-world views of numerous nearby domes, cliffs, ridges, and rims. Be sure to take photos of Lower Yosemite Fall from various places along the Merced River. From atop Eagle Peak, sprawling and gorgeous Yosemite Valley looks like a detailed, flat map.

Although you can camp along Yosemite Creek above the upper fall but at least 0.25 mile from the rim, most folks leave early and hightail it down well before dark. There's much more privacy atop Eagle Peak, but to evade the crowds at Yosemite Falls, go in midweek before Memorial Day weekend.

To get there, drive to and park in the westernmost part of Yosemite Lodge in Yosemite Valley. Better yet, take a park shuttle bus there. Follow signs for the trail through sections of Sunnyside Walk-In Campground.

From the get-go, there are dozens and dozens of switchbacks over talus slopes and past house-sized boulders, thankfully the route is shaded much of the way to the falls by canyon live oaks and occasional ponderosa pines, incense cedars, and California bay trees. After a bit over 1 mile, reach a rail-guarded viewpoint known as Columbia Rock showing off Half Dome (Hike 1), Mount Clark, and the distant Clark Range (Hike 99). Sentinel Rock occupies center stage across Yosemite Valley. After more ascent, you get

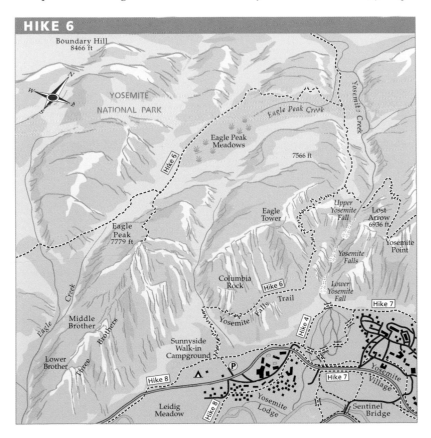

HIKE 6

inaugural views of 1430-foot Upper Yosemite Fall, framed by large manzanita bushes and canyon live oak branches. After a cold winter storm, there is significant ice and rockfall on the upper switchbacks here. The constant and invigorating mist of the fall support thriving little gardens of ferns and mosses wedged in the granite slab cracks.

Black oaks and evidence of previous rockslides accompany a refreshing descent that's about level with Lower Yosemite Fall to the east. Climbing resumes in more open country, and the warmer it is, the more you'll be reaching for your water bottles while admiring the improving, previously mentioned views. Enter a cool and shaded glen upon reaching the rim at 3 miles. From a seasonal creeklet amid Jeffrey pines and staghorn-lichen-coated white firs, follow the trail sign indicating Upper Yosemite Fall, but make note of the trail ahead, which is your route to Eagle Peak. Head south on the side trail that leads to an overlook of the fall. There are a couple of spots where it seems you could spit directly down on Yosemite Valley, so watch your step.

Double back and ascend northward for Eagle Peak via welcome shade from Jeffrey pines and white firs. Depart the Yosemite Creek drainage before leveling off in a bouldery region, which is a terminal moraine. Veer south on a gentle climb beneath red firs and lodgepole pines to boggy Eagle Peak Meadows. Eagle Peak holds snow longer than the rest of the area and sometimes water covers the trail up to a foot deep. Cross the meadow and the headwaters of Eagle Peak Creek and soon reach a hillside trail junction

Willows, Merced River, and Yosemite Falls

at 5.7 miles, where you turn left. From here, it's a moderate 0.7-mile climb to brushy Eagle Peak. Stick around to soak in the panorama, highlighted by the obtuse triangle of North Dome, Clouds Rest, and Half Dome to the east, garnished by Vogelsang Peak and Mount Florence way in the distance. The previously mentioned views are now clearer, and new views include Mount Hoffmann and its towering neighbors to the northeast.

7 YOSEMITE FALLS AND ROYAL ARCHES

Distance: 6.6-mile loop
Hiking time: 4–7 hours
High point: 4175 feet
Elevation gain: 600 feet
Difficulty: Easy to moderate
Season: Year-round
Maps: USGS Half Dome, USGS Yosemite Falls
Nearest campground: Sunnyside Walk-In Campground
Information: Yosemite National Park

Stare at the longest falling falls in America and stand beneath a vertical wall of sheer granite towering some 2000 feet above. Stroll a scenic meadow, and check out a wild river on this popular hike.

This is a unique trip, for you can hike to or near Yosemite Falls, Royal Arches, Ahwahnee Meadow, and the meandering Merced River and have lunch at a restaurant roughly halfway through. And just like Hike 11 (El Capitan), the constant streams of vehicles that border this trip are surprisingly out of sight and sound most of the way. Dodge both of these excursions during the blazing heat of summer, when crowds and temperatures are high. But take either one before Memorial Day weekend in spring when the river is swift and the waterfalls are full, or in the autumn when the dogwoods, black oaks, willows, and bigleaf maples are changing colors. Going on a weekday is probably the easiest way to explore the numerous photogenic sites rock-walled Yosemite Valley offers, minus the major crowds of tourists. Better yet, hike or snowshoe this route in the dead of winter, when even fewer folks are present.

The valley floor trails can be confusing and hard to follow and a good map is a great help. If you lose the trail, just continue in the right direction and enjoy the continually awesome views. Your course adjoins the easternmost, main valley roads where interpretive signs posted near turnouts tell you of the interesting geology of the area. The route alternates between busy, developed areas and sections of rapturous solitude.

To get there, follow all signs into Yosemite Valley. Get to Sentinel Bridge parking area (your starting point) by taking the shuttle bus from Curry Village (runs every 20 minutes) or by driving there if you can find an open parking spot.

Walk southeast away from Yosemite Village on the pedestrian path. At 0.2 mile, turn south, crossing Northside Road while heading out into a meadow. As you cross shallow, orange-bottomed Merced River via a footbridge, admire views of the river and Half Dome to the east. Behind the chapel at 0.5 mile, find the trail junction and turn east. Wander through an area of black oaks and big boulders, and soon enter an evergreen forest of incense cedar, Douglas fir, and ponderosa pine, a theme that recurs throughout the journey as you pick and choose your route around the outer edges of Yosemite Valley.

Reach the outskirts of Curry Village at 2.5 miles, pass the hamburger stand and then pass Upper Pines Campground to your left. Cross the Happy Isles Bridge spanning the Merced River, pass underneath a huge overhanging rock, and eventually reach a trail junction near the Tenaya

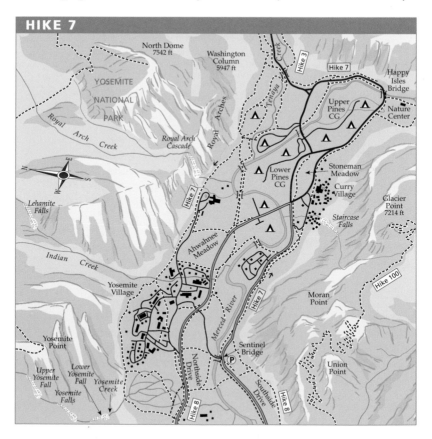

HIKE 7

Merced River and Cathedral Rocks

Bridge, where you turn left, crossing the road to Mirror Lake at 3.4 miles.

Fine views of steep and granitic Royal Arches are yours as you walk along Tenaya Creek, soon reaching the stables at 3.8 miles, where you bear sharply right near the sign for Yosemite Falls. As you angle west in light forest, note improved views of Royal Arches punctuating the sky as you drop down to skirt scenic Ahwahnee Meadow at 4.6 miles. Over the next 2 miles, consisting of a moderate descent, ascent, and then mostly level trekking, watch for views to the north of Yosemite Falls, which free-fall 2425 feet.

8 YOSEMITE VALLEY: EL CAPITAN AND BRIDALVEIL FALL

Distance: 11-mile loop
Hiking time: 5–8 hours
High point: 4065 feet
Elevation gain: 500 feet
Difficulty: Easy to moderate
Season: Year-round
Maps: USGS Half Dome, USGS Yosemite Falls
Nearest campground: Sunnyside Walk-In Campground
Information: Yosemite National Park

Here's the best way to explore Yosemite Valley, a prominent natural wonder of the world. This journey shows the photogenic splendor of a mammoth granite chunk of mountain called El Capitan, towering above shallow and scenic Merced River. Mix in views like Bridalveil Fall free-falling from the shoulder of massive Cathedral Rocks and the jaunt escorts you into an epic wonderland of continuous and striking picturesque highlights.

Your course adjoins the main valley roads where interpretive signs posted near turnouts tell you of the fascinating geology of the area. The valley floor trails can be confusing and hard to follow and a good map is a great help. If you lose the trail, just continue in the right direction and enjoy the continually awesome views. To evade the crowds, take the many spur trails that lead to the Merced River or viewpoints, and come in midweek. Better yet, snowshoe this route during the peace of winter, when snow occasionally blankets the Yosemite Valley and wedges in the stark and vertical granite walls. The key is good timing (there's enough snow perhaps 20 to 40 days a year).

To get there, drive to Yosemite National Park east from Interstate 5 by taking State Route 120 just south of Stockton, SR 140 in Merced, or SR 41 in Fresno. Once in the park (a $20 entrance fee is charged), follow all signs into Yosemite Valley. Get to Sentinel Bridge (your starting point) by taking the shuttle bus from Curry Village (runs every 20 minutes) or by driving there.

Head south by southwest on a mostly level grade, which stays that way to journey's end. Traipse in a light forest of incense cedar, ponderosa pine, Douglas fir, and black oak, an intermittent theme on this trek. Pass above Sunnyside Walk-In Campground, then head for and cross the main road. Admire Leidig Meadow at 1.2 miles as you skirt past it, then approach Merced River, which is mostly rock-bottomed and features a brownish orange cast. Find a good perch for looking east at a scene that includes North Dome, Royal Arches, Clouds Rest, and Half Dome.

Cross Eagle Creek via a wooden bridge and head for the small clearing that reveals a staggering view of precipitous El Capitan. This massive bulk

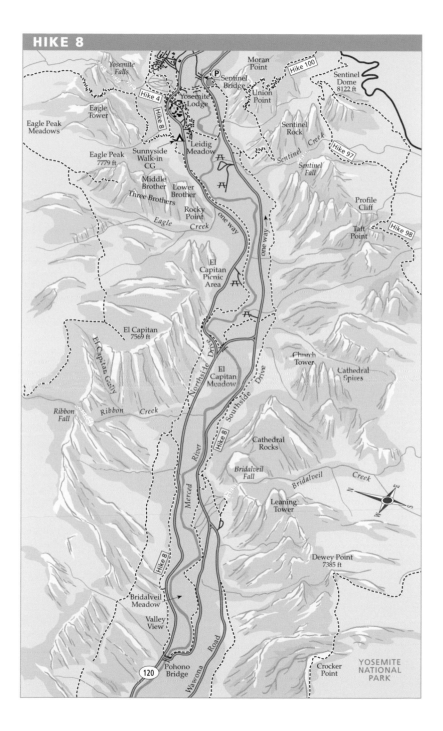

Yosemite Falls

Moran Point

P Sentinel Bridge

Hike 100

Sentinel Dome 8122 ft

Hike 4

Yosemite Lodge

Union Point

Hike 8

Eagle Tower

Sentinel Rock

Eagle Peak Meadows

Leidig Meadow

Sentinel Fall

Hike 97

Sunnyside Walk-in CG

Eagle Peak 7779 ft

Middle Brother

Lower Brother

Profile Cliff

Three Brothers

Rocky Point

Taft Point

Hike 98

Eagle Creek

one way

one way

El Capitan Picnic Area

El Capitan 7569 ft

Church Tower

Cathedral Spires

El Capitan Gully

Northside Drive

El Capitan Meadow

Southside Drive

Ribbon Fall

Ribbon Creek

Hike 8

Cathedral Rocks

Merced River

Bridalveil Fall

Bridalveil Creek

Leaning Tower

N

Dewey Point 7385 ft

Hike 8

Bridalveil Meadow

Valley View

Wawona Road

120 Pohono Bridge

Crocker Point

YOSEMITE NATIONAL PARK

El Capitan and ponderosa pines

of durable, unbroken granite soars 3000 feet into the sky. The Ahwahneechee Indian name for El Capitan is *Tutokanula,* the name for an inchworm that according to legend led bear cubs safely down the sheer cliff. Varying and arguably better views of El Capitan keep coming as you follow the peaceful course of alder- and willow-lined Merced River. Pass the El Capitan Picnic Area at 3.3 miles, trek beneath the looming mountain itself 1 mile farther, and then cross Ribbon Creek.

Plan on picnicking at a photogenic but typically crowded spot called Valley View at 5.4 miles. By wandering along the banks of a rapids section of Merced River, you can capture small Bridalveil Meadow topped in the same gaze by El Capitan, Clouds Rest, and Half Dome. Switch your stare to the south and spy slim but powerful Bridalveil Fall pouring and misting straight down a stark granite face. The Ahwahneechee called this place *Pohono,* "spirit of the puffing wind." The wind swirls about the cliff, occasionally lifting the spray as it eventually plummets several hundred feet.

Stand on the Pohono Bridge at roughly the halfway point, cross it, and continue counterclockwise. Close-up views of Bridalveil Fall occur at 6.7 miles as you crane your neck upward to take in the imposing Cathedral Rocks, massive granite rocks that are a darker gray than most found here. View El Capitan beyond close-by Merced River and El Capitan Meadow 1 mile farther. Just before reaching Sentinel Bridge at 11 miles, your attention will be fixed on Yosemite Falls to the northeast. It's the longest falling falls in America, fifth longest in the world, at 2425 feet.

9 | SOUTH FORK MERCED RIVER TO HITE COVE

Distance: 9 miles round trip
Hiking time: Up to 6 hours
High point: 1100 feet
Elevation gain: 1400 feet
Difficulty: Moderate to strenuous
Season: December into May
Maps: USGS El Portal, USGS Kinsley
Nearest campground: Hodgdon Meadow
Information: Sierra National Forest in Mariposa

Venture deep into a wild and rugged canyon that frames twisting and scenic South Fork Merced River. Find peace and seclusion on your quest for an old abandoned mining town called Hite Cove. Come during March and April and discover a riot of native wildflowers poking out of the scree in profuse colonies. Look for orange California poppies, purple owl's clover, and blue lupines as well as several endangered wildflowers.

Be advised that this river trail section is closed during fire season, which usually starts Memorial Day weekend and lasts until the fall rains arrive. Call the Sierra National Forest office in Mariposa to make sure it's open.

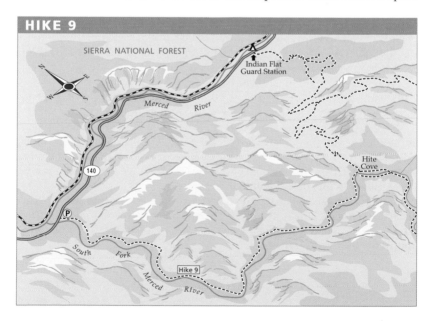

California poppies

The hot months are a bad time to be here anyway. The steep canyonsides are dry as a bone, the annual grasses that were cheery green in winter and spring are brown and stickery in summer, and rattlesnakes rule.

Wide, boulder-bottomed, and swift, this stretch of the South Fork Merced River is as gorgeous as it gets. The trail often rises high above the water, then gradually switchbacks down the canyon to reunite with it. The river roars as it swells with snowmelt starting in March and continuing into June, and it rotates between foamy rapids, swirling currents, and deep pools. You'll also find attractive views of spacious, gravel bar islands laced with willows.

To get there, take State Route 140 east of Mariposa, or west from El Portal to the union of Merced River and South Fork Merced River at a large bridge. Park for free in the turnout on the north side of the highway, then cross the road and head toward the river and several chalets.

The trail, used also by fishermen and miners, climbs right off, heading up the narrow canyonside. Lichen-coated rock outcrops gouged into the hillsides are a constant theme. The easy-to-follow trail is like a roller-coaster ride, with spur paths leading to picnic spots and swimming holes alongside the river each time it dips down to the canyon bottom.

In addition to spring's awesome wildflower display, the countryside is a mosaic of gray pines, canyon live oaks, black oaks, ponderosa pines, ceanothus, manzanita, and poison oak. There are patches of mountain misery ground cover and occasional redbud (magenta flowers in March) shrubs and buckeye (white flower spikes in May) trees.

Look for western fence lizards doing push-ups on the trail, while kingfishers zoom across the river and red-tailed hawks patrol above the canyon. Reach Hite Cove at 4.5 miles, where there's a nice swimming hole, then return the way you came.

Facing page: Porcupine Creek

TIOGA ROAD: TAMARACK CREEK EAST TO TENAYA LAKE

10 | TAMARACK CREEK AND CASCADE CREEK

Distance: 7.6 miles round trip
Hiking time: 3–5 hours
High point: 6000 feet
Elevation gain: 1300 feet
Difficulty: Moderate
Season: Year-round
Maps: USGS Tamarack Flat, USGS Yosemite Falls
Nearest campground: Crane Flat Campground
Information: Yosemite National Park

Witness profuse shrubbery, a dazzling spring wildflower show, and a metropolis of young conifers on this peaceful and secluded excursion to a pair of creeks that feature fishing, summer swimming, and splendid cascades. The exuberant plant show is courtesy of the lightning-caused A-Rock Fire of 1990 that cleared and opened up the forest floor so sun could strike gorgeous spring wildflowers such as showy wild irises and pink and yellow harlequin lupines. Birding is brisk here on the first third of the journey because of the numerous nesting sites in the charred and hollowed, burned trees that were left as snags. Look for white-headed woodpeckers, mountain bluebirds, and yellow-rumped warblers. The plentiful rodents

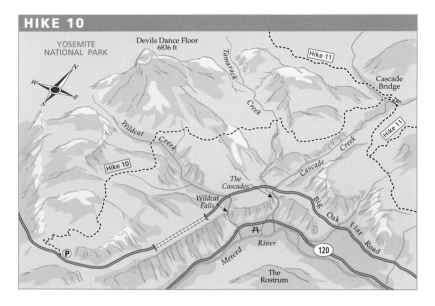

Cascade Creek tumbles over granite boulders

thriving in this burned area are hunted by red-tailed hawks and rattlesnakes.

Because this is a side, and not the main, route to places such as El Capitan, foot traffic is typically low, especially on weekdays. When Tioga Road is closed because of snow (generally from November through May), this trip to lovely Cascade Creek that connects with the trail to El Capitan is the only available route in winter and early spring to El Capitan (Hike 11). Call ahead for snow conditions if you plan to hike all the way to Cascade Creek in winter. March and April are the best times to climb this trail, when the flowers, including those from the whiteleaf manzanitas, are in full bloom.

To get there, from the junction of State Routes 120 and 140 at the west end of Yosemite Valley, it's a 4-mile drive north on SR 120 to the trailhead located 0.25 mile above the Forest Road junction. From Crane Flat, the trailhead is 6 miles east along SR 120.

The first 0.5 mile is a punishing 400-foot-in-elevation climb over a chaparral-clad slope to a ridge featuring a view of El Capitan and Half Dome. Thousands of ponderosa pines that sprouted in open areas in the early 1990s are thriving here. The path then traverses north 0.5 mile to a moist region with a seasonal spring. Cross several tributaries of Wildcat Creek, where western azaleas and dogwoods display whitish flowers in spring. Enter unburned forest and soon descend to Wildcat Creek.

Climbing resumes for almost 1 mile to a ridge sporting a view of the Merced River Canyon. It's a steep descent down to Tamarack Creek at 2.5 miles, where the huge leaves of Indian rhubarb turn showy yellow and orange come autumn. Tamarack Creek is usually too dangerous to cross during high water (typically May and early June). Climb another mile, drop briefly to then rock-hop a tributary of Cascade Creek, and then promptly reach old Big Oak Flat Road, which is closed to vehicles. Cross the creek here, where serviceberry shrubs hug the bank of a petite pool fed by a scenic cascade. Now on the road, wander down to the Cascade Bridge for a picnic. Camping is allowed as long as your site is at least 100 feet from the water. There are some legal though shadeless sites across the bridge. If the weather is warm, you'll be tempted to at least dangle your feet in crystal-clear Cascade Creek, which features warm and shallow small pools by summer.

11 | TAMARACK FLAT TO EL CAPITAN

Distance: 16 miles round trip
Hiking time: All day or overnight
High point: 7569 feet
Elevation gain: 1500 feet
Difficulty: Moderate
Season: May through November
Maps: USGS Tamarack Flat, USGS El Capitan
Nearest campground: Tamarack Flat Campground
Information: Yosemite National Park

Gleaming and polished, the sheer vertical wall of El Capitan looks like a gargantuan slab of gold when the sun hits it just right and it's viewed from down in Yosemite Valley. You see a totally different El Capitan when perched upon it. The top is rounded and domelike, more like a gradual hump and not flat as it appears from the valley floor, and it offers scintillating views of the Tenaya Creek and Merced River Canyons as well as corridors of classic Yosemite National Park ridges and peaks. Along the way of this route you can dip your toes in three major creeks and traipse across a meadow. This excursion is extra-popular on weekends in May and June. If you plan to backpack here in the month of August or later, call ahead to find out if Ribbon Creek—the only place to camp—is still flowing as a water source. Keep an eye out for where the trail leaves the old road. Although it's marked, some folks miss it.

To get there, from Crane Flat take Tioga Road (State Route 120) 3 miles east and take the Tamarack Flat Campground turnoff. Drive this road 3 miles southeast to its end.

Tamarack Flat was named for its dominance of erroneously dubbed tamaracks, which are actually lodgepole pines. But as you depart the flat and head across slopes on old Big Oak Flat Road (closed to vehicles), stately white firs take over. Note the huge, partially buried boulders strewn about—the ground around them was gradually removed, which took millions of years. The trail steadily descends past a conspicuous rock cluster toward Cascade Creek; it goes left at a trail junction at 2.2 miles, and then reaches a bridge over Cascade Creek. The next 0.1 mile is scenic, as Cascade Creek, adorned with large-leaved Indian rhubarb plants, tumbles down via cascades into petite pools that make ideal swimming holes in summer. The banks are decorated with western azaleas, dogwoods, willows, and serviceberries.

Climb sometimes steeply in a forest of white fir, ponderosa and sugar pines, and incense cedar to drier, more exposed slopes laden with evergreen greenleaf manzanita and huckleberry oak shrubs. Lodgepole pines

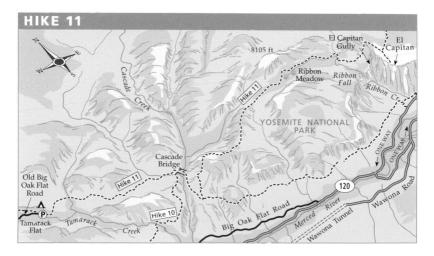

dominate again at 5.2 miles down in a damp meadow occupied by sedges, marsh marigolds, and shooting stars. After another mile, traverse Ribbon Meadow, which is dominated by lodgepole pines. Stroll the banks of Ribbon Creek, which is lined with the trail's only campsites (waterless by late season). It's a mostly ascending traverse east to the head of El Capitan gully, with inaugural views of El Capitan and the Yosemite Valley's rocky south wall through scattered Jeffrey pines. Ascend south from the gully and take the short spur trail that leads past dense shrubs to the broad summit of El Capitan. Take advantage of several vantage points to check out all

El Capitan and the Merced River in winter

the views, which include Yosemite Valley, spread out like a map full of major place-names, such as the Merced River, which snakes below Cathedral Rocks, while Half Dome and Clouds Rest take center stage to the east.

12 | HARDEN LAKE

Distance: 6 miles round trip
Hiking time: 3–4 hours
High point: 7800 feet
Elevation gain: 300 feet
Difficulty: Easy
Season: May through October
Maps: USGS Tamarack Flat, USGS Hetch Hetchy Reservoir
Nearest campground: White Wolf Campground
Information: Yosemite National Park

Here's a hike all about spectacular summer wildflowers, along with crashing cascades and swimming holes. There's also the potential for a glorious view of the Grand Canyon of the Tuolumne River. The pleasant stroll to shallow and warm, 9-acre Harden Lake parallels Middle Tuolumne River part of the way, traveling through a secluded and scenic pine forest. Late summer is the best time for wildflowers and swimming, and hiking during midweek or late afternoon are the best times to enjoy solitude.

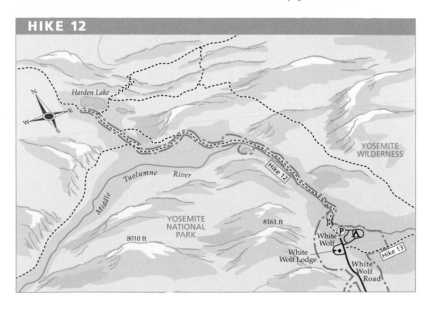

HIKE 12

Buttercups bloom in late spring on the way to Harden Lake

To get there, drive 14 miles northeast from Crane Flat up Tioga Road (State Route 120) to the signed White Wolf turnoff. Follow that road north for 1 mile down to the trailhead, across from White Wolf Lodge.

Get on the signed trail to Harden Lake, which is the original, historical, dirt Tioga Road built in 1883, now gated and closed to vehicles. Cross Middle Fork Tuolumne River via a bridge and follow the trail as it meanders along the river, passing a series of cascades that usually diminish to rapids by September. Choose a couple of favorite deep and clear holes for a refreshing swim. The course passes over unglaciated granitic terrain where lodgepole pines thrive amid meadow strips hosting lupine, columbine, yarrow, and senecio.

After 1 mile of gentle downhill, the trail ascends over a low ridge of glacial deposits, then drops into a shady grove of red firs and lodgepole pines. Bear right at a trail junction and traverse a slope of a large glacial moraine. In this well-drained area, Jeffrey pines combine with an interesting mix of quaking aspens and white firs, along with chinquapin shrubs and colonies of bracken ferns.

After two more successive right turns at trail junctions, reach tree-lined Harden Lake at 2.8 miles, occupying a small depression that formed between two lateral moraines. Since Harden Lake has no surface inlet or outlet, its water level begins to fall by midsummer, which warms up the lake nicely for swimming. Fishing is considered weak at best, however. Stroll the lakeshore, and if energy and/or time permit, ascend the slight rise on the far side of the lake and enjoy a nice view through tree openings of the Grand Canyon of the Tuolumne River.

13 | LUKENS LAKE

Distance: 5 miles round trip
Hiking time: 3 hours
High point: 8000 feet
Elevation gain: 200 feet
Difficulty: Easy
Season: May through October
Map: USGS Yosemite Falls
Nearest campground: White Wolf Campground
Information: Yosemite National Park

Traipse through tranquil lodgepole pine forests interspersed with wildflower-dotted meadows to placid Lukens Lake, which is adorned on the south and east sides with lush meadows and framed on the north and west sides with mixed forest. Anglers and families with small kids often take the shorter trail that leads 0.8 mile into a deep red-fir forest filled with leafless plants, such as pinedrops and snowplant, to the lake. Your described route crosses and follows the lovely and slender Middle Tuolumne River. The meadow sections of this popular lake hike stay soggy into late summer, and therefore are thick with mosquitoes, especially when the shadows

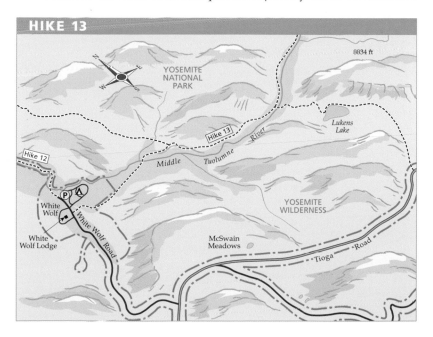

HIKE 13

8834 ft

YOSEMITE
NATIONAL
PARK

Lukens
Lake

Hike 13   River

Hike 12   Middle Tuolumne

P

White
Wolf

White Wolf Road

YOSEMITE
WILDERNESS

White
Wolf Lodge

McSwain
Meadows

Tioga Road

A pair of frogs

creep in. For the most privacy, come late in the day and/or on a weekday. Lukens Lake is very much like nearby Harden Lake (Hike 12). Both are warm, shallow, 9-acre swimming lakes that lack views of astounding peaks. Lukens Lake has a mostly grassy bottom.

To get there, drive 14 miles northeast from Crane Flat up Tioga Road (State Route 120) to the signed White Wolf turnoff. This trailhead is a turnout on the east side of White Wolf Road, 1.8 miles north of the turnoff to White Wolf.

The trail skirts the south edge of White Wolf Campground and stays in a lodgepole pine forest, where occasional views of the Middle Fork of the Tuolumne River exist before crossing it at 0.7 mile. Stay right at a trail junction 0.25 mile farther and walk in marvelous meadows that border the river. Purple shooting stars often grace these meadows in early summer. Look for deer, pocket gophers, Belding ground squirrels, shrews, mice, and the coyotes that hunt the rodents. May through July, sections of the trail can be sloshy from snowmelt and runoff from feeder creeks.

Enjoy the meadow, forest, and river scenery for 1 mile, then cross the river again at 2 miles just after going right at another trail junction. A moderate incline ensues, with occasional views through trees of a sloping meadow. You'll cross a few glacial moraines during this 0.4-mile ascent to

Lukens Lake. Just prior to reaching the lake, red firs, mountain hemlocks, and western white pines join lodgepoles in the forest and decorate much of the lake's shoreline as well.

Several logs extend into the water and serve nicely as fishing piers. Note that camping is not allowed, but strolling the entire shoreline is a pleasant, serene experience.

14 | YOSEMITE CREEK TO YOSEMITE VALLEY VIA TIOGA ROAD

Distance: 13 miles one way; 16 miles round trip for Yosemite Falls
Hiking time: All day or overnight
High point: 7350 feet
Elevation gain: 1100 feet
Difficulty: Moderate
Season: May through November
Map: USGS Yosemite Falls
Nearest campground: Porcupine Flat Campground
Information: Yosemite National Park

This is the easiest route to reach spectacular Yosemite Falls and take in top-of-the-world views looking down on wondrous Yosemite Valley. Witness two distinct landforms as you wander along the rolling uplands of Yosemite Creek to the steep, rock-walled Yosemite Valley. The falls are at their peak at the same time the mosquitoes are, in May and June, when snow patches may still linger in the upper hollows and valleys. To avoid the hordes of humanity, go on a weekday. If you backpack in (camping within 0.25 mile of the rim is prohibited; a permit is required), spend the night along scenic Yosemite

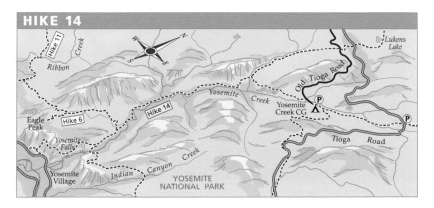

HIKE 14

Dogwoods and maples along Yosemite Creek

Creek 1 mile or so from Yosemite Falls, and then obtain the most seclusion by visiting the top of the falls in late afternoon or early evening. **To get there,** travel about 20 miles east of Crane Flat on Tioga Road (State Route 120) and park on either side in the lots. The trailhead is a few feet to the west along the narrow shoulder of the road where there's a sign for the trail next to brush. If you opt to start the hike from Yosemite Creek Campground, you can shave off 5.5 miles round trip, making the round trip for Yosemite Falls 10.5 miles. Get to this trailhead by driving 14.8 miles northeast of Crane Flat on Tioga Road. Turn right onto Old Tioga Road and follow it southeast 5 miles to its end.

Much of the journey is spent amid lodgepole pines, with red firs and western white pines along the shaded slopes and some picturesque Jeffrey pines thriving out of rock cracks in drier, more exposed areas. The trail meanders for 1 mile to the boulder-hop crossing (can be tricky when high and rushing in spring) of Yosemite Creek, and the next mile follows the east bank to Yosemite Creek Campground. Follow a dirt road through the campground, reach and get on rutted Old Tioga Road, and then head down canyon almost 0.5 mile to another crossing of the creek. Now back on the trail proper, trudge south through open forest, staying comfortably close to Yosemite Creek. At 1.5 miles farther, the path ascends up a ridge away from it. Barren bedrock takes over, where large boulders perched atop polished slabs evidences glaciation.

Descend the ridge via switchbacks, pass a trail junction that heads north, and then cross a tributary of Yosemite Creek where some good campsites exist. The smooth and rounded granite walls gradually force the creek and trail into a narrow canyon where the swirling aquamarine waters flow fast over smooth rock. More good campsites are situated a bit farther as the valley widens in forest along Yosemite Creek to the crossing of Blue Jay Creek 6 miles from the trailhead.

Cross two wide and sandy flats, reenter forest, and then meet the Eagle Peak Trail (see Hike 6) in a ferny glen 1.5 miles from Blue Jay Creek. Reach the junction for Yosemite Falls 0.5 mile farther and follow the signs east to the falls overlook. There are a couple of spots where it seems you could spit directly down on Yosemite Valley, so watch your step. By now, there are candid views across Yosemite Valley of Half Dome, Clouds Rest, Sentinel Rock, Cathedral Rocks, the Clark Range, and much more that stay with you for the next 2 miles of winding trail that leads into Yosemite Valley. The Merced River below looks like a big brown snake slithering through the middle of this broad, glacially carved canyon.

The final 3 miles down to Yosemite Valley is a steep roller-coaster ramble via dozens of switchbacks over talus slopes and past house-sized boulders, shaded much of the way by canyon live oaks, black oaks, and occasional ponderosa pines, incense cedars, and California bay trees. There are spots where you'll note the constant and invigorating mist of the falls that support thriving little gardens of ferns and mosses wedged in the granite slab cracks. A bit over 1 mile from Yosemite Valley, reach a rail-guarded viewpoint known as Columbia Rock, showing off Half Dome (Hike 1), Mount Clark, and the distant Clark Range (Hike 99). Sentinel Rock occupies center stage across Yosemite Valley.

15 | PORCUPINE FLAT TO NORTH DOME

Distance: 9.4 miles round trip
Hiking time: 5–7 hours
High point: 8100 feet
Elevation gain: 1050 feet
Difficulty: Moderate
Season: May through November
Map: USGS Yosemite Falls
Nearest campground: Porcupine Flat Campground
Information: Yosemite National Park

Domineering North Dome appears impossible to climb from the Yosemite Valley Floor, but it can be mounted rather easily from a solid trail that leads down to it from Tioga Road. Be forewarned—there's a 700-foot ascent on the return, so factor in the time and energy for it, along with enough water. Most hikers shoot a lot of film on North Dome, which offers a panorama of Yosemite National Park and unsurpassed vistas of the vast faces of Clouds Rest and Half Dome, along with a commanding view of Yosemite Valley.

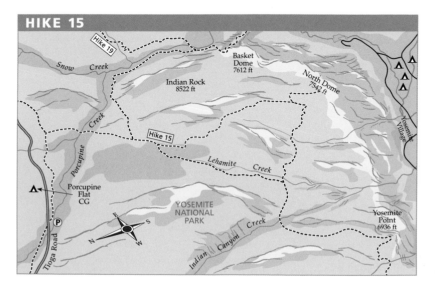

HIKE 15

Yellow-bellied marmot

For the most seclusion, climb this bald, rounded granite summit on a week-day offering high visibility. A 1.4-mile round-trip side tour to a rare natural arch on the flank side of Indian Rock is a bonus.

To get there, drive 24 miles east of Crane Flat on Tioga Road (State Route 120) and park on the south side of the road, 1 mile west of Porcupine Flat Campground. The trailhead is 13 miles west of Tuolumne Meadows.

The trail starts on a gentle grade downhill on the eroded remains of a road that leads to the former site of Porcupine Creek Campground. In 0.7 mile, cross aptly named Porcupine Creek, where there's a pure stand of lodgepole pines, the favorite food of porcupines who climb in their tops to eat tender growth tissues. The trail now contours for just over 1 mile to two consecutive junctions atop a shady saddle framed by regal red firs, where you keep straight. Traverse 0.3 mile to a spur ridge, contour past manzanita shrubs in another 0.3 mile, and then descend to a gully before climbing steeply to a junction signed for Indian Rock. Take this interesting side trip along brushy slopes to a delicate 20-foot arch just over 1 foot thick at the thinnest part of its span. You can easily climb it from the west side.

Return to the junction, climb to a red fir saddle, and head south for 1 mile along Indian Ridge, where western white pines and red firs give way to Jeffrey pines. The trail drops sharply to the left, then picks up the rocky ridgeline again. Soon, huckleberry oak shrubs dominate, allowing superb views ahead of North Dome and Half Dome farther away. Look for another spur trail that meanders right for an even grander view of North and Half Domes. By now, Yosemite Valley, highlighted by the swirling Merced River, is capped by El Capitan and Sentinel Rock. Imposing Half Dome and smoothly curved Clouds Rest dominate across the gorge.

Reach another junction and bear left for the 0.5-mile-long side trail out to North Dome. Notice V-shaped Tenaya Canyon, which is harshly glaciated, and follow your gaze clockwise to scan three other canyons: Merced Canyon, Illilouette Gorge, and Yosemite Valley, in that order. The 4000-foot-high face of Clouds Rest is imposing to the east, and frequently photographed Half Dome looms large farther southwest. Continuing this panorama clockwise, Mount Starr King farther away is a steep-sided dome. Glacier Point is just below and to the left of bulging Sentinel Dome. Peering into Yosemite Valley, note the near vertical north face of Sentinel Rock, backed by jagged Cathedral Rocks. On the north side of the big valley, El Capitan juts majestically behind the Three Brothers.

16 | MOUNT HOFFMANN MEADOW

Distance: 3-mile loop
Hiking time: 2–3 hours
High point: 8400 feet
Elevation gain: 100 feet
Difficulty: Easy
Season: May through October
Maps: USGS Tenaya Lake, USGS Ten Lakes
Nearest campground: Porcupine Flat Campground
Information: Yosemite National Park

Here's a little-known stroll around the edge of a subalpine meadow nestled beneath imposing Mount Hoffmann. This sensitive meadow has no trails through it—the idea is to appreciate its grassy splendor from a distance as you circumnavigate it. Slim and surprisingly deep streams flow smoothly and clearly through the meadow and along portions of its edges, tempting you to dip your feet. Take this hike to marvel at the impressive array of summer wildflowers or indulge in a snooze on a flat granite rock slab as the sounds of birds and buzzing insects carry on.

To get there, travel Tioga Road (State Route 120) some 27 miles northeast of Crane Flat and turn north onto signed Old Tioga Road. This junction is 3.7 miles west of the southwest parking area at Tenaya Lake.

Mount Hoffmann and Mount Hoffmann Meadow

Drive paved but bumpy Old Tioga Road (signed for May Lake) about 1 mile, then find a place to park off the side of the road.

Pick and choose your way easily, moving in a counterclockwise direction amid a scattered mix of lodgepole pine saplings and ancient specimens. This theme stays with you the whole way, with a bonus of a couple of quaking aspen groves to enjoy. If it's early summer, there will be soggy spots out on the meadow, and even some muddy spots in the pines. The mosquitoes may bug you, especially in the shadows during early morning or evening.

After about 0.75 mile, follow the meadow's edge away from Old Tioga Road, and from here on out, you're pleasantly alone with the birds. In June, the blue grouse moves down from the slopes of Mount Hoffmann to mate, so listen for the male's deep hoot. The dark-eyed junco is probably the most common bird occupying this meadow during summer. The Cassin's finch uses grass from the meadow to make its nest.

From the north edge of the meadow, Mount Hoffmann demands your attention and perhaps a photo with the meadow's greenery and a lodgepole sapling in the foreground.

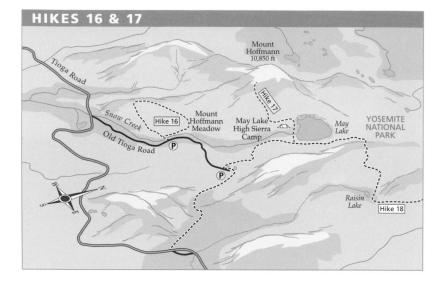

17 | MAY LAKE AND MOUNT HOFFMANN

Distance: 2.5 miles round trip for May Lake; 6.2 miles round trip for Mount Hoffmann
Hiking time: 3–7 hours
High point: 10,850 feet
Elevation gain: 2400 feet
Difficulty: Moderate to strenuous
Season: June through October
Maps: USGS Tenaya Lake, USGS Ten Lakes
Nearest campground: Porcupine Flat Campground
Information: Yosemite National Park

The dramatic visage of Mount Hoffmann imposes its reflection across the subalpine, clear, and deep waters of May Lake on late afternoons and early evenings. When the wind kicks up, the focused reflection in the lake gets fuzzy and even fades, sure to return when the breezes calm.

This journey offers that scene, plus many views of jagged, rounded, and pointed rocky mountains marching north to south. It's not necessary to claim the top of Mount Hoffmann to gather these views, for these High Sierra peaks unfold a mere 0.5 mile along the rugged trail from the lake.

Facing page: May Lake and red mountain heather

Centrally located in the park, Mount Hoffmann features some of the finest views of Yosemite's varied high-mountain landscapes from its summit. An unmaintained use trail leads to the top, where it's a rare treat to be able to admire large streaks and patches of snow lingering on all the peaks when you visit in late spring.

Although swimming isn't allowed, fishing for rainbow and brook trout in May Lake is relaxing. Because of the sheer beauty, the easy trail access, and the brief half-hour aerobic workout that's required to get to May Lake, the place is crawling with folks on warm weekends. For more privacy, explore it on weekdays or after Labor Day.

To get there, travel Tioga Road (State Route 120) some 27 miles northeast of Crane Flat and turn north onto signed Old Tioga Road. This junction is 3.7 miles west of the southwest parking area at Tenaya Lake. Drive paved but bumpy Old Tioga Road (signed for May Lake) 1.7 miles and park in the obvious dirt trailhead parking area.

Go to the southwest side of a small pond to gain the trail, which climbs right off in a moderately dense forest of lodgepole and western white pines, mountain hemlocks, and red firs. Soon the forest thins, and the western white pines, with their checkerboard-pattern bark on the trunks, become larger and more dominant. Red mountain heather and pinemat manzanita clusters of ground cover adorn the scene, along with pleasingly fragrant mountain pennyroyal.

The steady climb is soon rewarded with numerous sightings of distant Cathedral Peak above Polly Dome to the east and the Clark Range, Clouds Rest, and Half Dome behind you to the south. Continue walking past granite slabs until you reach May Lake at 1.2 miles, where you can camp just above the lake's south shore.

Factor in time to stroll the inviting shoreline, where an exposed, vertical, gray wall of granite dominates the west end. Red mountain heather blooms in July, beneath colonies of hemlock, lodgepole pine, and red fir. Toward the northeast shore, find a heather- and willow-lined pond, followed by a pair of meadow strips.

Get on the trail for Mount Hoffmann at the southeast corner of the lake, striking west. Traverse across metasedimentary rocks above the lake's southwest shore, then ascend south, eventually traipsing through a boulder-strewn wildflower garden accentuated by western chokecherry shrubs that feature white flowers in July.

After hiking 0.5 mile from the lake, follow rock ducks (cairns) as the trail snakes up the slope. After 0.25 mile of steady ascent, the climb intensifies as you strike west on the exposed east slopes of Mount Hoffmann. Make sure you've applied sunblock, and wear a hat and sunglasses, for the bright talus shines back in your face. Mat lupine and buckwheats eke out an existence low on the loose ground, and you'll find yourself alternating between gazing down at these cute flowers and up at the awesome rocky ridge that supports Mount Hoffmann. Stunted, windswept whitebark pines join the climb, and you'll soon notice Mount Hoffmann has several summits. Your trail leads to the western summit, which is also the highest. Virtually every prominent peak in Yosemite can be identified with a good map from the top.

18 OLD TIOGA ROAD TO TEN LAKES BASIN

Distance: 24 miles round trip
Hiking time: 3 days
High point: 9900 feet
Elevation gain: 4300 feet
Difficulty: Moderate
Season: June through October
Maps: USGS Falls Ridge, USGS Ten Lakes, USGS Tenaya Lake
Nearest campground: Porcupine Flat Campground
Information: Yosemite National Park

This romp is all about snagging several miles' worth of High Sierra views while getting up close and personal with several gorgeous, rock-encased, subalpine lakes. It's a privilege and honor to stare down into the Grand Canyon of the Tuolumne River after all the sweat and huffing that's required to achieve the Ten Lakes Basin, and you'll probably find that by the third day out you've built up enough fitness to hightail it back to the trailhead in 6 or 7 hours.

The trip can be shortened and varied by continuing on the trail from

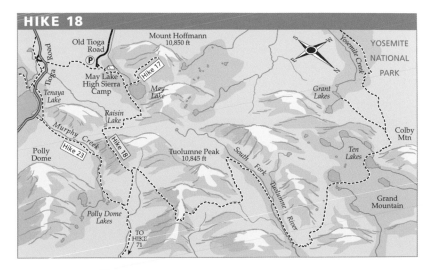

Ten Lakes Basin west and then south in forest via Yosemite Creek. All that's needed is a car shuttle at the Yosemite Creek trailhead or the intrepid can hitchhike 7 miles back to Old Tioga Road. But the scenic route is to retrace your steps back toward May Lake and recapture those numerous rocky mountain views in reverse.

To get there, travel Tioga Road (State Route 120) some 27 miles northeast of Crane Flat and turn north onto signed Old Tioga Road. This junction is 3.7 miles west of the southwest parking area at Tenaya Lake. Drive paved but bumpy Old Tioga Road (signed for May Lake) 1.7 miles and park in the obvious dirt trailhead parking area.

Find the trail by the southwest side of a small pond in a medium forest of red fir, mountain hemlock, lodgepole pine, and western white pine. A steady climb up open granite slabs flecked with lodgepole pines doesn't abate until precious May Lake is reached at 1.2 miles. But the work is refreshed by occasional views east of distant Cathedral Peak and west of nearby Mount Hoffmann, the geographic centerpiece of Yosemite National Park. After about 0.75 mile, look behind you for treasured sightings of the Clark Range, Clouds Rest, and Half Dome to the south.

Consider fishing for rainbow and brook trout at May Lake, where you can camp just above the lake's south shore. The imposing east flank of Mount Hoffmann reflects in the shiny clear waters late in the day. This mighty mountain has a trail to it (see Hike 17).

Your trail traces the eastern shore of the lake to the north end, then climbs promptly to a shallow pass decorated with large purplish-blue-flowered lupines in midsummer. The path now descends via switchbacks, showing off Polly Dome, topped by Cathedral Peak. Enter shady forest and cross four seasonal creeklets, then reach Raisin Lake at 3 miles. Shallow and warm, this cute little lake invites you to take a long and comfortable swim in its soothing waters.

Climb to another shallow pass and attain a panorama of the High Sierras, featuring Mount Conness to the northeast. Descend some rocky switchbacks and eventually cross a third shallow pass with a view beyond lodgepole pines of Tenaya Lake to the south. The forest now thickens with mountain hemlocks to a trail junction at 4.8 miles. Bear left and soon begin a long climb via moderately graded switchbacks to a crest and then a pond at 7.7 miles. Nearby Tuolumne Peak beckons to be climbed to the southwest.

Short, rocky switchbacks escort you toward the Cathedral Creek canyon floor, and when you cross it, several campsites are nearby. Climbing up a Sierra juniper–dotted slope ensues, where you can take a well-earned breather at vantage points that show off Mount Gibbs to the east. Follow the scant trail closely climbing up this basin. A bit more climbing places you in the Ten Lakes Basin at 10.2 miles, crowned by Colby Mountain, named after conservationist William Colby, the Sierra Club's third president.

Plan on spending a lot of time exploring the basin, which is situated in a light forest of hemlocks, western white pines, lodgepole pines, and

Red Mountain heather above May Lake

whitebark pines. The shores of most of the lakes are adorned with red mountain heather and Labrador tea shrubs. From the basin's largest lake, other lakes can be reached from its southwest corner, following its inlet stream upward.

Pressing on to the Grant Lakes, reach an open ridge called Ten Lakes Pass, where it's time to spend quality hang time photographing the long-distance views. The panorama extends from Mount Conness, past Tioga Crest, and across to Matterhorn Peak to the east. The Grand Canyon of the Tuolumne River severs a deep gash between the ridge in front of you and the dramatic High Sierra peaks beyond.

Take the signed trail south to Grant Lakes, where you'll drop into a bowl laden with summer wildflowers to isolated Grant Lakes at 12 miles.

19 | TENAYA LAKE TO SNOW CREEK AND MIRROR LAKE

Distance: 12 miles one way
Hiking time: 5–7 hours or overnight
High point: 8100 feet
Elevation gain: 500 feet
Difficulty: Easy to moderate
Season: May through November
Maps: USGS Tenaya Lake, USGS Yosemite Falls
Nearest campground: Porcupine Flat Campground
Information: Yosemite National Park

This epic one-way journey starts at deep and large Tenaya Lake and climaxes at small and shallow Mirror Lake (see Hike 3) at the east end of Yosemite Valley, where you hopefully meet your partner with the car shuttle. Be forewarned—it's a 4000-foot-in-elevation haul back up to Tenaya Lake. This is the easiest and one of the least visited routes from Tioga Road to Yosemite Valley.

To get there, drive to a bend in Tioga Road (State Route 120) near Tenaya Lake's southwest shore and park in the large lot. The trailhead is 8.5 miles southwest of Tuolumne Meadows Campground and 30 miles northeast of Crane Flat.

From the signed Tenaya Lake trailhead, your trail traverses southwest across a sometimes boggy meadow for 0.5 mile before reaching a side trail that promptly reaches nearby Tioga Road. Glance backward for views of Polly Dome towering above the lodgepole pine–ringed meadow, which is filled with sedges and dwarf bilberry ground cover. Stroll south 0.3 mile along the west edge of the meadow, enter level lodgepole pine forest for 0.2 mile, and then climb to a clearing for a view behind you of Medlicott Dome, Polly Dome, and the distant Mount Conness.

Reenter forest, now dominated by mountain hemlocks, and climb via switchbacks to a gap just below Olmstead Point, one of Tioga Road's most popular and scenic turnouts. The low knoll you're on is punctuated by erratic boulders and partly clothed with Jeffrey pines, western white pines, and lodgepole pines. The ensuing 0.5-mile winds around bedrock

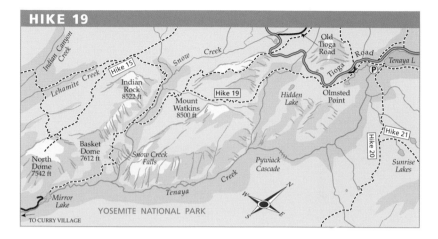

knobs, then the trail swings away from Tioga Road and switchbacks down into a damp-floored, forested, and glaciated canyon awash with corn lilies and yellow-flowered senecios. Cross two seasonal creeks and descend in this canyon, which is mosquito-infested in early summer, for 1 mile. Climb briefly to a crest strewn with erratic boulders, then switchback down into the forested canyon. If snow lingers here, follow the painted markers attached high on various conifers.

Traverse below a pair of smooth-sided domes, then reach a trail junction at 5.8 miles, where you stay left. Switchbacks continue in a forest of red and white firs and Jeffrey pines well into Snow Creek Canyon and after 1 mile you arrive at campsites nestled under white firs along Snow Creek. The trail crosses the creek and proceeds down canyon for 0.5 mile in forest, emerges on open slopes, and then snakes steeply down to Tenaya Canyon's floor. Check out inaugural views of the mammoth northwest face of Half Dome and the pinnacles of Mount Watkins. Continue down to a gully and a stand of conifers that includes Douglas firs and white firs. The trail follows the gully 1.4 miles down to a dry slope that you traverse past whiteleaf manzanita shrubs, paintbrush, and penstemon flowers and birds foot fern. Clouds Rest and Half Dome keep getting your attention on the descent, which includes a view of Tenaya Creek plunging over a long, vertical, rock wall below. Pass under a cliff, reenter forest dominated by canyon live oaks with a few occasional bay laurel trees, and then reach the wide bouldery bed of Tenaya Creek.

You then reach the Tenaya Creek Trail, where you walk 1 level mile to the west end of Mirror Lake, which is well on its way to becoming a meadow. Hundreds of years ago, huge boulders tumbled down the steep mountain and partially dammed Tenaya Creek, helping to form this large pool. Willow- and alder-lined Mirror Lake has a shapely shoreline to explore. Rocky crevices in the cliffs loom over the lake to the south, where

Granite outcrop

there are several prime nesting nooks for spotted bats and peregrine falcons, two of Yosemite Park's endangered species. Swifts, swallows, and ouzels also inhabit the steep, granitic flanks. It's another mile past incense cedars, ponderosa pines, and a lot of tourists to Curry Village.

20 | TENAYA LAKE TO CLOUDS REST

Distance: 14 miles round trip
Hiking time: 8–11 hours or 2-day backpack trip
High point: 9930 feet
Elevation gain: 2600 feet
Difficulty: Moderate to strenuous
Season: May through October
Map: USGS Tenaya Lake
Nearest campground: Porcupine Flat Campground
Information: Yosemite National Park

From atop the countless and amazing exfoliated granite slabs that grace expansive Clouds Rest, hikers acquire staggering views of nearby Half Dome from its most dramatic and compelling angle. To gain the airy summit for an unparalleled panorama of a metropolis of gray peaks, take a promenade across a narrow and precipitously edged ridge composed of piled sheets of granite resembling huge stacks of pancakes or a line of toppled dominoes.

While Clouds Rest isn't as visited as Half Dome, it's more rewarding to take this epic endeavor in midweek or after Labor Day weekend to enjoy more solitude. The entire ridge and summit is exposed, meaning a

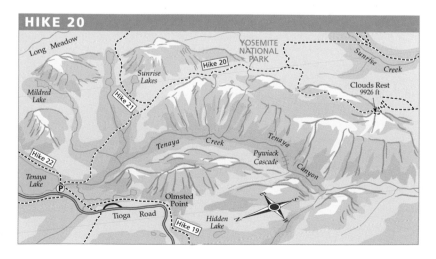

Clouds Rest during a cloudburst

windbreaker should be packed in case those typically fierce winds kick up, and extra sunblock should be applied. In case of lightning, a common occurrence during summer afternoons, hightail it on down pronto.

To get there, drive to the southwest end of Tenaya Lake (8 miles southwest of Tuolumne Meadows) on Tioga Road (State Route 120). You can also take the Tuolumne Meadows shuttle to Stop 10, Sunrise Lakes trailhead (your trailhead on the south side of Tenaya Lake), and take the signed trail near the restrooms.

Cross Tenaya Lake's outlet stream and enjoy some level strolling through mini meadows adorned with lupine and corn lily, and forest dominated by lodgepole pines. Scrappy mountain hemlocks join the open forest after you cross a second stream. The grade increases after 1.5 miles and climbs a rocky slope and eventually reaches the ridgeline at 2.3 miles, where you go right at a trail junction. The left turn goes to Sunrise Lakes (see Hike 21). Descend steeply for 0.5 mile, then enter an alpine meadow followed by a block-strewn ridge laden with chinquapin shrubs and quaking aspen trees. The trail then descends promptly to a tree-ringed pond, where adequate campsites exist nearby.

After another 0.5 mile, you cross the first of three Tenaya Creek tributaries, and these serve as your last reliable sources of water. You gently climb and soon reach the Clouds Rest Trail junction at 4.9 miles, where you bear right and proceed in an open forest of western white pines. By now, teasing glimpses of many of Yosemite National Park's major mountains keep appearing. Reach the base of the summit proper at 6.8 miles. The expansive 4500-foot-tall abrupt face of Clouds Rest, the largest granite face in the park, spreads below, as does spectacular and wild Tenaya Canyon. Now on a scant footpath, scramble steeply over rocks weathered to the shapes of countless flat slabs amid scattered, knee-high whitebark pines and Jeffrey pines.

After 300 yards, you're on the summit, where a predictably amazing panorama unfolds. Half Dome looms large to the southwest, guarding sprawling Tenaya Canyon across a deep green chasm. Bulbous North Dome and Basket Dome are gray twins farther southwest. Matterhorn Peak and the Sawtooth Ridge crowns vivid Tenaya Lake to the northeast. A trio of the park's tallest peaks, Mounts Florence, Lyell, and Maclure, cap the extensive Merced River Canyon to the east. The Clark Range to the south assists in making the overall view resemble a series of gray-ridged waves marching to the horizon.

21 | TENAYA LAKE TO SUNRISE LAKES

Distance: 8.5 miles round trip
Hiking time: 6 hours or overnight
High point: 9000 feet
Elevation gain: 1100 feet
Difficulty: Moderate
Season: May through November
Map: USGS Tenaya Lake
Nearest campground: Porcupine Flat Campground
Information: Yosemite National Park

Explore a threesome of small, round lakes that drain into Tenaya Canyon and obtain dramatic panoramic views that include Clouds Rest and Half Dome. By establishing one of the equally gorgeous Sunrise Lakes as a base camp, you can day hike north to Cathedral Lakes for an easy 8-mile round trip, or day hike southwest to mount Clouds Rest for a moderate 10-mile round trip. For solitude, visit Sunrise Lakes after Labor Day or during weekdays.

To get there, drive to the bend on Tioga Road (State Route 120) near Tenaya Lake's southwest shore. This often crowded trailhead parking area is located 8.5 miles southwest of the Tuolumne Meadows Campground and 30 miles northeast of Crane Flat. You can also take the Tuolumne Meadows shuttle to Stop 10, Sunrise Lakes trailhead (your trailhead on the south side of Tenaya Lake), and take the signed trail near the restrooms.

The wide trail leads to the crossing of the usually flowing outlet of Tenaya Lake and a trail fork. Leave the trail here so you can wander over to the lake's scenic and bouldery southwest shore. If it's hot, swim here. Tenaya Lake gets more sunshine than the Sunrise Lakes and is 800 feet lower in elevation, and therefore is a bit warmer. A trail here goes around the south shoreline of mile-long Tenaya Lake (Hike 22). Your trail heads south, away from the lake.

Enjoy some level walking through mini meadows featuring lupine and corn lily, and forest dominated by lodgepole pines. Scrappy mountain

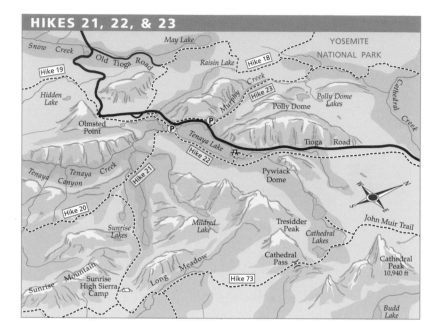

HIKES 21, 22, & 23

hemlocks join the open forest after a second stream crossing. The grade increases after 1.5 miles as the trail steadily climbs a rocky slope and eventually reaches the ridgeline at 2.3 miles, where you come to a trail junction for Clouds Rest (Hike 20). But first, take a brief unsigned trail to the right for 300 yards for a photogenic view of imposing Half Dome, wild Tenaya Canyon, and sprawling Yosemite Valley.

Back at the trail junction, bear east on the trail for the Sunrise Lakes, contouring through open forest of western white pine and mountain hemlock. Cross a low gap and then descend north to Lower Sunrise Lake, the most popular of the three lakes. Look for the unstable slabs of exfoliating granite above a large talus slope on the eastern shore. Several small campsites exist 50 to 100 yards from the lake. The trail climbs from this lake and soon reaches a crest at 4 miles where a spur trail leads north for about 100 yards to middle Sunrise Lake, which is the most secluded and is sprinkled with small rock islands. To reach upper Sunrise Lake, the largest of the trio, follow the main trail east and climb about 10 minutes to it. Good campsites are located a short distance from the north shore, away from the trail. Consider getting up at the crack of dawn and following the trail 0.5 mile east to aptly named Sunrise High Sierra Camp to catch the sunrise over rocky and jagged Matthes Crest.

Facing page: Flowering bitter cherry shrubs
on the slopes near Sunrise Lakes

22 | TENAYA LAKE

Distance: 3 miles round trip
Hiking time: 2 hours
High point: 8260 feet
Elevation gain: 200 feet
Difficulty: Easy
Season: May through November
Map: USGS Tenaya Lake
Nearest campground: Porcupine Flat Campground
Information: Yosemite National Park
See map page 82

This leisurely stroll along the southern, more remote shore of oblong Tenaya Lake is intimate, romantic, and photogenic. You'll be enticed to linger long at this easily accessible and very popular lake, where the best time to do this hike for privacy is early morning or early evening. There's also solitude in the middle of cold late spring and early autumn weekdays. Big, beautiful, and glacial Tenaya Lake was named after Chief Tenaya, who was driven from his Yosemite home with his people by the U.S. cavalry.

To get there, drive to the bend on Tioga Road (State Route 120) near Tenaya Lake's southwest shore. This often crowded trailhead parking area is located 8.5 miles southwest of the Tuolumne Meadows Campground and 30 miles northeast of Crane Flat.

The wide trail meanders to the crossing of the usually flowing outlet of Tenaya Lake and a trail fork. Leave the trail here and go over to the lake's bouldery southwest shore. If it's hot, swim here. You don't get the northeast shore's sandy beach, but you also don't get its strong upcanyon breezes or its crowds. Walk briefly east along the bedrock basin shore and soon relocate the trail. Note the impressive views across the grayish lake of huge Polly Dome and dwarfish Pywiack Dome. There will be several opportunities along the ensuing mile to adore these views, featuring the steep-sloped granite rock of Polly Dome rising 1600 feet above the lake, along with plenty of easy access points to the nearby southeast shore of mile-long Tenaya Lake.

Hike through garden after garden of summer wildflowers thriving naturally in open spots spaced between conifer groves and bordering babbling brooks. You're apt to find the most solitude in the midway portion of the excursion. The trail follows the gently curving shoreline to a sandy beach on the northeastern shore. On a hot summer afternoon, sunbathers will be out en masse, and even the parking lot, picnic area, and restrooms can be full. The beach is a prime place to watch rock climbers clinging to the bare rock of

Tenaya Lake, Polly Dome, and Tresidder Peak

the many domes across nearby Tioga Road. You can stroll a ways along the
north, sandy shore of the lake, near the bases of the domes, but for views
and solitude, it's best to return the way you came.

23 | MURPHY CREEK TO POLLY DOME LAKES

Distance: 6 miles round trip
Hiking time: 3–4 hours
High point: 8700 feet
Elevation gain: 600 feet
Difficulty: Easy to moderate
Season: May through November
Map: USGS Tenaya Lake
Nearest campground: Porcupine Flat Campground
Information: Yosemite National Park
See map page 82

This scenic and secluded journey is a rock-lover's heaven, with its array
of house-sized erratics and the shiny glacial polish and striations that
can be found on other scattered rocks. Along the route, which follows
modest Murphy Creek, look for crescent-shaped gouges in various rock

Northwestern flank of Polly Dome

faces—they're called chatter marks and were made by big boulders dragged by glaciers. The vast majority of hikers are congregated at popular and nearby Tenaya Lake, so solitude is a virtual shoe-in to Polly Dome Lakes, which is situated at the northwest base of massive Polly Dome.

To get there, drive to and then park at the picnic area on the south side of Tioga Road (State Route 120) about halfway along Tenaya Lake. Cross the road to the signed trailhead which is 8 miles southwest of the Tuolumne Meadows Campground and 30.5 miles northeast of Crane Flat.

Essentially the whole way, the trail ascends gently alongside slim and mostly quiet Murphy Creek, first through a forest of lodgepole pines, and then from about the midway point between and over rock slabs marked by ducks (man-made stone piles). There's glacier action galore here: look for glacier-polished bedrock slabs and boulders moved ever so slowly by glaciers.

Reach a pond on the right at the head of Murphy Creek, near the divide. Depart the trail here and do some easy cross-country trekking southeast for 0.4 mile to the largest of the Polly Dome Lakes. The others are more pondlike and warrant a visit only if time permits. One of the best things about shallow and lodgepole-ringed Polly Dome Lake is that the boulders scattered in the lake make for good sunbathing islands. Decent campsites exist along the west shore, and Mount Hoffmann (Hike 17) pokes above the lake to the southwest. On the return, look for grayish Tenaya Peak guarding mile-long Tenaya Lake, and consider strolling part of this attractive lake from the southeast side (Hike 22).

Facing page: Hetch Hetchy Reservoir

CRANE FLAT AND HETCH HETCHY RESERVOIR

24 | CRANE FLAT LOOKOUT

Distance: 3.2 miles round trip
Hiking time: 2–3 hours
High point: 6645 feet
Elevation gain: 500 feet
Difficulty: Easy
Season: December through March
Map: USGS Ackerson Mountain
Nearest campground: Crane Flat Campground
Information: Yosemite National Park

Crane Flat Lookout offers an enticing panorama of Yosemite National Park's upper reaches and other High Sierra mountains. Still manned during high fire-danger times, impressively built Crane Flat Lookout sits on a large plain that beckons a snowshoer or cross-country skier to venture to every corner to see what view's in store. Although some folks climb the paved road that's closed to traffic in warmer months, this journey should be set aside for when the road is snow-covered. At that time the lookout offers solitude, peacefulness, and heavenly, clear views of snowcapped mountains.

To get there, drive Big Oak Flat Road (State Route 120) 6.8 miles southeast from the Big Oak Flat Entrance or 9.3 miles northwest of the junction with SR 140. Park at the signed trailhead for Crane Flat Lookout.

The route begins with a steady 0.25-mile climb followed by a brief

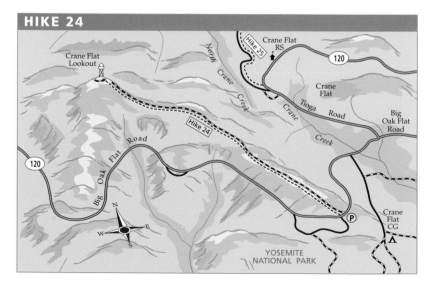

HIKE 24

Clark Range From Crane Flat Lookout

descent in a mixed forest of sugar pine, ponderosa pine, white fir, incense cedar, and Douglas fir. The sizes are an equal mix of small, medium, and tall, casting intricate and dappled shade patterns on the snow. Peaceful and steady ascent ensues in this lovely forest, where mule deer and coyote tracks occasionally are spotted on this old, snow-covered road.

A brief but intense climb occurs at 1.3 miles, near the summit. The terrain switches to open countryside with drifts of manzanita near and at the top.

As you wander the edges of Crane Flat Lookout's flat zenith while scanning the vast scenery, note that the best views are far off (bring binoculars). The most impressive view is the tall Clark Range and Half Dome to the southeast. Peruse the conifer-clad range that hides the Merced River Canyon to the south.

25 | TUOLUMNE GROVE AND HODGDON MEADOW

Distance: 6 miles one way; 2.2 miles round trip for
    Tuolumne Grove
Hiking time: 2–4 hours
High point: 6200 feet
Elevation gain: 500 feet
Difficulty: Easy to moderate
Season: Year-round
Map: USGS Ackerson Mountain
Nearest campground: Crane Flat Campground
Information: Yosemite National Park

Stand alone beneath the world's largest living things and sniff the air these mammoth sequoia conifers help purify. Tuolumne Grove is second to Mariposa Grove as the most popular of the three giant sequoia groves gracing Yosemite National Park. But by extending the journey 4 more miles downhill to Hodgdon Meadow and the Big Oak Flat Entrance Station (where you prearrange a car shuttle pick-up), you benefit from the most overall seclusion of the three grove hikes.

If it's snow season, consider an ultimate snowshoe or cross-country ski

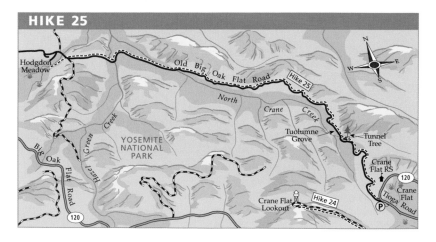

HIKE 25

Giant sequoias

trip downhill to admire these hulking and long-lived trees—among the rarest in America. Discover the bizarre-looking Dead Giant (tunneled in 1878). Time your visit just after fresh snowfall and these mighty evergreens wear mystical white beards.

To get there, drive to the junction of Crane Flat with Tioga Road, located 9 miles northwest of the junction with State Route 140 and 7.3 miles southeast of the Big Oak Flat Entrance Station. Follow Tioga Road (SR 120) 0.6 mile to the large parking area near the sign for Tuolumne Grove.

Downhill hiking in a pleasant mixed forest ensues right off. Note the varying sizes of young and old white firs. Gradually, incense cedars and sugar pines join the conifer forest and remain for the rest of the way. After numerous sharp bends along Old Big Oak Flat Road, you sweep around a hillside and enter Tuolumne Grove at 1.1 miles.

A short lateral spur trail to the right leads promptly to the Tunnel Tree, which reveals the cinnamon-colored trunks typical of sequoias. This quaint tree has a huge, teepee-shaped hole in its base and a top resembling a tuning fork. With your head tilted way back, wander through this cluster of about 25 sequoias, looking down occasionally to read the interpretive signs.

Once the vision of the sequoias' extreme girth is thoroughly etched into your memory, either climb the road back to your car or continue downhill along Old Big Oak Flat Road. Please take your time; this trail can be overly taxing during hot summers. Appreciate the groves of sizable white firs, while perhaps being watched by a great horned owl perched in the evergreen boughs above. Arrive at small but scenic Hodgdon Meadow at 5.5 miles, where it's another 0.5 mile to Big Oak Flat Entrance Station and Visitor Center.

26 | MERCED GROVE

Distance: 3 miles round trip
Hiking time: 2–3 hours
High point: 5840 feet
Elevation gain: 500 feet
Difficulty: Easy
Season: Year-round
Map: USGS Ackerson Mountain
Nearest campground: Crane Flat Campground
Information: Yosemite National Park

Attain deep peace and feel wonderfully small among the world's largest and longest-lived things on this tranquil trip down into Yosemite National Park's smallest of three sequoia groves. Among the rarest trees in America, these giant sequoias will most likely fill you with the same feelings of awe as being among their close relatives, the mammoth redwoods of the northern California coast.

If there's enough snow in winter or early spring, consider a quiet and isolated cross-country ski or snowshoe outing to these few clusters of stately sequoias called Merced Grove. Also, consider combining this route with nearby Tuolumne Grove (Hike 25) to admire about 25 more sequoias and to extend your endeavor by 3 miles. By far the most remote of the three groves, Merced Grove is a prime resource study area for learning more about sequoias.

To get there, drive to the parking lot for Merced Grove trailhead on the southwest side of State Route 120, about 4 miles south of the Big Oak Flat Entrance and 3.5 miles west of the junction at Crane Flat.

The easy-to-discern route follows a closed road all the way down to the grove in a scenic forest of incense cedar, ponderosa pine, and white fir. Look up into the boughs to see whether you can find a porcupine clinging to any of the main trunks. If there's snow, look for long-tailed weasel, mule deer, and raccoon tracks in the snow. Bear left at a Y junction at 0.6 mile, then follow the wide trail as it winds around and emerges into the drainage of Moss Creek. The route heads down to the tumbling creek, then reaches the first cluster of

Giant sequoias reach a maximum diameter of 35 feet

sequoias where the grade lessens. They're in a row of six, with a handful more scattered behind on the hillside.

It's possible for some of these trees to live up to 3000 years, perhaps eventually reaching heights of 250 feet and a trunk girth of 30 feet. Growing exceptionally fast throughout their lives, these big trees are resistant to death from fire, and some of these sequoias here have already survived lightning strikes. Fire suppression and logging from the past are the biggest contributors to the decline in sequoias.

The old road curves and reaches more sequoias with their tiny, gray-green leaves 100 yards farther at 1.5 miles.

27 TUOLUMNE RIVER TO PRESTON FALLS

Distance: 8.8 miles round trip
Hiking time: 4–6 hours
High point: 2900 feet
Elevation gain: 500 feet
Difficulty: Easy to moderate
Season: Year-round
Maps: USGS Lake Eleanor, USGS Hetch Hetchy Reservoir
Nearest campground: Carlon Campground
Information: Stanislaus National Forest

Here's a lazy journey that intimately traces the banks of meandering Tuolumne River below Hetch Hetchy Reservoir. Although the goal is precious Preston Falls, best seen in late winter through spring, you can roam as far as your heart desires, stopping to swim or fish at the numerous holes

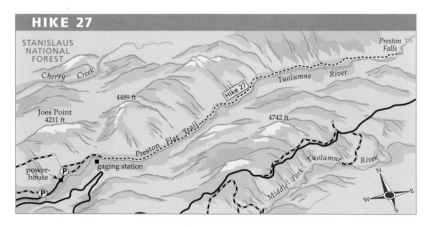

HIKE 27

Indian rhubarb along the Tuolumne River

along the way. Few folks know about the Preston Flat Trail, and sometimes on weekdays you may have the entire rugged and rocky canyon to yourself. If you go during a typical summer heatwave, try to leave at the crack of dawn to escape the high temperatures.

To get there, take Cherry Lake Road (Road 17) from State Route 120, about 13 miles east of Groveland. After 5.5 miles of paved but winding driving, go left and descend Road 17 for 3.1 miles. At the bridge crossing the Tuolumne River, turn right and climb a paved road 0.8 mile to the trailhead parking area next to a restroom and park here for free.

Well-built Preston Flat Trail starts as an old dirt road that goes 0.25 mile to a stream-gaging station. Staying mostly shaded beneath a tall canopy of live oaks, black oaks, ponderosa pines, and Douglas firs, the trail soon passes by a prime camp spot on a bouldery flat beside the Tuolumne River, and 1 mile farther it reaches the base of a granitic slab featuring mortar holes drilled by Native Americans. The campsites (permit required) keep appearing, as frequently as the fishing and swimming holes.

Large lupines bloom in June in the occasional, scattered open areas, and huge manzanita specimens are glorious in dry spots. Buckeye trees bloom in May in moister places. Occasional incense cedars and bay laurel trees offer pleasing fragrance. The ground cover shrub with sticky, finely divided leaflets is mountain misery.

After 3.5 miles of occasional brief ups and downs, reach a meadow that features a spring waterfall toppling down toward it. At 0.8 mile farther, the trail peters out at an ideal campsite next to a granitic slab. From here, check out Preston Falls across a long pool, and watch its 15-foot plunge into the river. If the river isn't raging unsafely, you can swim to the base of this thunderous waterfall.

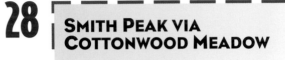

28 | SMITH PEAK VIA COTTONWOOD MEADOW

Distance: 16 miles round trip
Hiking time: 11 hours or 2–3 days
High point: 7751 feet
Elevation gain: 2900 feet
Difficulty: Moderate
Season: May through November
Map: USGS Hetch Hetchy Reservoir
Nearest campground: Carlon Campground
Information: Yosemite National Park

The ultimate way to spy on Hetch Hetchy Reservoir, the Grand Canyon of the Tuolumne River, and the marching, curved rows of mountains in the northwestern portion of Yosemite National Park is via Smith Peak. The ideal

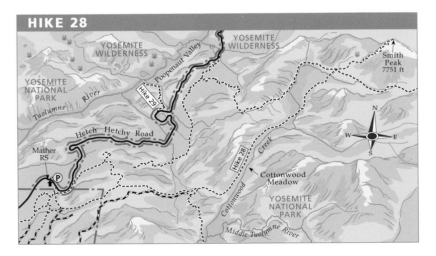

HIKE 28

Crag near Smith Peak rises above Hetch Hetchy Reservoir

way to get atop this wide-girthed crest is from the slopes of Lookout Point, traveling east to lovely Lower Cottonwood Meadow and then going northeast to the brush-coated and view-filled mountain.

Oh sure, there's less climbing heading northwest from White Wolf in the park, but you'd encounter more hikers and miss lower and upper

Cottonwood Meadow. Beware that snow often lingers on the upper flanks of Smith Peak through spring, and it's best to wear sturdy, broken-in boots with good-gripping soles. This area is one of many bear havens in the park, so if you're backpacking, see the information on bears in the "Wilderness Ethics" section in the Introduction. There are several brushy sections on this trail because of recent fires.

To get there, drive to just less than 1 mile west of the Big Oak Flat Entrance Station on State Route 120. Turn north on signed and paved Evergreen Road and drive about 7 miles. Go right onto paved Hetch Hetchy Road and drive 1.3 miles to Mather Ranger Station, where you can park for free. Ask a ranger where to park and where to find the nearby trailhead.

From the station's east side, follow a trail briefly south past ponderosa pines, black oaks, and incense cedars to a junction where you turn left and parallel Hetch Hetchy Road. The path roller-coasters over rocky slopes that support a bevy of spring wildflowers. The trail levels above a gully and promptly reaches two junctions, where you head right (east) both times. The well-graded trail climbs 0.5 mile to an extensive saddle, where you traverse east another 0.5 mile past a junction with the Base Line Camp. In another 0.5 mile begin a moderate climb to a lateral moraine at the top of an expansive ridge.

Enter a forest of white firs and Jeffrey pines just prior to entering Lower Cottonwood Meadow at 2.7 miles, which is bordered by lodgepole pines and quaking aspens. At 0.5 mile beyond the meadow, note a slab on your left with numerous mortar holes. The nuts from nearby sugar pines were relished by the Native Americans long ago, and they likely ground them here.

Reach Upper Cottonwood Meadow at 4.3 miles, cross Cottonwood Creek, and then climb to a broad ridge. After a brief descent, enter Smith Meadow, which, like the peak, is named after a sheep rancher who grazed his sheep here into the 1920s. Just beyond the meadow, in forest cover, this trail unites with the trail coming from White Wolf. Backpackers can find decent campsites a couple hundred yards west of this intersection, so they can day-hike to the peak.

A steep and direct climb to enticing Smith Peak ensues in a white fir forest featuring some sugar pines and incense cedars, then pass through a trio of boggy little meadows. Red firs take over near and on the crest, where the final climbing burst can be made by any of many brush-lined paths. To gain the best viewpoint atop pitted rocks of granite, crash through dense huckleberry oak shrubs. From next to the pocketed boulders, peer down to Hetch Hetchy Reservoir and the meandering, steep Grand Canyon of the Tuolumne River some 4000 feet below. Surveying the northeast skyline, check out Mount Hoffmann, glacier-dominated Mount Conness, and jagged Matterhorn Peak. The rugged and scenic mountains south of Sonora Pass sprawl to the north.

29 | TUOLUMNE RIVER AND POOPENAUT VALLEY

Distance: 2.8 miles round trip
Hiking time: 3–4 hours
High point: 3500 feet
Elevation gain: 1300 feet
Difficulty: Strenuous
Season: Year-round
Map: USGS Hetch Hetchy Reservoir
Nearest campground: Carlon Campground
Information: Yosemite National Park

This challenging hike features myriad crystalline pools for swimming and fishing, although the water is always cool because the river drains from nearby Hetch Hetchy Reservoir's cold waters. There are also plenty of granite ledges and perches for picnicking, sunning, and jumping into the river, which is safer for swimming than Preston Falls (Hike 27) downstream because this area stays flat over a large expanse. Stable knees get worked big-time during the descent, and the steep climb during the return will burn your quadriceps, take your breath away, and make you sweat. If you camp way below, you can beat the heat by escaping up the canyon in early morning.

To get there, drive to just less than 1 mile west of the Big Oak Flat Entrance Station on State Route 120. Turn north on signed and paved Evergreen Road (Road 17) and drive about 7 miles. Go right at Camp Mather onto signed, twisting but paved Hetch Hetchy Road. Stop at the park entrance station (where wilderness permits are obtained) in about 1 mile, then proceed just under 3 miles to a clockwise turn in the road. There's limited parking on the right side of the road here.

This very old trail starts across an open spread of granodiorite with manzanita and incense cedars poking through. Watch for western fence lizards doing push-ups or

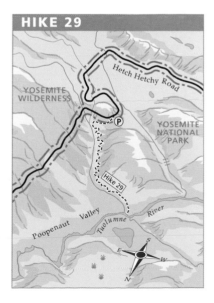

Douglas squirrels scurrying over rocks. The trail veers north and commences a steep descent past some sugar pines and white firs, which soon give way to ponderosa pines, Douglas firs, black oaks, and incense cedars. The path nears a swift seasonal creek, mellows its gradient, and leads to a large, grassy meadow at 1.1 miles.

You can traverse west through the meadow (skirt the edge of the meadow if it's wet, which is common in late winter and early spring), heading for the woodpecker-visited gray pines nestled along the base of a granitic ridge. This rocky obstruction with a lot of ledges constricts the

Granite boulders and Tuolumne River swimming hole

river, cutting a deep channel, whereas the willow-lined channel above the meadow is noticeably shallow. If you plan to fish and/or camp, it's best to start a traverse north along the meadow's edge, keeping close to the base of a granitic rise. By heading upcanyon across low ridges, you'll find plenty of camping and fishing spots. Look skyward for the red-tailed hawk patrolling for rodents, and gaze along the Tuolumne River's rocky shoreline for warblers and purple finches.

30 WAPAMA FALLS AND RANCHERIA FALLS

Distance: 13 miles round trip
Hiking time: All day or overnight
High point: 4720 feet
Elevation gain: 1500 feet
Difficulty: Moderate
Season: Year-round
Maps: USGS Lake Eleanor, USGS Hetch Hetchy Reservoir
Nearest campground: Carlon Campground
Information: Yosemite National Park

Yosemite country brims with awesome waterfalls, and Wapama Falls and Rancheria Falls fit the bill splendidly. Photogenic views abound most of the way along this route, which is highlighted by the lofty flanks of Smith Peak towering over deep and dark Hetch Hetchy Reservoir and a close encounter with obtrusive Hetch Hetchy Dome. You'll also get close enough to spit

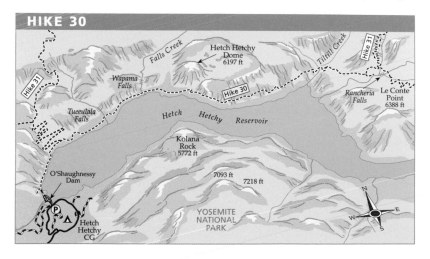

Hetch Hetchy Reservoir

down on a wild and raging section of world known as the Tuolumne River and have the chance to stare blankly at the sheer face of Kolana Rock, a huge outcrop that closely guards the mid-south segment of the 8-mile-long reservoir, which furnishes drinking water to San Francisco residents. Swimming isn't allowed, but the fishing is brisk. All told, you'll get personal with nine major Yosemite place-names, with Tueeulala Falls as a bonus from midwinter through spring.

In springtime, the trail to Rancheria Falls is among the most bountiful in wildflowers of all Yosemite trails. Because of the relatively low elevation of this journey, during hot spells it's prudent to tackle this endeavor at dawn or just past. If it's too hot, or if time and/or energy forbids, consider making Wapama Falls your destination, which makes for a 4.8-mile round-trip hike. Typically, the bridges crossing Falls Creek below Wapama Falls are closed at the height of late spring and early summer runoff. Call ahead.

To get there, drive to 1 mile west of the Big Oak Flat Entrance Station on State Route 120. Turn north on signed and paved Evergreen Road (Road 17) and travel about 7 miles. Go right at Camp Mather onto signed, twisting but paved Hetch Hetchy Road. Stop at the park entrance station (where wilderness permits are obtained) in about 1 mile, then proceed 8 miles to Hetch Hetchy Reservoir, where backpackers park in the large lot and walk 0.5 mile to O'Shaughnessy Dam. Day hikers get to use the other paved lot a few yards southwest of the dam.

Absorb the jaw-dropping views of Tuolumne River cascading into Poopenaut Valley to the west as you cross O'Shaughnessy Dam, named for the engineer who headed the controversial Hetch Hetchy Reservoir project that started in 1914. There's an obvious picturesque view of Wapama Falls and Hetch Hetchy Dome, framed by the reservoir. Cross the dam, walk through a long, cool tunnel, and then follow the worn roadbed to a trail sign 0.3 mile from the day hiker's parking lot.

A pleasing mix of gray pines, canyon live oaks, manzanita shrubs, and California bay trees accompany you along the roadbed, offering countless views of tadpole-shaped Hetch Hetchy Reservoir. Poison oak, which adorns the trailside most of the way, turns flashy crimson in fall. In springtime, purple brodiaea and bright farewell-to-spring wildflowers keep showing up in little patches. Spring and early summer wildflowers dominate soon after turning right at 1 mile onto the trail signed for Rancheria Falls. The slender and rocky path leads in and out of colorful dells laced with native bunchgrasses, mariposa lilies, white flowering yampah, and yarrow.

Tueeulala Falls at 1.5 miles tumbles over the trail. Expect to get wet feet early in the season as you admire the heavy flow of white, frothy water streaming over granite. But by mid-June the falls and its feeder creek are often bone dry. Proceed along the trail, which passes over an exfoliating granitic nose, gaining a vista at 1.9 miles for an inaugural sighting of Wapama Falls.

Reach Wapama Falls at 2.4 miles, where a long rivulet of white water crashes over the stark canyon lip high above, then drops in bounding leaps over monstrous boulders. Sniff the cool mist of the falls as you cross on a series of steel bridges. Past the falls, the trail heads up around the base of a sheer bulge of striated and glacier-polished granite filtered with canyon live oak and occasional, scrubby mountain mahogany. Bay and wild grape vines thrive in the shady spots. Imposing Hetch Hetchy Dome looms to the left, and soon your path descends to the live oak and ponderosa pine–dotted gorge sliced by Tiltill Creek. Cross two bridges and climb via tight switchbacks, eventually emerging in gray pine and manzanita chaparral.

At 5.2 miles, cross a stream and climb steadily for 0.5 mile to hear and see Rancheria Creek, where water slides and pools invite a frolic, especially if you're sweaty. An unsigned trail forks to the right at 6 miles and leads to a stately grove of incense cedars and pines at a campsite. There are a lot of bears here, so store all your food in a canister. From here, there's a grand view up the shady canyon of Rancheria Falls. Back on the main trail, a bridge spans Rancheria Creek just above the falls at 6.5 miles.

31

HETCH HETCHY TO LAKE VERNON AND TILTILL VALLEY

Distance: 30-mile loop
Hiking time: 3–4 days
High point: 7700 feet
Elevation gain: 3800 feet
Difficulty: Moderate
Season: May to November
Maps: USGS Hetch Hetchy Reservoir, USGS Kibbie Lake, USGS Tiltill Mountain, USGS Lake Eleanor
Nearest campground: Carlon Campground
Information: Yosemite National Park

Get wide open views of scenic and shapely Hetch Hetchy Reservoir, climb to tree-lined Laurel Lake and rock-encased, subalpine Lake Vernon, and stroll through verdant green fields on this varied journey. For fantastic wildflowers, visit this lower elevation area with a high country feel in May and early June. Both lakes are touted for their abundance of rainbow trout and good swimming. The climax of the route features a bench-to-bench traverse just

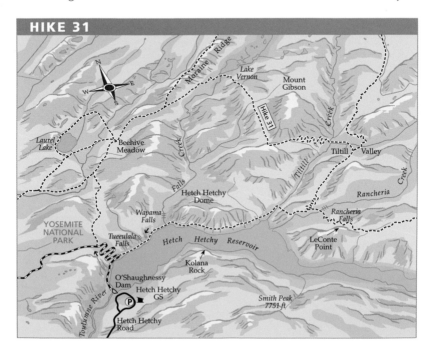

HIKE 31

Hetch Hetchy Reservoir and Kolana Rock

above the dark and clear waters of Hetch Hetchy Reservoir, furnishing changing vistas of Hetch Hetchy Valley. This is an ideal early season backpack loop when higher areas are still covered with snow and the two waterfalls roaring into the reservoir are full and powerful. See the information on bears in the "Wilderness Ethics" section of the Introduction.

To get there, drive to 1 mile west of the Big Oak Flat Entrance Station on State Route 120. Turn north on signed and paved Evergreen Road (Road 17) and travel about 7 miles. Go right at Camp Mather onto signed, twisting but paved Hetch Hetchy Road. Stop at the park entrance station (where wilderness permits are obtained) in about 1 mile, then proceed 8 miles to Hetch Hetchy Reservoir, where backpackers park in the large lot and walk 0.5 mile to O'Shaughnessy Dam. Day hikers get to use the other paved lot a few yards southwest of the dam.

Check out the views of Tuolumne River cascading into Poopenaut Valley to the west as you cross the 200-yard-long dam. You may see a flock of acrobatic swallows and/or bats swooping in and out of a low-lit, drippy tunnel that spans 500 feet. Back in 1938, when the original dam was raised 85 feet, crews blasted through solid granite to make the tunnel you're passing through.

Continue along the level road, which is decorated by canyon live oak, California bay, bigleaf maple, gray pine, Douglas fir, and whiteleaf manzanita. California wild grape, shiny poison oak, and dainty giant chain ferns thrive in the shady seeps and were harvested here by the Miwok Indians. In late spring, tiny trickles of water pour from cracks in the rocks to boost buttercups, columbines, and monkeyflowers. If it's May, perhaps you'll witness the migration of brown-and-orange California newts slithering over the trail in large numbers.

At 1.5 miles from the backpacker's parking lot, reach a solid rusted sign at a trail junction, where you go left on the old roadbed and climb steeply along lengthy but mostly shaded switchbacks, eased by improving views behind you of Le Conte Point and the Grand Canyon of the Tuolumne River. Reach a junction at 3.6 miles with the path to Miguel Meadow. Stay right (north) and climb beneath ponderosa and sugar pines and fragrant incense cedars and soon get to a level stretch that winds through manzanita chaparral, where you'll need to watch alertly for rock ducks that keep you on the trail.

Reenter forest and keep ascending, passing a pair of small meadows that are emerald green in the spring and highlighted by white meadow foam and yellow monkeyflowers. Stay right at another junction at 6.5 miles, then reach a soggy meadow called Beehive within 1 mile, where a couple of good campsites exist. The trail to Laurel Lake takes off here for a mere 1.3-mile-long rolling traverse west. You're apt to enjoy a night of privacy at this often overlooked, rather large lake.

Back at Beehive Meadow, head northeast and soon gain Moraine Ridge, and then drop down a rocky slope to enter Lake Vernon basin. Look for the faint trail 3.5 miles from Beehive Meadow that leads you to shallow Lake Vernon. Several campsites exist, mostly on exposed, flat rock slabs that make hanging your food away from bears challenging.

Some three dozen switchbacks of climbing take you away from the lake, but the views keep improving with each gasp. The views vanish some 700 feet in elevation above the lake in a small hanging valley laden with red firs. The trail gently descends into a long meadow 2.3 miles from Lake Vernon, where a grove of aspens provide leaves for deer to munch in summer.

The trail departs the meadow and climbs up to a crest, where you promptly descend along the brushy hillside and eventually reach Tiltill Creek 3.5 miles from Lake Vernon. Along the west bank at the crossing sits a nice campsite under incense cedars and ponderosa pines. A cluster of mortar holes in bedrock where the Miwok Indians ground their acorn meal is located nearby beneath towering black oak trees.

The trail lingers close to the base of Tiltill Valley's lofty north wall once past the creek. After 0.5 mile, the trail turns south and crosses a seasonally soggy meadow. When it's dry, the meadow sports tall native bunchgrasses that harbor rodents and rattlesnakes.

The trail heads south in Tiltill Valley to the base of steep bluffs, then passes a lush stand of alders, willows, quaking aspens, mountain dogwood trees, and American dogwood shrubs shading thimbleberry, lady fern, and currant. Skirt a dinky pond sporting pond lilies and lined with spring blooming western azaleas. Descend via switchbacks through chaparral to the trail junction with Rancheria Falls (see Hike 30) some 25 miles into the journey. Turn right and follow Hike 30 in reverse to the trailhead.

32 KIBBIE RIDGE AND MIGUEL MEADOW VIA LAKE ELEANOR

Distance: 3 miles round trip to Kibbie Ridge; 5 miles round trip to Miguel Meadow
Hiking time: 2 days
High point: 5300 feet
Elevation gain: 800 feet
Difficulty: Easy to moderate
Season: March through November
Map: USGS Lake Eleanor
Nearest campground: Cherry Valley Campground
Information: Stanislaus National Forest; Yosemite National Park

The northwest corner of Yosemite National Park is a seldom-explored wild land of profuse rock and ample native foliage. Here's a rarely accomplished journey where you can stroll to and then spend a therapeutic, solitary night at spacious and shapely Lake Eleanor, and then take two contrasting but easy day hikes.

No question though, emerald blue, 27,000 acre Lake Eleanor is the highlight. With its generous shoreline, rocky outlet creek, and series of short spur paths, this deep, swimming and fishing lake should be rightly

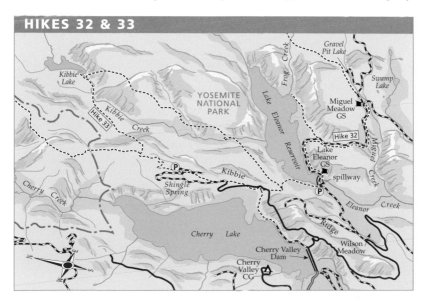

HIKES 32 & 33

considered a retreat. The existing lake was raised 35 feet by the city of San Francisco in 1918 to form a reservoir. The best seasons to visit this low-elevation area are spring and fall.

To get there, take Cherry Lake Road from State Route 120, about 13 miles east of Groveland. Although paved and very scenic, it's narrow and it twists for 24 slow miles to Cherry Lake. Drive across Cherry Valley Dam and proceed right on a decent dirt road. Go right again after 1 mile, then left after another mile at forks. At 1 mile farther, stay straight and proceed to the free parking in the gravel lot after a total of 5 miles of dirt-road driving.

Follow the dirt road trail 0.3 mile south to Lake Eleanor's curving spillway, a 60-foot-high concrete dam where numerous large logs are trapped (viewable from the dam's walkway). By using the middle of the spillway as a vantage point, you can look down on Eleanor Creek way below and absorb the dense greenery that clothes an otherwise rugged ridge across the lake. The backpack campground is nestled beneath trees at the east end of the spillway. A rocky spur trail leads down to cascading Eleanor Creek, where a soul can spend a lot of quality hang time sitting in its many pools.

The first and easiest day hike leads west from the west end of the spillway on a good trail that ascends moderately about 300 feet in elevation to access Kibbie Ridge. The climb is mostly shaded by black oak, incense cedars, ponderosa pines, and canyon live oak, with an understory of manzanita and mountain misery. The ridge is reached in just over 1 mile, where you wander

Lake Eleanor

on it a ways just to snag the clearest views of Cherry Lake sprawling to the west and Lake Eleanor to the east, revealing whitecaps when the breezes kick up. You can continue northward to reach Kibbie Lake (see Hike 33).

Day hike option number two takes off from the eastern end of the spillway and gently climbs 600 feet in elevation over a 2.5-mile span to Miguel Meadow, which is golden brown come autumn. The route stays in mostly shaded forest of oak and pine. The edge of forest and meadow is where you're apt to hear and see the most birds, including mountain chickadees, dark-eyed juncos, warblers, and purple finches. Expect company from golden-mantled ground squirrels and yellow pine chipmunks.

33 | CHERRY LAKE TO KIBBIE LAKE

Distance: 8 miles round trip
Hiking time: 5–8 hours
High point: 6800 feet
Elevation gain: 1200 feet
Difficulty: Moderate
Season: April through October
Map: USGS Lake Eleanor
Nearest campground: Cherry Valley Campground
Information: Stanislaus National Forest; Yosemite
    National Park
See map page 107

This rhythmic and peaceful stroll takes you through deep forest to isolated, granite-bound but shallow Kibbie Lake, where the swimming is comfortable and the fishing is relaxing. Tucked in the far northwest corner of Yosemite National Park, Kibbie Lake is sometimes free of people on cool spring or fall weekends. Therefore, that's the best time to be alone, avoid the mosquitoes, and beat the summer heat.

The 106-acre Kibbie Lake, named for a pioneer who established small cabins in the north Yosemite backcountry, is bounded on the west by gently sloping granite, and the east shore is epitomized by steep, broken bluffs. The sandy bottom is algae-coated, which sports a good population of California newts, and helps give the lake, along with the surrounding conifers, a greenish glow. Kibbie Lake is a mini-version of its neighbor, the much deeper Cherry Lake, which features good fishing and a fine campground just west of it, and also merits a visit.

Kibbie Lake has seen a dramatic increase in visitation, with frequent crowding on summer weekends. Because of the impact from this use, fires are no longer permitted within 0.25 mile of the lake. Hikers often get lost on the roads to the trailhead, so call ahead.

Cherry Lake

To get there, take Cherry Lake Road from State Route 120, about 13 miles east of Groveland. Although paved and very scenic, it's narrow and it twists for 24 slow miles to Cherry Lake. Drive across Cherry Valley Dam and continue north on decent dirt roads. After 0.5 mile, go left (north) at a junction, go up then down, and pass several signed trail junctions that you can ignore until you reach the one indicating the way to the Kibbie Ridge Trail. Park for free near a corral, some 4 miles from Cherry Valley Dam.

A slim path climbs northeast to the nearby Kibbie Ridge Trail. Visit Shingle Spring, a mere 100 yards down from the main trail, where graceful dogwoods take center stage and a few shaded camps exist. Steady climbing ensues on the main trail heading north, then eventually going east into cool and densely forested Deadhorse Gulch. At 1.3 miles, reach a small, grass-lined pond and then turn right onto the trail signed for Kibbie Lake.

Just below an open ridge, you walk through a flowery ground cover of mat lupine, brodiaea (eaten by the Miwok Indians), and buckwheat. Enter a chaparral belt lightly treed with Jeffrey pines, and soon reach the canyon bottom occupied by white firs and lodgepole pines. Yampah, violet, bleeding heart, bracken fern, and shooting star flourish in the shadows here.

Climb out of the forest onto granite slabs dappled with huckleberry oak shrubs to the saddle at 3 miles. Descend to and then follow the smooth green pools highlighting Kibbie Creek along with western azalea and willow shrubs. An ascent over blasted granitic ledges ensues, where you follow rock ducks past lagoons to labrador tea–lined Kibbie Lake.

Facing page: Mono Lake

EMIGRANT AND HOOVER WILDERNESS AREAS

34 | PINECREST LAKE

Distance: 4-mile loop
Hiking time: 2 hours
High point: 5600 feet
Elevation gain: 400 feet
Difficulty: Easy
Season: Year-round
Map: USGS Pinecrest
Nearest campground: Pinecrest Lake Campground
Information: Stanislaus National Forest, Summit
Ranger District

Trace the rugged and scenic shoreline of gently curving and deep Pinecrest Lake and see a wide variety of native plants and birds on this ideal and mostly remote family outing. This shapely, 1.5-mile long picturesque lake features three huge granite outcrops that are plainly visible from most places along the shoreline. This popular fishing lake is very busy on summer weekends and is jammed on Memorial Day and Labor Day.

To get there, head northeast from the town of Sonora on State Route 108 toward Sonora Pass. At the Pinecrest Lake turnoff, turn right onto signed Pinecrest Lake Road at the ranger station and continue on the paved

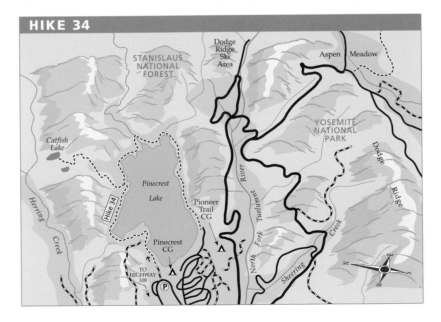

Pinecrest Lake

road for 1 mile. Park for free at the large, paved parking area on the western shore of the lake.

The journey will be filled with solitude in due time, but first you must take the trail past the waterfront dock and some cabins, heading clockwise. Your eyes will feast on the tempting, swimming lake that shimmers in the breeze as you wander in mostly open forest that adorns the banks. Walk under ponderosa pines, incense cedars, and canyon live oaks, and past colonies of mountain misery ground cover and huckleberry oak and manzanita shrubs. In sunny spots, admire the lupines and paintbrush flowers.

At 0.4 mile, reach the first granite outcrop, where the path twists along boulders wedged in the ground and continues around the bulky mass to a grand, photogenic view of the lake and the second granite outcrop punctuating Pinecrest Lake's eastern edge. There are several flat rocks at 0.6 mile for sunning and picnicking, with great views across the water. At 1 mile, a slender path veers to the left and goes 0.75 mile to shallow and small Catfish Lake surrounded by old-growth forest—a nice way to extend your trip by 1.5 miles.

At 1.9 miles, reach the far eastern shore and Pinecrest Lake's inlet, which is the South Fork Stanislaus River. The trail now negotiates the second granite outcrop. Bird life abounds in the area where outcrop and river meet the lake. Look and listen for woodpeckers, Steller's jays, white-crowned sparrows, juncos, and kingfishers.

Linger along this eastern shore as long as possible, for the solitude is blissful. Eventually, continue along the shoreline trail that reaches the final granite outcrop at 2.7 miles, where more picnic spots exist. The shoreline trail becomes paved through the campground and continues that way back to your car.

35 | KENNEDY MEADOW TO RELIEF RESERVOIR

Distance: 6.5 miles round trip
Hiking time: 3–5 hours
High point: 7200 feet
Elevation gain: 1200 feet
Difficulty: Moderate
Season: May through October
Map: USGS Sonora Pass
Nearest campground: Baker Campground
Information: Stanislaus National Forest, Summit
Ranger District

Take a view-filled journey to the western edge of Emigrant Wilderness to a vista of nearly 2-mile-long Relief Reservoir. It's a short scramble down to this long and narrow, sky blue lake, which features superb trout fishing and is part of Summit Creek. Wide, meandering, and swift Middle Fork Stanislaus River is nearby for the first third of the way, featuring plenty of swimming and fishing holes and gentle current strips for brief floats on your back. Its banks are lined with black cottonwoods, willows, and alders.

Because this trail is popular with horses and kids, you'll attain more

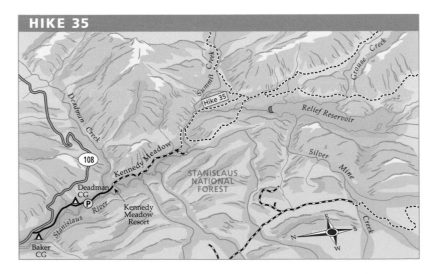

HIKE 35

solitude by going on weekdays or on September and October weekends after Labor Day.

To get there, drive northeast from Sonora toward Sonora Pass on State Route 108 past the towns of Strawberry and Dardanelle. Just beyond the village of Douglas, 5.5 miles southeast of Dardanelle, turn right into Baker

White fir in winter

Campground onto paved Kennedy Meadow Road. Go 1.1 miles, passing an initial trailhead for backpackers after 0.5 mile. Day hikers should continue to Kennedy Meadow Resort and park for free in the designated public parking area next to Middle Fork Stanislaus River.

Pass a gate and climb gently in a dense forest, mainly of incense cedar and Jeffrey pine, but also some sugar pines, Sierra junipers, and white firs. Cross a small ridge to broad Kennedy Meadow, where the trail, lined with sagebrush, manzanita, and goldenrods, offers sweeping views of these grasslands. Reach a sign marking the boundary of Emigrant Wilderness at 1.1 miles and cross a sturdy footbridge 0.2 mile farther, crossing the Middle Fork Stanislaus River. There are spots to visit the river here.

The route, now a trail blasted out of the granite, takes you up the gradually narrowing canyon as the views improve along the base of a granite dome. The forest gets sparse as the views down on Middle Fork Stanislaus River increase. In late spring, look for several precipitous cascades near the union of Summit Creek and stony Kennedy Creek. Spring and early summer cascades highlight the crossing of Summit Creek via a footbridge.

Keep climbing beneath sharp-edged cliffs and past canyon live oak, Sierra junipers, sagebrush, and occasional elderberry bushes and mules ears to a junction with the Kennedy Lake Trail, which veers to the left. Go right and reach a fantastic viewpoint of Relief Reservoir 0.5 mile farther, passing a PG&E dam maintenance station along the way. For more views of this large lake, continue climbing south on a good trail. Otherwise, sit on your sweatshirt (if it's cool enough), take out your binoculars, and look for ducks cruising the lake or red-tailed hawks hunting overhead. It's a steep but worthwhile 0.3-mile-long descent to the water's edge.

36 | SAINT MARYS PASS TO SONORA PEAK

Distance: 5 miles round trip
Hiking time: 4 hours
High point: 11,460 feet
Elevation gain: 2000 feet
Difficulty: Strenuous
Season: July through October
Map: USGS Sonora Pass
Nearest campground: Baker Campground
Information: Stanislaus National Forest, Summit Ranger District

At 11,459 feet tall, bulky and brownish Sonora Peak is the highest mountain north of Tower Peak in Yosemite National Park and south of Mount

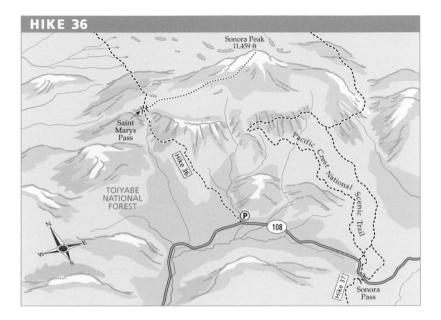

Shasta. Although ascending this volcanic peak is no cakewalk, it's still one of the easiest peaks over 11,000 feet to climb in California.

This is a land of windswept and scrubby whitebark pines, profuse and low-growing summer wildflowers, and loose brown cinders. It's a stark and harsh environment, where the mouselike pikas leave round droppings on rocks and noisy Clark's nutcrackers and colorful Cassin's finches flutter about.

Expect to encounter snow patches into August and frequent lightning storms during late afternoons in summer. It's best to do this hike early in the day, wear sunglasses, bring a lot of water, and carry a windbreaker.

To get there, drive over Sonora Pass, which is 16 miles west of State Route 395 on SR 108. Continue 0.8 mile northwest down Highway 108 to a road sign indicating Saint Marys trailhead. Park for free on the shoulder of SR 108.

Pass a boundary sign for the Carson-Iceberg Wilderness and ascend through an open forest of lodgepole pines and fragrant, gray sagebrush. Assorted patches of corn lily, fragrant mountain pennyroyal, and Brewers lupine add color splashes. When the grade steepens, look for mules ears, scarlet gilia, and paintbrush flowers, as picturesque whitebark pines replace the lodgepoles.

Reach a saddle called Saint Marys Pass at 1.2 miles. At 10,400 feet in elevation, you'll enjoy a photogenic panorama, highlighted by The Dardanelles to the northwest. This pass was part of the first pioneer trail spanning this region, and it went to the Clark Fork of the Stanislaus River.

A handful of scant footpaths wander east to the top of Sonora Peak, but it's basically a cross-country pick-and-choose route that follows the ridgeline upward. The incline is abrupt and the terrain is rugged, eased by the presence of mid- and late-summer wildflowers, including lupine, alpine buckwheat, and monkeyflower.

Get to the top of the first knoll at 1.8 miles, descend a bit, and then ascend across a broad expanse of scree to the final, nearly vertical slope of Sonora Peak's summit. From here, contour left and gain the ridgeline just above, then traipse on it toward the summit on the right. Though steep, footing is secure. Reach the summit at 2.5 miles, pull out a good map of the region, and identify several prominent peaks, such as Leavitt Peak to the south and Mount Lyell in Yosemite National Park farther south.

37 | SONORA PASS AND PACIFIC CREST TRAIL

Distance: 9 miles round trip
Hiking time: 5–6 hours
High point: 10,840 feet
Elevation gain: 1500 feet
Difficulty: Moderate to strenuous
Season: July through October
Map: USGS Sonora Pass
Nearest campground: Baker Campground
Information: Toiyabe National Forest, Bridgeport
Ranger District

Stroll a high ridge where the air is thin and the panoramas are plentiful. This is another photogenic segment of the Pacific Crest Trail, where the subjects are the brownish, volcanic mountains neighboring Sonora Peak, and the grayish, granitic mountains of the north Yosemite National Park high country.

At 9626 feet in elevation, Sonora Pass, your starting point, is second highest to Yosemite National Park's Tioga Pass of all highway crossings in the extensive Sierras. This also means that spacious snowfields often linger into July, making footing treacherous in some steep places, so call ahead. This is a land of wide open spaces, stunted and bushlike whitebark pines, and a variety of summer wildflowers. Bring a windbreaker and plenty of water, and wear sunglasses, a wide-brimmed hat, and sunblock.

To get there, drive 16 miles west on State Route 108 from U.S. Highway 395. Spot the sign just west of Sonora Pass indicating the Sonora Pass

Facing page: Sonora Peak

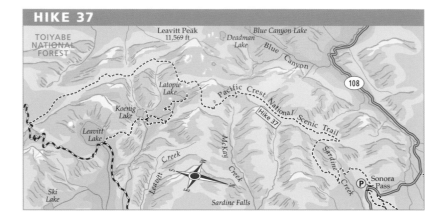

Trailhead. There are toilet facilities here as well as ample free parking. Climb gently about 150 yards back along SR 108 to reach the signed trailhead on the south side of the road.

Ascend briefly, then drop a bit across a sunny slope awash in lupine, blue flax, and mountain pennyroyal. Later, yarrow, pussypaw, and alpine monkeyflower join those native wildflowers to add more charm to the trail, which was an old wagon road opened to pack animals in 1862 and completed as part of the Pacific Crest Trail in 1977.

Look east, down on a slender waterfall, and soon cross a handful of consecutive gullies—your only sure water sources of the trek. As you pant while climbing the mountainside, note the improving views, especially of Stanislaus Peak and Sonora Peak (Hike 36) to the north, the West Walker River canyon to the east, and Peak 10,641 to the southwest.

Note during the climb that the two-needled lodgepole pines are quickly being replaced by the five-needled-to-a-bunch and squatty whitebark pines that epitomize harsh winters. At 2.3 miles gain the ridgeline and breathe easy, for the brunt of the ascent is done. Now's the time to savor the panoramas of seemingly endless mountains and the colorful mix of wildflowers, including alpine gold, rock fringe, and penstemon.

Reach a saddle at 3.8 miles, where Sardine Meadow (Hike 38) sprawls to the east below. Descend mildly as you skirt across the open mountainside, then make a final but brief climb to journey's end at 4.5 miles, an impressive saddle standing at 10,800 feet. Lewitt Peak towers to the west. A trio of deep blue lakes glistens below to the east: Latopie Lake, Koenig Lake, and the larger Leavitt Lake (Hike 39), sitting a bit farther to the southeast. If the breezes are brisk, there are a lot of large rocks to snuggle behind to gaze at Tower Peak to the south in Yosemite National Park. This trail goes there, if you're backpacking. See Hike 70 in reverse.

Facing page: View east from Leavitt Peak

38 | SARDINE MEADOW TO SARDINE FALLS

Distance: 2 miles round trip
Hiking time: 2–3 hours
High point: 9200 feet
Elevation gain: 400 feet
Difficulty: Easy to moderate
Season: Mid-May through October
Maps: USGS Sonora Pass, USGS Pickel Meadow
Nearest campground: Leavitt Meadow Campground
Information: Toiyabe National Forest, Bridgeport
      Ranger District

Traipse across a flower-dotted, high mountain meadow en route to little-known Sardine Falls. Short and easy hikes with a lot of visual highlights are always great for children—this one fills the bill. This journey also features open views of sprawling, gray and brown mountaintops and ridges that hem this basin that features enticing and meandering McKay Creek. Plan on three or four creek wades in May and June. If you're coming in May, call ahead to be sure State Route 108 is free of snow and open.

To get there, drive SR 108 some 2.7 miles east of Sonora Pass or 14 miles west of U.S. Highway 395. Pull off onto the shoulder of the highway and park for free when you notice Sardine Meadow on the south side of the road.

Ten yards wide and 20 yards long in late spring, Sardine Falls can be seen from the road, past Sardine Meadow and beneath the snowy, north-facing flanks of Leavitt Peak (Hike 37). The trail begins as an old dirt road (closed to vehicles) that splits the meadow, which is adorned with yellow prim-rose monkey—flower, blue gentian, scarlet gilia, and white yarrow. Watch also for wild iris and lupine. Wade Sardine Creek and begin a steady but mostly gentle climb along the west banks of McKay Creek amid scattered lodgepole pines.

At 0.6 mile, check out a series of cascades streaming over exfoliating, rusted rock slabs. As the meadow narrows, ranger buttons, mountain pennyroyal, larkspurs, and corn lilies show up. Climbing eases at

Monkeyflowers and Leavitt Peak

0.8 mile, at a bench laced with willows and quaking aspens that line swirling and colorful McKay Creek. By now you can hear the roar and crash of Sardine Falls, and in another 0.2 mile, you're at its base, which is dominated by huge rocks. A torrent of white, frothy water tumbles down a sheer vertical rock cliff, contrasting wildly with the dark rock wall.

If you came from US 395, consider the short drive to Sonora Pass, which features spectacular views.

39 | LEAVITT LAKE

Distance: 6 miles round trip
Hiking time: 3–5 hours
High point: 9600 feet
Elevation gain: 1200 feet
Difficulty: Moderate
Season: June through October
Map: USGS Pickel Meadow
Nearest campground: Leavitt Meadow Campground
Information: Toiyabe National Forest, Bridgeport
    Ranger District

Here's a little-known, secluded hike to a scenic, subalpine lake encased by brownish mountains that hold snow on their north faces through July.

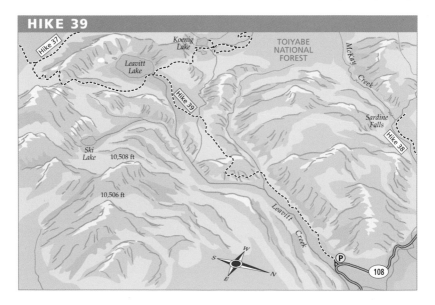

HIKE 39

Aspen leaves

Rounded and large Leavitt Lake is known for trout fishing, but it's also photogenic and makes an ideal destination for an early evening stroll around its rocky shore.

Your route is actually a bumpy, dirt, very rough, old road still used occasionally to access remote mining claims. The climb is moderate but relentless the whole way, but the views of high mountains accompany you across a volcanic and wild wonderland. Be forewarned: it's possible to get passed by an ORV during the hike.

To get there, drive 13 miles on State Route 108 from U.S. Highway 395. Forest Service Road 077 (your trailhead) is signed on the left, but it is hard to see from the winding road. It's approximately 5 miles east of Sonora Pass, at a hairpin turn. Park for free in the small dirt clearing. The hike starts by going around the brown gate nearby.

There are superb views right off of the desertlike, smooth, and whitish mountains stretching north to south beyond US 395. At first you'll be traipsing past an odd mix of drought-tolerant Sierra junipers and riparian quaking aspens, both with gorgeous trunks. Soon, this trailside scene is replaced with more open forest consisting of lodgepole pines, mountain mahogany, and sagebrush.

This scenario continues the whole way, as you climb steadily on the east side of the canyon, down low and just above slender Leavitt Creek, which features a rust-colored, rocky bottom. You cross it at 1 mile and again at 2 miles into the journey. Straight-ahead views of the shoulders of Peak 10,850 and Peak 10,866 tempt you to keep climbing. These brownish peaks reflect their ominous faces over Leavitt Lake when winds are calm. Nearby Leavitt Peak (Hike 37) is visible above the Leavitt Creek canyon from turnouts along Highway 108.

Your trail intersects with the Pacific Crest Trail at Leavitt Lake, furnishing the most direct route into Emigrant Basin.

40 | LEAVITT MEADOW AND WEST WALKER RIVER

Distance: Up to 18 miles round trip
Hiking time: All day or overnight backpack trip
High point: 8500 feet
Elevation gain: 1400 feet
Difficulty: Moderate
Season: June through October
Maps: USGS Pickel Meadow, USGS Tower Peak
Nearest campground: Leavitt Meadow Campground
Information: Toiyabe National Forest, Bridgeport
Ranger District

The spirited West Walker River swirls, crashes, and meanders down one of the grandest canyons just outside of Yosemite National Park on Forest Service land. This remote journey gets you up close and personal with this well-known fishing river along a stretch of it that's not so known and actually quite wild and view-filled.

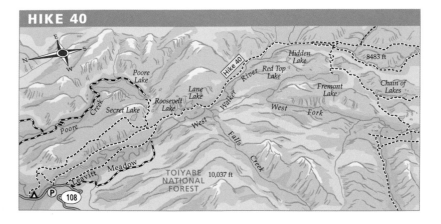

West Walker River and Forsyth Peak

The trip starts in and above lovely and long Leavitt Meadow, and it stays near the river most of the way, passing several rock-rimmed swimming holes. The views of mighty Forsyth Peak within Yosemite National Park are frequent, and the steady ascent never gets steep. As described, the trip visits five high-mountain lakes. For the ambitious with more time, this route provides ideal access to the Pacific Crest Trail and the upper, northerly regions of Yosemite National Park, a mere 5 miles away from this hike's destination, Fremont Lake. See the first two-thirds of Hike 70 in reverse for an ultimate car-shuttle hike through Yosemite National Park high country.

To get there, from north of Bridgeport on U.S. Highway 395, head west onto Sonora Pass State Route 108. Reach the Mountain Warfare Training Center after 3.6 miles, and continue to Leavitt Meadow Campground's backpacker's area to park for free, 7.2 miles from US 395.

Cross a metal bridge spanning the West Walker River and ascend briefly on the trail to a junction at 0.3 mile. Go right onto the West Walker River Trail on a dry, sagebrush-covered low slope. The trail drops to spacious Leavitt Meadow, where the river canyon ahead frames an awesome view of 11,180-foot-tall Forsyth Peak, which sometimes holds snow into September on its steep north face.

Mountain mahogany, relished by residing mule deer, pokes above the sagebrush as you ascend gently, taking in views down on the river. Pass Leavitt Meadow and a pond at 2.2 miles, then note the trail on the left—it leads 0.5 mile to long and curvaceous Poore Lake, worth visiting on the return trip, along with neighboring Secret Lake.

The main trail promptly climbs gently to Jeffrey pine-dotted and algae-bottomed Roosevelt Lake, where campsites can be set up on the west side. The trail heads over a granite shoulder to Lane Lake, a clone of Roosevelt Lake, then soon levels along a strip of quaking aspen groves, which often shimmer in the late-afternoon wind.

The trail drops to the willow-lined river at 3.4 miles, where you climb mildly for 0.25 mile in a shaded forest of aspens, cottonwoods, and mixed conifers. The climb steepens as the trail swings away from the river and gets rocky and dusty. The trail climbs to a saddle adorned with Jeffrey pines and Sierra junipers and opens to another vista of the upper reaches of West Walker River capped by Forsyth Peak. Pass the signed junction with Red Top Lakes and continue the moderate climb along the scenic east bank of the river, where swimming and fishing holes abound. The river often erupts into mini waterfalls and cascades over white granite flecked with black spots as it makes its way through this area that's hemmed in by the metavolcanic canyon walls of yellow, red, gray, and black.

The trail to Fremont Lake likely involves a log crossing of the river to reach the abundant campsites on the west side. The signed Fremont Lake Trail starts just downstream. Climb to a saddle featuring fine views of Tower Peak in Yosemite National Park. Descend to Fremont Lake at 9 miles, where lodgepole pines and junipers dominate. Fish for eastern brook and rainbow trout and consider a layover day, where you can explore nearby Chain of Lakes, Long Lakes, and the Pacific Crest Trail.

41 | PICKEL MEADOW

Distance: Up to 5-mile loop
Hiking time: 3–4 hours
High point: 6760 feet
Elevation gain: 100 feet
Difficulty: Easy
Season: Year-round, especially snowshoe season
Map: USGS Pickel Meadow
Nearest campground: Leavitt Meadow Campground
Information: Toiyabe National Forest; Bridgeport
Ranger District

An otherwise ordinary area transforms into an enchanted land when snow covers it. Families in snowshoes or on cross-country skis frolic along this simple route around the edges of expansive Pickel Meadow, making a few detours to its middle to admire the pure, rushing waters of meandering West Walker River.

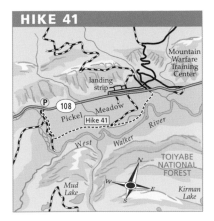

Something's bound to be at its peak, no matter what time in winter you visit. It could be a heavier than normal snowpack tightly hemming the curving banks of the West Walker River. Or it could be a thin coating of snow, interspersed with frozen native bunchgrasses, dormant but heaving. Or perhaps it's the swollen, gleaming orange clusters of willows, standing naked in late winter with their new leaf buds about to burst.

Because there's a substantial river flowing through the meadow, with

Pickel Meadow and willows

colonies of willows in the middle and patches of forest on the edges, this route is ideal for spotting wildlife. If you're quiet and still, maybe a wily coyote will trot along an edge of a clearing. Porcupines sometimes cling to the main trunks of conifers, high up. The great horned owl resembles a big squatting cat, camouflaged in the evergreen boughs. Mountain chickadees flit in the low limbs while Steller's jays squawk and rustle loudly in the branches. Deer herds come out late in the afternoon.

Novice snowshoers can let their guard down in the flat expanse of Pickel Meadow, while the more accomplished snowshoer can delve into the forest edges and explore the banks of the West Walker River a mere 0.25 mile away. Customizing wanderings to fit your fancy is easy here.

To get there, drive north of Bridgeport on Highway 395. Turn west onto Sonora Pass Highway 108. Reach the Mountain Warfare Training Center after 3.6 miles, which is generally as far as Caltrans plows the highway in heavy snow seasons. But chances are you can drive another 1.3 miles to park for free near the locked gate that closes the highway. Just park alongside the highway as conditions allow.

Stroll into Pickel Meadow and let your heart's desires dictate the route. If you can find a safe way to cross gorgeous West Walker River at the west end of the meadow, you can explore 1 mile or so up scenic Poore Creek before terrain gets steeper. This can add another 2 miles to the trip. Photo opportunities abound in this meadow that's rimmed by snow-clad ridges rising some 1500 feet above it, especially when the sun partially sinks behind the mountains in late afternoon, casting dramatic shadows across the meadow.

42 | BARNEY LAKE, PEELER LAKE, AND KERRICK MEADOW

Distance: 22.5-mile partial loop; 8.4-mile round trip for Barney Lake
Hiking time: 2–3 days; 5–6 hours for Barney Lake
High point: 10,100 feet
Elevation gain: 4100 feet
Difficulty: Moderate to strenuous
Season: July through October
Maps: USGS Twin Lakes, USGS Matterhorn Peak
Nearest campground: Mono Village Campground
Information: Toiyabe National Forest; Bridgeport Ranger District; Yosemite National Park

Here's one of those visual-highlight-package hikes, where hikers have the opportunity to admire flowers along Robinson Creek, visit granite-ringed Barney Lake, explore a subalpine meadow, and swim or fish in up to six gorgeous lakes. This trek to Barney Lake will be shared with a few folks, especially on weekends, but the spectacular, rocky country beyond features scenic seclusion.

To get there, from the town of Bridgeport on U.S. Highway 395, turn southwest onto signed Twin Lakes Road and drive about 13 miles, passing Twin Lakes to Mono Village Campground. Park inside the village for $5.

Traipse through the camping area, following signs for Barney Lake. Reach an old fire road and promptly go right on the signed Barney Lake Trail in a quiet forest of Jeffrey pines, Sierra junipers, white firs, and aspens. The high-pitched purr of Robinson Creek accompanies you on a gentle climb past open areas sprinkled with sagebrush and mules ears. Reach beaver ponds lined by aspens and the Hoover Wilderness sign at 2.7 miles, where there's a premium view to the south of rugged Little Slide Canyon.

The contrasting aromas of wild rose and mountain pennyroyal accompany you on an ardent climb away from Robinson Creek, eased by views behind you of Twin Lakes. The final ascent consists of several switchbacks over a granite slope, then a brief entry into cool forest before reaching 14-acre Barney Lake at 4.2 miles. With a sandy beach for wading and for viewing 11,346-foot-tall Crown Point, Barney Lake at 8290 feet in elevation makes for a prime picnic spot. There are beautiful campsites among junipers above the lake's east side.

Pressing on, alternate between open, rocky sections and light forest dominated by graceful mountain hemlocks in a switchbacking climb to a trail junction at 6.3 miles, where you head right. In another 0.7 mile of climbing along the now slim Robinson Creek, you reach 0.5-mile-long Peeler Lake, which is jammed into the lower flanks of Crown Point to the southeast and Cirque Mountain to the northeast. The deep azure lake is engulfed in glaciated and frost-shattered granite and features several

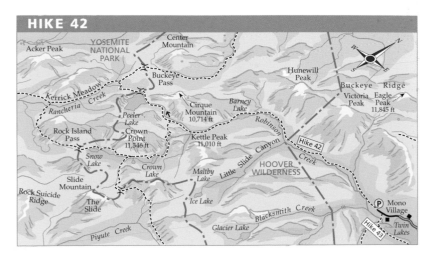

HIKE 42

intimate campsites nestled a safe distance along the north shore, beneath clumps of conifers. Granodiorite boulders block the outlet.

Past the lake, the trail climbs gently to a granitic bench littered with wind-sculpted, dwarfed lodgepole pines and occasional ocean spray shrubs. A brief descent leads into Yosemite National Park and you soon reach pocket meadows sprinkled with sedges and bilberry, which flashes in crimson come

Robinson Creek

late September. The theme continues into spreading, 1.5-mile-long Kerrick Meadow, at 8.2 miles, where photogenic, meandering Rancheria Creek accompanies you. Bear left at a signed trail fork, cross the creek at 9.7 miles, and commence a moderate, 1.5-mile-long climb to Rock Island Pass. Make a point to capture a twilight view from this scenic pass of jagged Kettle Peak rising above shapely Snow Lake. This is a superb area for spending the night.

It's all downhill from here, past rock-littered Snow Lake, equally scenic Crown Lake, and finally to a signed trail fork, where you veer right back to Barney Lake.

43 | TWIN LAKES

Distance: Up to 9.5-mile loop
Hiking time: 4–6 hours
High point: 7200 feet
Elevation gain: 200 feet
Difficulty: Easy
Season: December through March
Map: USGS Twin Lakes
Nearest campground: Twin Lakes Campground
Information: Toiyabe National Forest; Bridgeport
    Ranger District

This matching pair of deep and attractive lakes transforms into a tranquil and remote wonderland when snow-covered in winter. Filled with folks

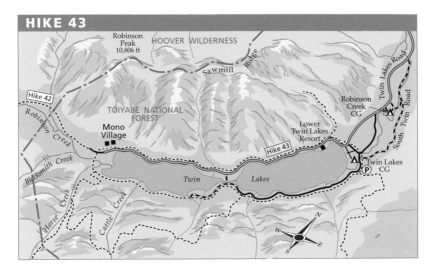

HIKE 43

Crater Crest and Twin Lake

all summer, this lightly forested shoreline route is scenic and pleasant the whole way, and it's ideal for novice snowshoers and cross-country skiers. Dramatic peaks rise suddenly above the lakes in all directions but east, some towering up to 4000 vertical feet with snow pockets gouged into the rocky crannies.

Blue grouse hide in the bushes while Steller's jays squawk in the lower conifer limbs. Look for the gray-crowned rosy finch flitting in the pines or a wily coyote sneaking along the lake's edge. The scattered trees and shrubbery and the open lakes offer ideal patrolling grounds for red-tailed hawks. Try to spot animal tracks, such as those of the long-tailed weasel, on the snow in the open areas.

You can trudge along the southern shore for up to 4.5 miles and retrace your steps, especially if snow levels are low enough. The trip can be reduced to a 4-mile loop in heavy snow by circumnavigating the lower lake. Since the course is predictable and easy to follow, it can be negotiated while snow is falling or if the skies are low overcast.

To get there, from the town of Bridgeport on U.S. Highway 395, turn southwest onto signed Twin Lakes Road. After 9.5 miles on this paved road, reach the left turn onto South Twin Road. Mono County periodically plows this road a short ways, so park for free on the side of the road or at the end of the plowed section as conditions allow.

Cross-country ski or snowshoe along the extension of the roadway across the bridge over rust- and orange-bottomed Robinson Creek and glide through Twin Lakes Campground. Stroll slowly along the east end of Lower Twin Lake and check out the jagged peaks forming Sawtooth Ridge to the southwest. Sagebrush is the dominant plant in open areas, while tall specimens of Jeffrey pines outnumber white firs and the occasional Sierra juniper.

Angle clockwise around the south shore of Lower Twin Lake. The stark visage of Robinson Peak to the northwest opens up as you wind westward, and 2 miles into the journey, 11,732-foot-tall Victoria Peak farther west rules the landscape, backed with Hunewill Peak. Matterhorn Peak and Crater Crest to the east take center stage from the north shores.

44 | HOOVER, GREEN, AND WEST LAKES

Distance: 16 miles round trip; 10 miles round trip for
  Hoover Lakes; 4 miles round trip for Frog Lakes
Hiking time: 10 hours or 2 days
High point: 11,110 feet
Elevation gain: 3200 feet
Difficulty: Strenuous
Season: July through October
Maps: USGS Dunderberg Peak, USGS Matterhorn Peak
Nearest campground: Trumbull Lake Campground
Information: Hoover Wilderness

Dunderberg Peak looks like a crumbling castle, its reddish flanks guarding a large colony of lakes all above 9000 feet in elevation. This journey swings

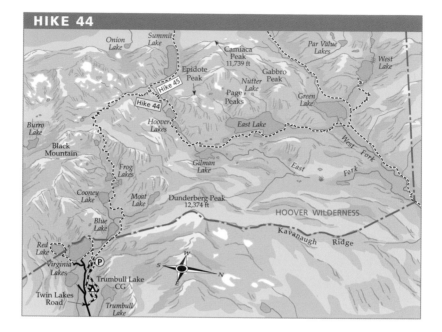

around and beneath this metamorphic, 12,374-foot-tall mountain so you can visit a dozen swimming and fishing lakes while taking in the barren and ever-changing visages of the ominous peak.

The easternmost Sierra peaks bordering Yosemite National Park are particularly laden with lakes, and this hike is the best way to get a good feel of what these photogenic lakes are all about. Hoover and Gilman Lakes in the middle of the trip offer the most privacy. Of the two, Gilman Lake is the best bet for camping because it has more trees and offers more privacy owing to its location off the main trail. This way, you can day-hike to East, Green, and West Lakes.

To get there, drive U.S. Highway 395 to Conway Summit north of Mono Lake, and take Virginia Lakes Road west for 6 miles. Follow signs for Virginia Lakes trailhead beyond Trumbull Lake Campground, and park for free in the large lot.

The trail starts with a gentle climb around the north shores of Virginia Lake and smaller, aspen-lined Blue Lake in open, semi-desert scenery featuring rabbitbrush and sagebrush. The rocky landscape includes gray granite ridges and the contrasting reddish Dunderberg Peak hovering to the north. Aptly named Black Mountain adds more color to the south.

The ascent intensifies beyond Blue Lake in a light forest of lodgepole and western white pines. Pass an old miner's cabin at 1 mile, then come to photogenic Cooney Lake 0.4 mile farther. By hiking around the lake to the talus on the southwest shore, you can capture an ideal view of Dunderberg

Peak across the shimmering lake. A great view east across the lake can be had from the granite outcrop above the western edge of the lake. The trail flattens out as it crosses a stream and winds through a meadowy basin, at 2 miles, that holds small but attractive Frog Lakes, named for the once numerous mountain yellow-legged frogs.

Steep switchbacks up the canyon ensue, and if it's early to midsummer, there may be lingering snowfields. The easily weathered, mineral-rich, water-retaining metavolcanic soil here supports profuse summer wildflowers, such as sulfur flower, penstemon, and alpine gold. Reach a broad, flat, and rocky bench perched below the western flanks of Black Mountain, known as Burro Pass, at 3.5 miles. From this 11,110-foot-high vantage point, stare at sky blue Summit Lake lying on a shelf below and stacks of Yosemite National Park peaks just to the west. Descend via switchbacks past wind-stunted whitebark pines, heading right at a trail fork at 4.6 miles.

The Green Creek Trail promptly leads down to a superb overlook down to the tree-scant Hoover Lakes, then over orange, cobbly schist around the north shore of larger, upper Hoover Lake. Carefully cross the sometimes slippery Gilman Lake inlet and head for Gilman Lake at 5.5 miles, which is situated in a pocket to the east. At 0.3 mile farther along Green Creek Trail, photogenic and tiny Nutter Lake is decorated by a smooth rock outcrop. The lake is framed by red mountain heather and the bright red Sierra bilberry in fall. A bit farther lies spacious East Lake, with its man made dam. Gabbro Peak reflects in its azure waters.

Dunderberg Peak and Cooney Lake

Descend in a lodgepole pine forest to reach Green Lake's log-strewn outlet. Traverse west through forest 0.2 mile on a trail to the scenic north shore of Green Lake, then climb via switchbacks 1.2 miles to isolated, view-filled West Lake.

45 | VIRGINIA LAKES TO SUMMIT LAKE AND MILLER LAKE

Distance: 26 miles round trip; 9.8 miles round trip for Summit Lake; 4 miles round trip for Frog Lakes
Hiking time: 3 days
High point: 11,110 feet
Elevation gain: 4300 feet
Difficulty: Strenuous
Season: July through October
Maps: USGS Dunderberg Peak, USGS Matterhorn Peak
Nearest campground: Trumbull Lake Campground
Information: Yosemite National Park; Hoover Wilderness

Visual highlights will be on constant overload on this trip as you visit four high-mountain lakes right off and then climb to a view displaying most of Yosemite National Park. A pleasant ramble takes you down into the park via Virginia Canyon. The views are so special in both directions during

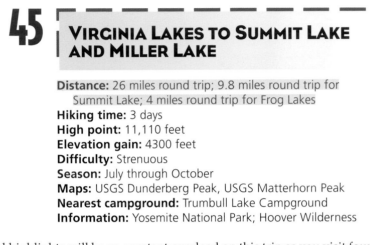
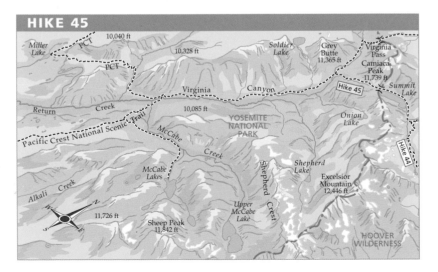

Facing page: Blue Lake

most of this ambitious journey that you will look forward to retracing your steps to enjoy them again from different vantage points.

Lush Virginia Canyon is the easiest to reach, classic, glacier-smoothed subalpine gorge in Yosemite country. Sunset views from unsheltered, whitebark pine–dotted Summit Lake can be dramatic, and that's enough reason to spend two nights there in order to day-hike into Virginia Canyon and perhaps go all the way to Miller Lake for a swim in its shallow waters.

To get there, follow the trail description for the first 4.6 miles of Hike 44, Hoover, Green, and West Lakes. At the trail fork at 4.6 miles, bear left.

Dip your feet in the brooks meandering through a lush meadow of alpine timothy grass, purple-mist grass, paintbrush, and monkeyflowers, then climb near Summit Lake's outlet stream. You soon reach pristine Summit Lake, elevation 10,205, which usually isn't crowded even on busy weekends. There are good campsites behind you, beneath the mountain hemlocks. Trace the shore of sagebrush and reed-grass-lined Summit Lake, watching for ground squirrels, and quickly gain Summit Pass at the park boundary.

Descend gradually into Virginia Canyon past tall lodgepole pines and fragrant sagebrush. One mile from Summit Lake, turn left at the trail junction and head into remote Virginia Canyon, promptly cross Return Creek, and then traipse carefree in a lodgepole pine forest for nearly 4 miles of virtually flat trekking. A trail leads left to McCabe Lakes, which are tucked beneath the rocky flanks of Shepherd Crest and Sheep Peak—the dramatic crags that have captured your attention for quite a while. Your trail continues right for a final 3-mile climb to Miller Lake, or you can turn back anytime.

46 | VIRGINIA LAKES

Distance: Varies; 8–14 miles round trip
Hiking time: 6–9 hours
High point: 9780 feet
Elevation gain: 1500 feet
Difficulty: Moderate
Season: December through March
Maps: USGS Dunderberg, USGS Lundy
Nearest campground: Lundy Lake Campground
Information: Toiyabe National Forest; Bridgeport Ranger District

A scattering of quaking aspens, with their bare limbs and white trunks getting ever brighter above a sunlit snow layer, presents an overwhelming scene on this serene and isolated route. On the way in to these subalpine lakes, the stark, snow-clad easternmost Sierra peaks and ridges greet you head on, punctuating the broad canyon bottom.

Make a steadfast but mostly mellow ascent along snow-covered Virginia Lakes Road to a cluster of frozen-solid, small lakes. The pleasant scenery along most of the easy-to-follow course is wide open, desert-motif terrain, where fragrant sagebrush dominates and is sometimes packed in white during periods of heavy snowfall. The dramatic backdrops of Black Mountain and Dunderberg Peak make for superb photos from the lakes. Because of exposed terrain and extra-high elevation, this snowshoe or cross-country ski trip should be canceled when foul weather and heavy winds kick up.

To get there, drive to Conway Summit on U.S. Highway 395, which is 12 miles north of Lee Vining and 13 miles south of Bridgeport. Turn west on signed Virginia Lakes Road and follow it to the snow line, then park on the side of the road for free. Mono County often plows the road almost all the way to the lakes in early spring, which allows cross-country skiers and snowshoers to venture farther up the Virginia Lakes canyon to explore gorgeous Cooney and Frog Lakes.

Follow the bending, gently to moderately climbing road, as it displays views to the northeast of Bridgeport Valley fronting the Sweetwater Mountains, south of Lee Vining Peak and to the west of Dunderberg Peak. Pass through typical eastside Sierra vegetation, mainly sagebrush and dead-looking (but alive) rabbitbrush amid scattered lodgepole pines and sporadic clusters of aspens.

Approach Virginia Creek at 1.5 miles and continue climbing a good ways above the north side of the stream. Pines and aspens fill in the scene more and more as Dunderberg Peak looms larger past the junction with Dunderberg Meadow Road. Stay on Virginia Lakes Road past cabins to the largest of the Virginia Lakes at 5.7 miles. Open but rugged slopes rise up to 11,797-foot-tall Black Mountain to the southwest, making this lake scene dramatic. From here, Blue Lake is a mere 0.25 mile to the northwest, with Cooney and Frog Lakes just beyond.

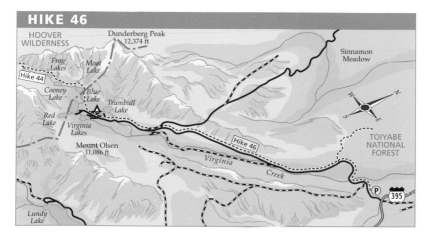

HIKE 46

Dunderberg Peak

47 | LUNDY CANYON TO 20 LAKES BASIN

Distance: 14 miles round trip; 4–10 miles round trip
for Lundy Canyon
Hiking time: All day or overnight
High point: 10,900 feet
Elevation gain: 3100 feet
Difficulty: Moderate to strenuous
Season: July through October and snowshoe season
Map: USGS Dunderberg Peak
Nearest campground: Lundy Lake Campground
Information: Inyo National Forest; Bridgeport
Ranger District

A view-filled area, 20 Lakes Basin is a mostly flat highland of few trees
and plenty of rock punctuated by a cluster of small lakes that reflect stark

visages of nearby stalwart peaks in their crystal-clear waters. Your mission is to explore all of them and pick your favorites. Although it's shorter and less strenuous to get here via huge Saddlebag Lake (Hike 55), you'd miss out on frolicking in gorgeous Lundy Canyon, which is lush with summer wildflowers and dominated by steep canyons and numerous waterfalls. You could always start from Saddlebag Lake and have a car shuttle arranged at Lundy Lake.

Snowshoeing up Lundy Canyon in wintertime is exhilarating. Fishing the lakes is relaxing, and swimming is refreshing on warm summer afternoons.

To get there, travel U.S. Highway 395 some 18 miles south of Bridgeport to the junction with State Route 167. Turn west on the paved road signed for Lundy Lake and reach the lake at 2.1 miles. Drive around the lake, then continue on a bumpy road for 1 mile to the trailhead, and park for free near the pit toilets and past the resort.

Head up Lundy Canyon on a mild grade past a long array of white-trunked quaking aspens adorning Mill Creek. Admire a steep wall that sports a waterfall, and soon cross a pair of side streams. Pass a pond and continue in a light forest of red fir, lodgepole pine, and more aspen. You soon reach a large clearing at 1.1 miles where waterfalls tumble down the cliffs on both sides of the canyons. Perennial bunchgrasses, yarrows, columbines, and monkeyflowers grace this opening.

As you continue along the bottom of the canyon, pause often to gaze northeast at Mount Olsen, north for ominous Black Mountain, and northwest for 12,446-foot-tall Excelsior Mountain. Climbing intensifies at the head of Lundy Canyon, where snowdrifts often linger along the snaking trail through midsummer and should be negotiated carefully.

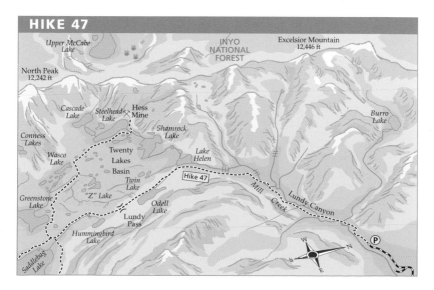

HIKE 47

Lundy Canyon and sulfur buckwheat

Lake Helen's outlet stream, a branch of Mill Creek, flows over solid rock in spots during the final 0.5-mile climb. The stream finally rushes through a narrow slot and then you reach Lake Helen at 4.7 miles. From this high basin, views to the west unfold rapidly. North Peak rises above a permanent snowfield and Mount Conness shades Conness Glacier just behind it.

Occasionally the trail system circumnavigating the numerous lakes in 20 Lakes Basin is hard to discern, but most of the time a trail isn't really necessary. Negotiate your way in a west, then south, counterclockwise direction and soon reach Shamrock and Steelhead Lakes, the region's largest of the small lakes at 10,300 feet elevation. Enchanting Shamrock Lake is deep and features scenic rock islands. Campsites are located an environmentally safe distance from the lakes, but campfires are not allowed here or in Lundy Canyon.

Grassy patches, slender beaches, and rock slabs for jumping into the lakes abound, as well as summer wildflowers such as paintbrush, ranger buttons, monkeyflowers, corn lilies, and alpine goldenrod. Be sure to stroll the lakeshores to gain the best views of North Peak and Conness Peak towering above them. Blocked and unblocked mines are situated among the lakes.

48 | LUNDY LAKE TO ONEIDA LAKE

Distance: 9 miles round trip
Hiking time: 5–7 hours
High point: 9700 feet
Elevation gain: 2000 feet
Difficulty: Moderate
Season: June through October and snowshoeing season
Maps: USGS Lundy, USGS Dunderberg
Nearest campground: Lundy Lake Campground
Information: Toiyabe National Forest; Inyo National Forest

Hike or backpack to a quartet of high-mountain lakes tucked into a confined cleft and capped with towering peaks reaching up to 2000 feet above. Along the way, discover a bit of California mining history. This is also an ambitious and gorgeous snowshoe trip in winter, but call ahead for trailhead accessibility and avalanche conditions.

To get there, travel U.S. Highway 395 some 18 miles south of Bridgeport to the junction with State Route 167. Turn west on the road signed for Lundy Lake and continue 2.1 miles to the closed gate just before Lundy Lake, and park for free near the restrooms.

To begin, stroll to the Lundy Lake dam and beach, where splendid photo opportunities await. Commence a steady and moderate climb on the slim, dirt, mining-road trail above the south shores of Lundy Lake. Pass by an

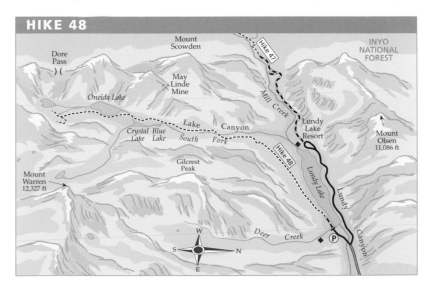

Lundy Lake, looking west

extensive colony of quaking aspens, then note how the route weaves in and out of desert chaparral that includes mountain mahogany, sagebrush, tobacco brush, and currant. The abundant summer wildflowers include mules ears, sulfur buckwheat, rabbitbrush, and fragrant mountain penny-royal. You'll pass through occasional moist seeps where deciduous shrubs, including elderberry, chokecherry, and willows, thrive. Over the first mile especially, constant views of snow-clad, metamorphic mountains loom over long and lean, gray-green Lundy Lake. Orange-colored, 11,086-foot-high Mount Olsen dominates to the northwest, and the tip of aptly named Black Mountain juts behind it. The sheer north face of Mount Scowden frowns at you from the west.

As the route abruptly veers south into Lake Canyon at 1.2 miles, you enter a forest of western white pine and red fir. The steady climb continues up this view-filled canyon, as you cross South Fork Creek at 2.3 miles beneath lodgepole pines. The terrain now alternates between conifer forests and open meadow areas. When the road levels, wander east to briefly check out tiny Blue Lake, at 3.3 miles, set in an open basin near the bottom of steep canyon walls.

A bit farther along the route, you reach a Y in the mining-road trail. Take the left branch, which promptly leads to narrow Crystal Lake perched beneath sensational, steep cliffs. Scout the mining equipment and dilapidated structures scattered around the basin. Ore cars, rock walls, and huge tubs are among the extensive artifacts.

Back on the main road-trail, make a brief climb past a pile of tailings to the actual mine and take a set of tracks that still lead into an old, boarded-up shaft. Pick and choose your way from here to large and lovely Oneida Lake. Rolling terrain, sprawling beyond the far shore, climaxes with the stark and steep canyon walls of the Tioga Crest, which forms a spectacular backdrop to the frozen expanse of rectangle-shaped Oneida Lake at 3.9 miles. An indistinct but easy-to-follow trail continues around the east shore of Oneida Lake and then heads up to a nearby, scenic and secluded lake that marks the headwaters of South Fork Mill Creek.

49 | BLACK POINT

Distance: 3 miles round trip
Hiking time: 2–3 hours
High point: 7000 feet
Elevation gain: 600 feet
Difficulty: Strenuous
Season: March through November
Map: Mono Lake Tufa State Reserve brochure
Nearest campground: Lundy Lake Campground
Information: Mono Lake Scenic Area Visitor Center

Climb what is said to be earth's only fully exposed underwater volcano and peer into several 15-yard-deep fissures atop cinder- and ash-covered Black Point. As a bonus, the views you get after this tough climb are priceless. From the Black Point summit, Mono Lake, Mono Craters, the Mammoth Area Mountains, and the steep and stark easternmost 12,000- and

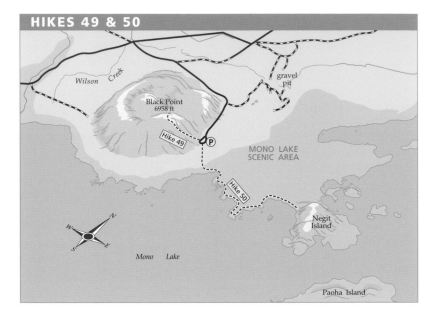

13,000-foot-tall mountains of Yosemite National Park are very photogenic.

The climb and the price you pay in effort and dealing with potentially challenging elements is steep. Each footstep during the incessant ascent sinks and slips a smidgeon in cinder and ash. This remote trek is treeless, which means a windbreaker, water, sunblock, sunglasses, and hat are essential.

To get there, from U.S. Highway 395 some 5 miles north of Lee Vining, take the paved road east that's signed for the county park. Drive 3.4 miles (the road soon becomes a decent dirt road), then turn right onto another dirt road signed for Black Point. Go 3 miles to road's end at the lot signed for Black Point, and park for free.

There's no need for a path, so just choose and pant your way up Black Point's east face to the top, pausing often to gasp from breathlessness and in admiration for the desertlike Bodie Hills to the north and ancient Anchorite Hills to the east. It's a glorious panorama at the top. The imposing bulks of Mount Dana, Mount Gibbs, and Mount Lewis dominate the southwest. Below to the southeast, Mono Lake, which has no outlet, looms large and displays two contrasting islands. The black island, which the local Kuzedika Indians named Negit, meaning "blue-winged goose," erupted about 1700 years ago. The Kuzedika called the white island Paoha, meaning "spirits of the mist," and it erupted about 250 years ago.

From the top, wander southwest to find the fissures, which are only a

Facing page: Mono Lake from base of Black Point

couple of feet wide. Note the layers of tufa, ash, and sediment inside them. When Black Point, a cinder cone, erupted about 13,000 years ago, the lava and cinders cooled quickly and hardened, and then the top split open to form several hundred-yard-long cracks.

Back at the trailhead, consider doing part of Hike 50 (North Mono Lake Beach), an easy, view-filled stroll. Treat yourself to a cleansing swim in ancient and sky blue Mono Lake, where you'll float effortlessly because of its extremely high salt content.

50 | NORTH MONO LAKE BEACH

Distance: Up to 10 miles round trip
Hiking time: 2–6 hours
High point: 6400 feet
Elevation gain: 100 feet
Difficulty: Easy
Season: March through November
Map: Mono Lake Tufa State Reserve brochure
Nearest campground: Lundy Lake Campground
Information: Mono Lake Scenic Area Visitor Center
See map page 148

Here's a view-filled, remote hike where a soul can get lost in a daydream while walking in rhythm to the often loud and choppy waves of Mono Lake and the noisy accompaniment of screeching gulls. The treeless setting is active with ducking, diving, and darting water birds, especially California gulls, eared grebes, phalaropes, and snowy plovers.

Although Mono Lake's salty and alkaline water is inhospitable to most creatures, the few species that thrive here are found in astronomical numbers, and they're easy prey for the birds. The alkali flies are so numerous, you can stand in a muddy flat and be literally engulfed by them, yet none will touch you. Feeding on algae and actually capable of swimming in the lake to lay their eggs, these tiny flies aren't attracted to you at all. The local Kuzedika Piute Indians ate the flies in their pupa stage. Trillions of 0.5-inch-long brine shrimp join the flies in feasting on the bountiful algae along water's edge.

As is the case with all fully exposed and therefore shadeless areas, sunblock, sunglasses, and a hat are essential. A windbreaker protects you from wind gusts. You'll see several craggy tufa castles from afar. Explore a city of these calcium towers by taking Hike 52, Mono Lake Tufa Castles and Navy Beach.

To get there, from U.S. Highway 395 some 5 miles north of Lee Vining, take the paved road east that's signed for the county park. Drive 3.4 miles (the road soon becomes a decent dirt road), then turn right onto another dirt road signed for Black Point. Go 3 miles to the road's end at the lot signed for Black Point, and park for free.

Traipse 0.3 mile straight to Mono Lake. Pass through rabbitbrush and sagebrush on the way to the beach, which features stands of alkali seepweed and salt grass. Head northeast and at 1.2 miles reach a slender peninsula with close-up views of large Paoha Island and cinder Negit Island with gray-brown Mono Craters beyond Mono Lake to the south.

At 2 miles, reach pure white flats, where you could throw a stone to Negit Island, if only there were any to throw. As you continue strolling, now in a northerly direction, consider temporarily departing the beach to spend a couple of miles a bit higher in the cinder dunes. For prime photos, it's best to be near water's edge on the return trip. The steep, vertical escarpments of Yosemite National Park's easternmost mountains plunge dramatically to meet a desert transition zone. Stretching from north to south, you can identify Lee Vining Peak, Mount Dana, Mount Gibbs, and Mount Lewis. A swim in Mono Lake, one of America's oldest lakes at more than 700,000 years, is an unforgettable adventure. The salt content is so heavy that you can float motionless on it.

Mono Lake and tufa castles

51 | BURGERS ANIMAL SANCTUARY

Distance: Up to 6 miles round trip
Hiking time: 3–5 hours
High point: 8550 feet
Elevation gain: 1300 feet
Difficulty: Moderate
Season: December through March
Map: USGS Mount Dana
Nearest campground: Lee Vining Creek Campground
Information: Inyo National Forest; Bridgeport Ranger District

Mount Dana and Mount Gibbs, two of Yosemite National Park's most recognizable tall mountains, are prominently displayed throughout most of this snowshoe or cross-country ski route that encompasses a variety of eastern Sierra environments. View these picturesque peaks past quaking aspen groves, low sagebrush, large boulder outcrops, or lush vegetation along a scenic creek.

The climb is steady but gentle, and chances are you'll enjoy the area all to yourself. The course follows the obvious, snow-covered road all the way, so routefinding is simple and staying with the route when it snows is doable. You may have to lug snowshoes a short distance if snow is scant.

The uncommon pinyon pine is common on this route. Admire these shrubby, gray-green pines, they're the only ones around featuring single needles. Bighorn sheep have been relocated to this general vicinity, so look for their pointed, deerlike tracks in the snow.

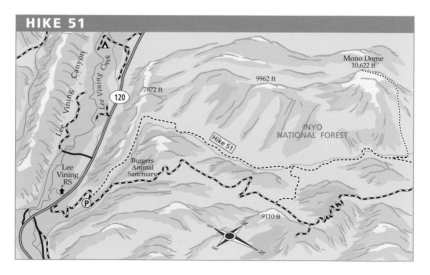

Mount Dana and Mount Gibbs

To get there, drive U.S. Highway 395 just south of Lee Vining. Turn west on Tioga Road (State Route 120), drive for 1.2 miles, and turn right on Log Cabin Road. If conditions permit, you can drive a short distance up to the shoreline and park for free on the side of the road. Otherwise, park for free in the Forest Service Ranger Station lot across the highway.

The route begins with a moderate grade as it heads up a sagebrush-covered and pinyon pine–dotted slope. The views alternate between part of spacious Mono Lake to the east and rugged Mount Gibbs, Koip Crest, and 13,057-foot-tall Mount Dana to the southwest. At 0.8 mile from the highway, reach a road fork. Going right takes you some 3 miles to an awesome view of Mono Lake, but this course veers left and heads straight toward the picturesque east face of the High Sierra and Mono Dome.

Several signs along the way tell you the history of Burgers Animal Sanctuary. The grade mellows as the trail passes along a willow-lined creek. The road bends sharply to the north around a rock cliff at 1.6 miles, and the views of Mounts Gibbs and Dana vanish. Promptly enter an extensive grove of quaking aspen called Robins Grove. Arrive at the cabins of the sanctuary 0.5 mile farther, where signs tell you of the fauna and flora seen in this region.

Trudge into a moderate forest of fir, pine, and aspen as the snow-covered trail parallels a lushly vegetated creek. Reach an old dam across the creek—as good a place as any to turn around. But from here, you can proceed up the road for another couple of bends, then pick and choose the safest cross-country route steeply up view-filled Mono Dome, which features direct views of Mounts Gibbs and Dana.

52 | MONO LAKE TUFA CASTLES AND NAVY BEACH

Distance: 2–7 miles round trip
Hiking time: 2-4 hours
High point: 6400 feet
Elevation gain: 100 feet
Difficulty: Easy
Season: March through November
Map: Mono Lake Tufa State Reserve brochure
Nearest campground: June Lake Campground
Information: Mono Lake Tufa State Reserve

A visit to the tufa castles that colonize a southern shoreline segment of huge Mono Lake is like being on another planet. These oddly contorted gray spires are incredible examples of what nature can do with only a couple of basic elements. The carbonates of salty Mono Lake water mesh with the calcium of freshwater springs to gradually form these extraordinary-looking knobs and spires. The limestone towers here at South Tufa are between 200 and 900 years old and ceased growing after the lake level dropped below them.

Strolling Navy Beach just east of the castles is an extraordinary experience, like being on the ocean's edge, except the views are of waves of cinder cones, volcanic craters, jagged granitic mountains, and reddish metamorphic mountains off in the distance.

To get there, drive east on State Route 120 from U.S. Highway 395, some 5 miles south of Lee Vining. After 5 miles, turn north onto a good dirt road signed for the tufa castles. Travel 1 mile, then park in the large lot near the bathrooms. A fee is charged. Note that although you can sometimes get here in winter, SR 120 east of US 395 is not plowed of snow, so call ahead.

Take the mile-long trail in a clockwise direction. The surface starts off paved, then changes to wood, and finally converts to dirt as you weave around the clusters of tufa castles. When you're surrounded by them, it's like being in the middle of a sci-fi dream city. Several native shrubs occupy thickets around the castles, especially green rabbitbrush, big sagebrush,

Facing page: Mono Lake tufa castles at Navy Beach

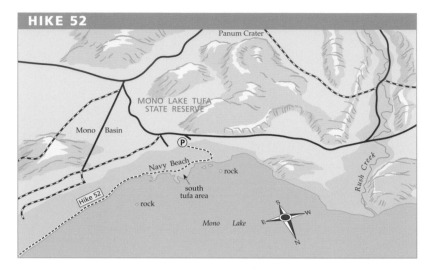

and caterpillar greasewood. Come in July and August to photograph the profusion of yellow flowers.

Numerous informative signboards explain scientific facts about the zillions of alkali flies all over that avoid you, the plethora of miniscule brine shrimp that the multitudes of water birds easily devour, and the tufa castles themselves. From points on Mono Lake's ever-curving sandy shoreline, tufa towers joined together look like bizarre islands dominated by minarets.

Just before the loop path winds away from Mono Lake, a clearing offers easy access to Navy Beach. Take it and leave the crowds behind for ultimate solitude. Walk in rhythm to the dancing miniwaves that lap quietly over the soft shore edge. The low vegetation just inland includes alkali seepweed, salt grass, and Russian thistle. Out across the lake, shapely Paoha Island sits invitingly. With a wilderness permit and a canoe, you can paddle out to and spend a quiet night under the stars on volcanic Paoha Island's beach.

When you're ready to return to the tufa castles from Navy Beach, admire the east-facing escarpments of several prominent mountain placenames within Yosemite National Park, including Mount Dana, Mount Gibbs, Mount Lewis, and Koip Peak.

Facing page: Mount Dana

TIOGA ROAD: SADDLEBAG LAKE WEST TO TUOLUMNE MEADOWS

53 | ELLERY LAKE

Distance: 2.2 miles round trip
Hiking time: 2 hours
High point: 9523 feet
Elevation gain: 300 feet
Difficulty: Easy to moderate
Season: May into November
Map: USGS Tioga Pass
Nearest campground: Ellery Lake Campground
Information: Inyo National Forest

Because of the multicolored peaks and ridges that tower over elegant Ellery Lake, the clear water displays extraordinary, photogenic reflections during sunrises and sunsets. The metamorphic rock outcrops surrounding this well-shaped lake furnish a flush of color no matter where you are on the hike, but they also make negotiating the route a challenge since there is no true trail. Avid fishermen have patterned scant paths that disappear and reappear, and they're all you need. Tioga Peak to the north and Peak 11,582 just above to the south share your attention throughout.

Since State Route 120 is so close, and Ellery Lake is crammed with tourists

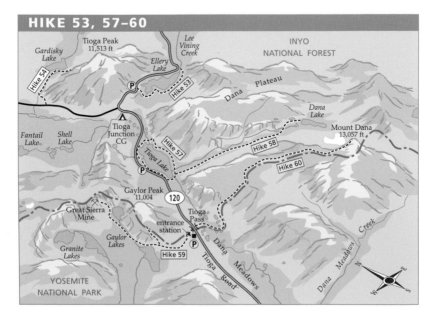

HIKE 53, 57–60

Willows and lodgepole pines at Ellery Lake

on summer weekends, this hike is best taken instead on a weekday before Memorial Day or after Labor Day. Consider doing it in early morning or at twilight, when traffic noise is sparse and dramatic shadows are cast across the lake. Another idea is to hike this lake and then stroll around Tioga Lake located a mile or so up the highway.

To get there, drive SR 120 west from U.S. Highway 395 just south of Lee Vining for 10 miles, then park for free in the Ellery Lake Campground lot.

Admire rust- and orange-bottomed Lee Vining Creek as you head south around one of many colorful rock outcrops as Ellery Lake disappears for a bit. Many of these rock outcrops form peninsulas that punctuate the contorted shoreline. Willows adorn the numerous waterways and lodgepole pines and occasional Sierra junipers occupy the forest strands. Trek along a steep, red talus slope on the shore at 0.8 mile and stare across the lake at reddish brown Tioga Peak (see Hike 54). Continue east beneath the chalky white incline of Peak 11,582 to the spillway at 1.1 miles. Turn around here and retrace your route of ups and downs, where you get to see entirely different views, such as White Mountain and North Peak to the southwest.

54 | GARDISKY LAKE AND TIOGA PEAK

Distance: 4.4 miles round trip
Hiking time: 4–5 hours
High point: 11,513 feet
Elevation gain: 1800 feet
Difficulty: Strenuous
Season: July through October
Maps: USGS Dunderberg Peak, USGS Tioga Pass
Nearest campground: Sawmill Campground
Information: Inyo National Forest; Bridgeport Ranger District

Here's a place where fierce winds whip the whitebark pines into stunted and twisted shapes and cause whitecaps to form on shallow and wide open Gardisky Lake. If the winds are calm, Gardisky Lake and Tioga Peak that guards it from the south are peaceful and secluded spots. When breezes kick in, you'll need a windbreaker and to seek shelter among the white-barks in this high country.

This is barren, sprawling country, hidden from the masses, with rocky beaches and sometimes awesome sunrises over Lee Vining Peak to the east and shimmering Gardisky Lake. The obvious cross-country route up to Tioga Peak presents unforgettable views of Mono, Saddlebag, Tioga, Gardisky, and Ellery Lakes. Fishing is typically superb at Gardisky Lake,

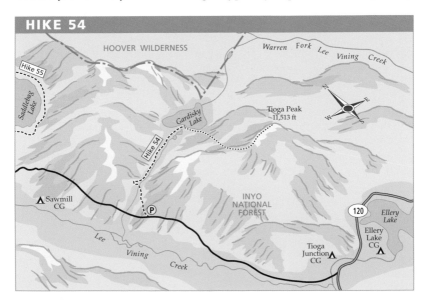

Lee Vining Peak from Gardisky Lake

especially in September and October. The steady climb on this route is relentless and lacks shade, turning this hike into a grueling, sweaty, literally
breathless task in the middle of the day during a summer heat wave. Dogs
are no longer allowed on this trail to protect the Sierra Nevada bighorn
sheep that roam here.

To get there, take State Route 120 west from its junction with U.S. Highway 395, just south of Lee Vining. Drive 10 fabulously scenic miles to just
beyond Ellery Lake, then turn north onto the unpaved road signed for
Saddlebag Lake. Drive 1.1 miles to the small, dirt lot signed for Gardisky
Lake on the west side of the road and park for free.

Cross the road and begin climbing on the trail in a lodgepole pine forest
with a gooseberry shrub understory. Straddle a slender, perennial, rocky
stream in a clearing at 0.5 mile to glimpse Mount Conness Glacier at the
boundary with Yosemite National Park to the west. Dome-shaped Mount
Dana stands to the south. The trail snakes up the willow-lined stream a
couple hundred yards, then swerves north to a wide open view at 0.7 mile
of Mount Conness and aptly named White Mountain to the west.

Reach a sloping meadow framed by whitebark pines at 0.9 mile as the
intense ascent finally eases. Arrive at the gap that holds Gardisky Lake at
1.5 miles. From here, you can safely head straight up Tioga Peak over
loose, brownish red rocks. The views are tremendous, particularly looking west over Yosemite National Park. Cathedral and Unicorn Peaks
feature crowning spires that jut into the western sky. Mount Lyell towers
to the south. The other peaks above 11,000 feet tall are too numerous to
count.

55 | SADDLEBAG LAKE TO SHAMROCK LAKE

Distance: 8.4-mile loop; 3-mile loop for Saddlebag Lake
Hiking time: 5–7 hours
High point: 10,400 feet
Elevation gain: 500 feet
Difficulty: Moderate
Season: July through October
Maps: USGS Tioga, USGS Dunderberg Peak
Nearest campground: Lee Vining Creek Campground
Information: Inyo National Forest; Bridgeport
      Ranger District

Explore a huge lake, surrounded by vibrant summer wildflowers, and then
visit a cluster of other alpine wonderland lakes on this popular hike loaded
with heavenly views of major Yosemite country place-names. This route

also puts you on the back porch of a classic cross-country course into Yosemite National Park via McCabe Lakes.

You'll wander under and near numerous high mountains that typify the ultimate eastern High Sierra backcountry. Often laden with fishermen, the many lakes can be highly populated, so escape the crowds by going on weekdays or after Labor Day. You can cut off 3 miles from the trip by taking a shuttle boat across Saddlebag Lake for a nominal fee. An amazing, nearly all downhill, one-way journey can be completed by arranging a car shuttle at the trailhead for Lundy Lake (Hike 47).

To get there, take State Route 120 west from its junction with U.S. Highway 395 just south of Lee Vining. Drive 10 fabulously scenic miles to just beyond Ellery Lake, then turn north onto the unpaved road signed for Saddlebag Lake. Drive 2.7 miles and watch for "trailhead parking" signs to the designated hiker's parking lot, then park for free.

Walk downhill toward the dam and set out on the rocky trail along the western shore of sprawling Saddlebag Lake. Stick with the upper path, for the lower one is a use trail for fishermen. Ominous Shepherd Crest to the north reflects across the lake in the early morning. An impressive variety of wildflowers adorn the crumbly, metamorphic rock slope. Metamorphic bedrock fractures into smaller pieces than granitic bedrock does, thus producing a greater water-storage capacity for wildflowers. It is also much richer in dark minerals, making for a more nutrient-rich soil. Metamorphic rocks are darker than granitic rocks, and they therefore absorb more heat, which is favored by the plants at these cool and high altitudes. Look for alpine goldenrod, ranger buttons, columbine, buckwheat, elephant heads, and paintbrush.

Stay with the trail as you ascend away from the lake and soon take in a

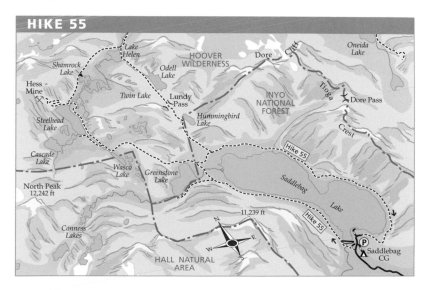

Mount Conness

lovely view of Greenstone Lake at 1.5 miles. From here until the return to Saddlebag Lake, as you progress slowly in a clockwise circle at each of these small lakes, the trail peters out and returns over and over, but routefinding is a cinch in this open country. Check out views from Greenstone Lake of Mount Conness to the south, with pointed Mount Dana protruding in the distance.

Head uphill amid lodgepole and whitebark pines via an old mining road to the entry sign for Hall Natural Area, then descend to Wasco Lake. Reach long and lean Steelhead Lake at 3.4 miles where a cross-country route veers west to McCabe Lakes. Stop for a picnic at shapely Shamrock Lake 0.5 mile to the northeast. This deep lake is highlighted with a handful of tiny rock islands.

Cross a creek lined with corn lilies and monkeyflowers, skirt along a rocky slope, pass through more whitebark pines, and then follow rock ducks to Lake Helen at 4.2 miles. The wildflowers keep appearing as you proceed past Odell Lake up to Lundy Pass. Descend through a green valley past Hummingbird Lake and soon regain sight of Saddlebag Lake. When you reach the lake, continue left along an old dirt road along the eastern shore for 1.7 miles past sagebrush to the trailhead.

56 | MINE CREEK TO FANTAIL AND SPULLER LAKES

Distance: 5.5 miles round trip; 2.4 miles round trip
    for Shell Lake
Hiking time: 3–4 hours
High point: 10,200 feet
Elevation gain: 600 feet
Difficulty: Easy to moderate
Season: July through October
Map: USGS Tioga Pass
Nearest campground: Tioga Junction Campground
Information: Inyo National Forest; Bridgeport
    Ranger District

The journey to remote and scenic Fantail and Spuller Lakes is filled with constant and staggering views of Yosemite National Park's major mountains. Summer wildflowers grace the path that follows cute Mine Creek and leads to a pair of historic mines. As bonuses, fishing and swimming in these shallow and clear lakes are refreshing pursuits. This is an ideal hike for those who want wondrous, open, high-mountain scenery on busy summer weekends while escaping the crowds.

To get there, drive 10 miles west on Tioga Road (State Route 120) from its junction near Lee Vining with U.S. Highway 395. Turn right into the Tioga Junction Campground just past Ellery Lake and northeast of the Yosemite National Park boundary. Park near the entrance to the campground across from the pit toilets and next to the plaque that tells the story of Bennettville and its mine.

HIKE 56

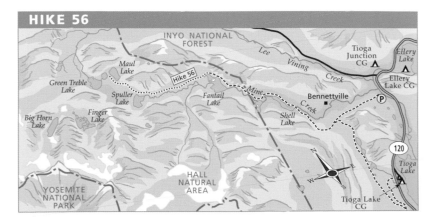

North Peak and Fantail Lake

The trail that promptly reaches Mine Creek skirts up the hillside above the campground and climbs gently but steadily along a rocky slope lined with a mix of youthful and ancient lodgepole pines. Wildflowers such as sulfur flower and nude buckwheat thrive in the dry, rocky pockets. Cross two streams and then walk above and near rushing Mine Creek. Each time you pause to catch your breath, look at red-topped Mount Dana behind you for a foretaste of what you'll see much of upon returning.

Level strolling ensues amid a riot of wildflowers, including ranger buttons, paintbrush, sulfur flower, cinquefoil, and mariposa lily. Arrive at two wooden structures at 0.9 mile called Bennettville Mine, where you can ascend stairs to a quaint loft. In 1882, some enthusiastic businessmen brought 8 tons of mining equipment to this tiny settlement called Bennettville. They hauled it via Saddlebag Lake from the nearby town of Lundy (Hike 47), but in the eight years the mine was in existence, no silver was ever harvested.

Continue on to slender and curvaceous Shell Lake via a gentle climb along Mine Creek for another 0.3 mile. Bilberry (purple leaves in early fall) and red mountain heather ground covers adorn the lake's shoreline, and there are grand views of Mount Dana to the south and North Peak just inside Yosemite National Park to the north. Frog-laden Fantail Lake another 0.7 mile along the slim trail has identical features, except the lake is twice the size.

Trout-loaded Mine Creek begins a twisting course up the rocky and grassy slope, past some small waterfalls to secluded Spuller Lake at 2.8 miles. Just follow the scant trail, and consider making the easy climb to Peak 10,493 that guards this photogenic lake. More petite lakes can be visited via easy cross country a bit farther to the north and west.

57 | TIOGA LAKE

Distance: 3 miles round trip
Hiking time: 2–3 hours
High point: 9800 feet
Elevation gain: 200 feet
Difficulty: Easy
Season: May into November
Map: USGS Tioga Pass
Nearest campground: Tioga Lake Campground
Information: Inyo National Forest, Bridgeport Ranger District
See map page 158

Tioga Lake joins neighboring Ellery Lake as the two highest lakes along State Route 120, including Yosemite National Park, which they border. At 9734 feet in elevation, Tioga Lake is a crown jewel set in an open high basin surrounded by 11,000- to 12,000-foot-high peaks. Follow the faint trail for this leisurely stroll that goes most of the way around the lake to the spillway and back.

Swimming, fishing, and picnicking can be enjoyed along the hike, which includes an option for exploring the meadow along Tioga Lake's inlet creek. Tioga Peak to the south stands in full view for the entire hike, while Gaylor Peak to the west captures interest during most of the return route.

Since State Route 120 is so close, and Tioga Lake is crammed with tourists on summer weekends, this hike is best taken instead on a weekday before Memorial Day or after Labor Day. Consider doing it in early morning or at twilight when traffic noise is sparse and dramatic shadows are cast across the lake. Another idea is to hike this lake and then stroll around Ellery Lake (Hike 53) a mile or so up the highway.

To get there, drive State Route 120 west from U.S. Highway 395 just south of Lee Vining for 11 miles, then park for free in the paved Tioga Lake Overlook lot above the campground, next to the picnic tables and restrooms.

Read the informative signboards, then proceed steeply downhill amid lodgepole pines to a slim meadow and the lake's inlet, where you can walk west in a lovely green meadow that turns golden by late summer. The

Thunderstorm brewing over Tioga Lake

southern shore skirts dense lodgepole pine forest and features a slender, sandy beach to walk that stretches for 0.4 mile. Continue close to the lake's edge to the spillway, where you turn around and check out views of Gaylor Peak and other neighboring ridges and passes previously unseen.

58 | GLACIER CANYON TO DANA LAKE

Distance: 4.8 miles round trip
Hiking time: 4–5 hours
High point: 11,200 feet
Elevation gain: 1300 feet
Difficulty: Moderate to strenuous
Season: May through October
Maps: USGS Tioga Pass, USGS Mount Dana
Nearest campground: Tioga Lake Campground
Information: Inyo National Forest; Bridgeport Ranger District
See map page 158

Rockbound Dana Lake is surrounded by steep and colorful ridges and peaks, including 13,057-foot-high Mount Dana. Because this highly scenic lake is just outside the Yosemite National Park boundary, and because several other popular hikes are nearby, this climb straight up remote and alpine Glacier Canyon is little known and seldom visited. Sky blue Dana Lake is a scene straight out of a sci-fi movie, with boulder chunks, metamorphic scree, and loose talus dominating the region. Avoid or reduce altitude sickness by climbing slowly and patiently. The entire journey is in open high country, so wear dark sunglasses, apply sunblock, pack a windbreaker, and bring plenty of water.

Most of the hike is above tree line and is easily impacted, so use only a stove and build no campfires if you're spending the night. Your route leads up to the headway of Glacier Canyon and the bouldery shores of glacier-fed, caterpillar-shaped Dana Lake.

To get there, drive State Route 120 west from U.S. Highway 395 just south of Lee Vining for 11 miles, then park for free in the paved Tioga Lake Overlook lot above the campground, next to the picnic tables and restrooms.

Read the informative signboards, then proceed steeply to the right and downhill amid lodgepole pines to a slim meadow and Tioga Lake's inlet. Make a mental note to picnic at and explore this lake (Hike 57) after returning from Dana Lake. A footpath (stay on it to minimize impact) meanders across this subalpine meadow and skirts several ponds that are worthy of bathing in come late summer. If you're lucky, you may see a mountain bluebird along the meadow edge or a pika darting over the scattered rocks.

Rocks along Dana Lake

From here, moderate but steady climbing ensues straight up the drainage of Glacier Canyon. Soon the lodgepole pines disappear, and you find yourself in exposed backcountry littered with boulders and filled with views of the steep side of reddish brown Mount Dana looming above. The unmaintained path enters Ansel Adams Wilderness and continues climbing. The higher you go, the more the way turns into rock and rubble, as you follow and eventually cross the creek that drains Dana Lake.

Pass a pond, then reach the north shore of the lake at 2.3 miles, featuring a good view across the lake of the gleaming white glacier embedded in the north-facing flank of Mount Dana. A brief but careful climb up the ridge a couple hundred feet in elevation reveals awesome views. Plan on scurrying around the entire lakeshore. You may hear the noisy, large, gray-and-black Clark's nutcracker along the way.

59 | GAYLOR LAKES AND GAYLOR PEAK

Distance: 4 miles round trip
Hiking time: 4–6 hours
High point: 11,004
Elevation gain: 1300 feet
Difficulty: Moderate to strenuous
Season: July through October
Map: USGS Tioga Pass
Nearest campground: Tioga Lake Campground
Information: Yosemite National Park
See map page 158

The open alpine country that encases the Gaylor Lakes looks more like a moonscape than High Sierra backcountry. Sloping meadows sprawl to the lakes' edges. Stunted and contorted whitebark pines punctuate the landscape and the lakes plunge dramatically from southern shores to display the multi-pointed Cathedral Range poking above. The snaking trail tops out on an expansive, open saddle on broken metamorphic rock. To the southeast, angular Mount Dana thrusts upward above pond-dotted Dana Meadows. From this spot, it's best to mount 11,004-foot-tall Gaylor Peak for one of the most impressive panoramas of red metamorphic peaks and white granitic peaks in Yosemite National Park. Because of its immense beauty and fishing and swimming opportunities, this hike is popular on warm summer weekends.

To get there, take State Route 120 west from its junction with U.S. Highway 395 just south of Lee Vining. Drive 12 fabulously scenic miles to a few

Facing page: Gaylor Lake and Cathedral Range

yards beyond the Tioga Pass entrance station, where you park on the north side of the road in a small paved lot next to restrooms.

Begin climbing immediately in a lodgepole pine forest that gives way in spots to sloping pastures dominated by native bunchgrasses. The moderate to steep climb doesn't ease until you reach the saddle at 0.6 mile that renders a dazzling view down on the southernmost and largest Gaylor Lake. From here you can study the obvious route straight up the enticing north flank of Gaylor Peak. Reach the lofty top, less than 0.5 mile of steady climbing farther, and soak in the amazing views. Spacious Saddlebag Lake resembles a pair of large, blue glasses to the north. North Peak and Mount Conness are nearby, and Tioga Peak sits in front of Lee Vining Peak to the east. Mount Gibbs to the south equals the girth of Mount Dana in front of it. Tuolumne Meadows spreads out to the southwest.

Return to the saddle and descend to the southernmost Gaylor Lake past scattered whitebark pines, red mountain heather, and patches of Sierra bilberry ground cover. Bilberry leaves turn flashy crimson in September and October, and they feature small but tasty berries that are typically devoured by rodents before you even notice them.

The trail climbs gradually north beneath the west-facing flank of Gaylor Peak and skirts the west end of the northernmost Gaylor Lake, which is more secluded than and just as shadeless as its neighbor. It's worth the continued climb to another ridge top farther north where the old Great Sierra Mine awaits. This is the spot of a failed silver-mining operation and another photogenic view. The walls of the old mine shafts are unstable, so use caution.

60 | MOUNT DANA

Distance: 6 miles round trip
Hiking time: 5–6 hours
High point: 13,053 feet
Elevation gain: 3100 feet
Difficulty: Strenuous
Season: July through October
Maps: USGS Mount Dana, USGS Tioga Pass
Nearest campground: Tioga Lake Campground
Information: Yosemite National Park; Inyo National Forest
See map page 158

Here's a classic climb to the second tallest peak in Yosemite National Park, where the views are incomparable, becoming more stupendous the higher

Facing page: Mount Dana

you get. Along the way, a riot of summer wildflowers adorns pond-dotted Dana Meadows and the rocky scree above it.

The entire journey to reddish brown Mount Dana passes through open high country, so wear sunglasses, pack a windbreaker, and bring plenty of water. Avoid or reduce altitude sickness by climbing patiently. If an afternoon lightning storm brews, get down the mountain right away. To evade the heavy crowds, go on weekdays or after Labor Day weekend.

To get there, take Tioga Road (State Route 120) west from its junction with U.S. Highway 395 just south of Lee Vining. Drive 12 miles to a few yards west of the Tioga Pass entrance station, where you park on the north side of the road in a small paved lot next to restrooms.

Cross Tioga Road and follow the unsigned path for Mount Dana's summit into scenic Dana Meadows, which, like most high meadows in the park, turns to golden amber by September. The trail meanders southeast past a pair of ponds that are among about two dozen that formed when the last primary glacier retreated. As you depart the flower-filled meadow, broadleaf lupine is replaced by paintbrush, alpine goldenrod, monkeyflower, and cow parsnips along the tumbling creeks. Meanwhile the ascent gets noticeably steeper, although a nice break comes in a petite alpine pasture at 1.2 miles. Corn lily, columbine, cinquefoil, and phlox eventually vanish as the occasional blue sky pilot appears along the rocky climb via an occasionally faint trail.

About 1 mile from the summit, already way above tree line, note a series of unmaintained use paths that head up the summit. Perhaps the best one heads east to a shallow saddle, then works its way southeast up the rubbly, ancient slopes to the windswept top. Pause often to gaze east down to lovely Dana Lake and admire the clusters of tall peaks that poke from all directions.

Plan on spending quality hang time with your map, figuring out which peaks are which as you delight in the fantastic panorama. Looking north and scanning counterclockwise, emerald blue and large Saddlebag Lake is backed by serrated Shepherd Crest. North Peak points to the sky next to mighty Mount Conness with its glacier. Tuolumne Meadows, capped by bald Lembert Dome, is punctuated by Tuolumne Peak and Mount Hoffmann, which is climbed about as often as Mount Dana. The craggy cliffs of the Cathedral Range are spiked by Cathedral Peak, Unicorn Peak, and the Echo Peaks. Johnson Peak and Rafferty Peak lead to Mount Lyell, the park's highest peak and largest glacier. At 13,114 feet, it is only some 60 feet higher than where you stand. Mount Ritter and Banner Peak poke above the Koip Peak glacier to the south, and Parker Peak and Mount Wood stand past nearby Mount Gibbs. Spacious Mono Lake sprawls to the northeast.

Consider altering your return route with a visit to broad, gently sloping Dana Plateau, featuring rare, ground cover snow willows and the sheer rock cliff called Cape Royal.

61 DANA MEADOWS TO SPILLWAY LAKE AND MONO PASS

Distance: 9.8 miles partial loop
Hiking time: 5–8 hours
High point: 10,600 feet
Elevation gain: 1000 feet
Difficulty: Moderate
Season: July through October
Maps: USGS Tioga Pass, USGS Koip Peak, USGS Mount Dana
Nearest campground: Tioga Lake Campground
Information: Yosemite National Park

Sparkling emerald lakes, green flower-filled meadows, and a lot of red rock comprise a color scheme unsurpassed in Yosemite National Park subalpine and alpine country on this journey loaded with views of hulking mountains. Along the way, you get well acquainted with rocky Parker Pass Creek while roaming beneath the imposing flanks of Kuna Crest, Mammoth Peak, and Mount Lewis, all towering at more than 12,000 feet tall. Evade the crowds by hiking in very early morning, or go on weekdays or after Labor Day. Most folks stay on the trail to Mono

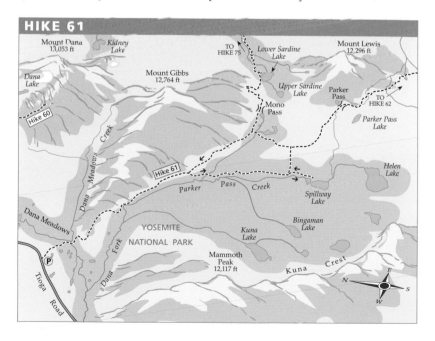

HIKE 61

Autumn views of Mount Gibbs

Pass and forget about Spillway Lake, one of this trip's prime stop-offs.

Mono Pass used to be a major trade route through the High Sierra between the Piute Indians on the east and the Miwok tribes on the west. It was also the site of the Golden Crown Mine operating in the early 1880s. By wandering around at Mono Pass, you will likely see several old mine structures still standing.

To get there, drive about 6 miles east of Tuolumne Meadows and almost 2 miles south of Tioga Pass on Tioga Road (State Route 120). The signed trailhead, toilets, and parking lot are on the southeast side of the road.

Depart the trailhead beneath a dense canopy of lodgepole pines and wander out on Dana Meadows, which dries to golden amber come September. At 0.5 mile, cross Dana Meadows Creek and Dana Fork a bit above their confluence. As you near Parker Pass Creek, note the ruins of a pioneer log cabin. Sagebrush shows up as you wander past creekside meadows to a junction at 2.3 miles, where you escape the majority of hikers by turning right for Spillway Lake (no camping).

The mostly open trail crosses a fork of Parker Pass Creek on its 1.4-mile-long climb to meadow-bordered Spillway Lake. Spend some quality, quiet hang time here at this scenic high-mountain lake, swimming the shallow waters or watching from the shore for California gulls flying over from Mono Lake. Get to the eastern shore and gaze across the lake to Kuna Crest stretching to the massive bulk of Mammoth Peak to the northwest.

Follow the outlet a hundred yards and veer east back on the trail. After 0.5 mile of climbing, turn north onto the trail that climbs 0.7 mile to Mono Pass. The trail continuing southeast leads to Parker Pass. Pass an odd-shaped lakelet as you draw near Mono Pass, set in open high country dotted with whitebark pines. Small Summit Lake sits atop Mono Pass, where the views across Yosemite National Park are treasured. Consider continuing steeply down to the Sardine Lakes to the east (Hike 75).

62 | DANA MEADOWS, PARKER PEAK, AND SILVER LAKE

Distance: 21 miles one way; 14 miles round trip for Mount Lewis
Hiking time: 2–3 days; 8–11 hours for Parker Pass
High point: 12,861 feet
Elevation gain: 3700 feet
Difficulty: Moderate to strenuous
Season: Late July through October
Maps: USGS Tioga Pass, USGS Koip Peak, USGS Mount Ritter
Nearest campground: Tioga Lake Campground
Information: Inyo National Forest; Yosemite National Park

Roam in some of the highest country described in this book, and feel satisfied that you've witnessed a lot of precious views and open space. This ambitious journey takes you to rock-dotted meadows, scree-coated fellfields, a trio of passes, a wondrous panorama atop easy-to-scale Parker Peak, and at least seven gorgeous lakes.

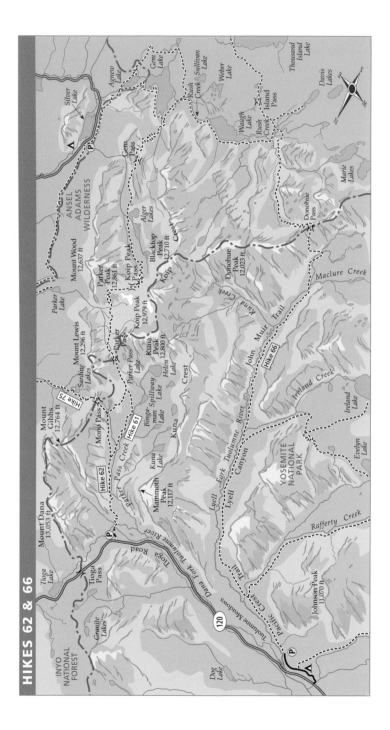

INYO
NATIONAL
FOREST

Granite
Lakes

Tioga
Lake

Mount Dana
13,053 ft

Tioga Pass

Mount
Gibbs
12,764 ft

Hike 75

Mono Pass

Parker Pass Creek

Tioga Road

Dana Fork Tuolumne River

120

Dog
Lake

Tuolumne Meadows

Mount Lewis
12,296 ft

Sardine
Lakes

Parker Pass

Parker
Lake

Parker Pass

Hike 61

Hike 62

Binga-
man
Lake

Spillway
Lake

Kuna

Mammoth
Peak
12,117 ft

Kuna
Lake

Kuna
Peak
12,800 ft

Helen
Lake

Crest

Lyell Fork Tuolumne River

Lyell
Canyon

Lyell

Pacific Crest
Trail

Johnson Peak
11,070 ft

Rafferty Creek

Parker
Lake

Mount Wood
12,637 ft

ANSEL
ADAMS
WILDERNESS

Parker
Peak
12,861 ft

Koip Peak
Pass

Koip Peak
12,979 ft

Blacktop
Peak
12,710 ft

Koip

Kuna Creek

Donohue
Peak
12,023 ft

John Muir Trail

Hike 66

Ireland Creek

Ireland
Lake

Evelyn
Lake

YOSEMITE
NATIONAL
PARK

Maclure Creek

Donohue
Pass

Marie
Lakes

Agnew
Lake

Silver
Lake

Gem
Pass

Gem
Lake

Algor
Lakes

Rush Creek

Sullivan
Lake

Weber
Lake

Waugh
Lake

Rush
Creek

Island
Pass

Thousand
Island
Lake

Davis
Lakes

This is mostly treeless land with lingering snow and thin air. Walk slowly to savor the fabulous scenery and avoid altitude sickness. This is mountain boot, hat, sunglasses, and sunblock country to the max. If lightning is imminent and you're perched at a pass or peak, get down to lower ground pronto. The hordes of humanity will be with you over the first and last 5 miles, so if solitude is your quest, linger long at Parker Pass, Parker Peak, Koip Peak Pass, Alger Lakes (good camping), and Gem Pass.

To get there, drive about 6 miles east of Tuolumne Meadows and almost 2 miles south of Tioga Pass on Tioga Road (State Route 120). The signed trailhead, toilets, and parking lot are on the southeast side of the road. If a car shuttle is planned, drive to Silver Lake via U.S. Highway 395 south of Lee Vining. Road 158, signed for June Lake, has two accesses west of US 395. Either one goes a little over 7 miles to the signed Rush Creek trailhead, where you park for free.

The trail wanders beneath lodgepole pines out on pond-speckled Dana Meadows. At 0.5 mile, cross Dana Meadows Creek and Dana Fork a bit above their confluence. As you near Parker Pass Creek, note the ruins of a pioneer log cabin. Sagebrush shows up as you wander past creekside meadows to a junction at 2.3 miles, where a right turn heads for Spillway Lake (no camping) described in Hike 61. Your route stays straight and climbs steadily but moderately for 1.7 miles to a view-filled, broad, deep, and sometimes windy fell-field called Mono Pass, where small Summit Lake and a larger, unnamed lake take center stage. From here, there's always the option to head steeply east down to Sardine Lakes and eventually Walker Lake (see Hike 75).

This route doubles back 0.3 mile to a large whitebark pine near a trail junction, where you head south by southwest 200 yards across a meadow, following ducks (rock cairns) that return you to noticeable tread. Climbing ensues past stubby whitebark pines, yellow-flowered cinquefoils, and eventually alpine willows, a summer host to white-crowned sparrows. Adore the views down on Spillway Lake nudged into the base of Kuna Crest. Approach detectable Parker Pass 1 mile before you get to it, wandering past Sierra wallflowers and Brewers lupines. A couple hundred yards prior to attaining Parker Pass, dart south by southwest a couple hundred yards along cross-country scree and bathe your toes in scenic, secluded, and teardrop-shaped Parker Pass Lake at the base of a sheer cliff.

Retrace your steps and promptly reach Parker Pass 6.4 miles from the trailhead, where you can take a few more minutes to climb 12,296-foot-high Mount Lewis to the northeast to gaze upon Walker Lake. Typical of the easternmost mountains in the Sierras, such as Mount Lewis and Parker Peak just to the south, the east faces are steep, ominous, and usually unsafe to climb, but the west faces are generally easy and safe to scale, as is the case for this pair of peaks.

You're now out of Yosemite National Park and in Inyo National Forest as you traverse southeast back on the trail toward a series of switchbacks

Metamorphic rock graces the slopes near Parker Peak

ascending the northwest flank of Parker Peak. Just less than 1 mile beyond Parker Pass, cross Parker Creek, which gets its vigor here from a permanent snowfield embedded in the northeast flank of Koip Peak directly west of Parker Peak. Koip Peak is climbable from here, but save your time and strength for Parker Peak, which is easier to mount. Reach a tarn where spacious Grant Lake is clearly seen to the east. From here, it's a steep 0.5-mile ascent on snaking tread to Koip Peak Pass. As you gasp for breath, let large, alkaline Mono Lake take your breath away along with Mount Conness rising above Parker Pass. Shallow Koip Peak Pass, which at 12,280 feet is one of the Sierra's highest trail passes, is the doorway to Parker Peak. Merely scramble up its scree slopes.

Back on the trail, you soon look ahead to see the Alger Lakes, June Lake, and volcanic Mammoth Mountain. Cross and then parallel Alger Creek for 0.8 mile, then descend past cairns to the long, tree-lined Alger Lakes. Nestled beneath the towering cliff face of Blacktop Peak, these shapely lakes warrant an easy stroll around them. You can camp on the bedrock land mass that separates the pair among whitebark pines.

From the outlet, climb a bit over 1 mile past two lakelets hosting yellow-legged frogs to lightly treed Gem Pass. Stare southward at the famous pair of peaks called Banner Peak and Mount Ritter (Hike 80), then descend under first whitebarks and then lodgepoles for 2 miles to good campsites at Gem Lake. Rush Creek Trail traces the northern shoreline of Gem Lake, then drops briefly to overlook Agnew Lake. The trail traces above its north shore, then commences a steep plunge for about 1 mile. The tread levels, revealing loving looks at Silver Lake, Grant Lake, and Mono Lake, all to the northeast. If a car shuttle or hitchhike is planned, keep walking the final 1.5 miles to the Rush Creek trailhead. Otherwise, this marks a final, glorious view before heading back to Dana Meadows.

63 | LEMBERT DOME

Distance: 4 miles round trip
Hiking time: 3–4 hours
High point: 9450 feet
Elevation gain: 900 feet
Difficulty: Moderate to strenuous
Season: June into November
Map: USGS Tioga Pass
Nearest campground: Tuolumne Meadows Campground
Information: Yosemite National Park

The panorama over Yosemite National Park from a football field-size granite slab known as Lembert Dome doesn't get any better anywhere. Nearby

Tuolumne Meadows looks dramatically magical when shadows from cumulus clouds are cast across it. As far as the eye can see, scattered and pointed peaks and rows of ranges reach skyward. The most prominent mountains include Pothole Dome, Cathedral Peak, Unicorn Peak, Johnson Peak, Mount Florence, Mount Lyell, Mammoth Peak, Mount Gibbs, Mount Dana, White Mountain, and Mount Conness, sweeping from west to east in a counterclockwise direction.

Go when visibility is high and the crowds are low, which is early summer mornings and weekdays after Labor Day. Because you'll be one of the tall objects atop the dome, zip down this bulging showcase of Tuolumne Meadows if lightning is near. The last 30 yards of doable rock climbing to reach the top requires a bit of hand use with your head down, so wear shoes with good gripping soles and avoid this part when it's wet from rain.

To get there, drive to the base of signed and obvious Lembert Dome, which is located on the north side of Tioga Road (State Route 120) at Tuolumne Meadows. You can also ride the Tuolumne Meadows shuttle bus to the paved Lembert Dome parking lot, which has restrooms.

From the Lembert Dome trailhead sign, wander north amid lodgepole pines and promptly cross an expansive rock slab gouged into the ground that has been finely polished by glacial ice. As you climb, following signs for first Dog Lake and then Lembert Dome, gaze east to behold the gigantic, smoothly polished, and lopsided mound of granite hovering over you.

Swing right at a trail junction at 1 mile and soon skirt a round pond that reflects the visage of the dome. Get to another junction at 1.6 miles,

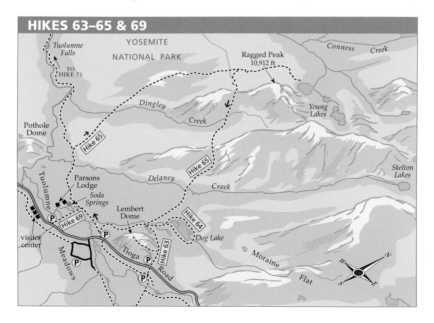

Cathedral Peak and Lembert Dome (photo by Dionne Soares)

where you bear right and climb steeply in deep woods. Reach a sheer rock saddle 0.2 mile farther and follow the layered, black-flecked, exfoliating granite slabs that form a natural staircase to the top. A few handfuls of stunted, leaning whitebark pines and mountain hemlocks adorn the upper slope of Lembert Dome. There are a few spots that offer shelter from the at-times fierce winds, where you can have a picnic and admire the breathtaking views simultaneously.

64 | DOG LAKE

Distance: 3.5 miles round trip
Hiking time: 3 hours
High point: 9200 feet
Elevation gain: 600 feet
Difficulty: Moderate
Season: June into November
Map: USGS Tioga Pass
Nearest campground: Tuolumne Meadows Campground
Information: Yosemite National Park
See map page 182

Here's one of the easier-to-reach high-country lakes in Yosemite National Park—a gently curving, clear gray lake that beckons you to wade in its water. Along the way, you'll crane your neck to stare at the stark east face of ominous Lembert Dome while climbing moderately in the pleasant shade of lodgepole pines.

The shallow lake's sunny edges sometimes warm up nicely during summer heat waves, making for a refreshing late afternoon swim. Popular with families, Dog Lake can range from secluded to overloaded on a summer weekend. If you're not visiting on a weekday or after Labor Day, you're apt to obtain more solitude and improved scenery by embracing the dramatic shadows cast over the medium-size lake just past dawn or at twilight. Make the hike more varied and view-filled by including the steep climb to Lembert Dome, which adds about 1.5 miles and ninety minutes to your excursion.

To get there, drive to the base of signed and obvious Lembert Dome, which is situated on the north side of Tioga Road (State Route 120) at Tuolumne Meadows. You can also ride the Tuolumne Meadows shuttle bus to the paved Lembert Dome parking area, which has restrooms.

From the Lembert Dome trailhead sign, head north in a lodgepole pine forest and promptly cross a large rocky slab embedded in the dirt that has been polished to a shine by glacial ice. Follow signs for Dog Lake at a couple of signed trail forks, and keep looking east for the sheer granite face of towering Lembert Dome. After crossing a petite creek, the climbing lessens. A spur trail takes off to the right at 1.5 miles, and 150 yards farther, you've reached Dog Lake at its outlet.

Head right on a scant but easy-to-follow path around the scenic shore. Many of the lodgepole pines at lake's edge have been exposed to fierce winds and heavy snows that have caused their trunks to gradually bend into a twisting shape. They accentuate the views eastward of a pair of

Dog Lake features a view of Mount Conness (photo by Dionne Soares)

reddish hulks called Mount Dana and Mount Gibbs that poke above a deep green forest slope. Whitish Mount Conness also graces the scene across the lake and beyond a meadow. Skinny, sandy beaches adorn the shoreline, which also includes patches of sedges. On the forest edges, red mountain heather and fragrant labrador tea shrubs thrive.

Continue to circumnavigate the lake and soon reach a colorful small meadow that is boggy into midsummer. Mosquitoes can be relentless here, so cover up and/or use repellent.

65 | YOUNG LAKES

Distance: 14-mile loop
Hiking time: 8 hours or overnight
High point: 10,000 feet
Elevation gain: 1500 feet
Difficulty: Moderate
Season: July through October
Map: USGS Tioga Pass
Nearest campground: Tuolumne Meadows Campground
Information: Yosemite National Park
See map page 182

Alpine wildflower meadows and a trio of lakes are photogenic features on this varied loop journey. A lot of backpackers and day hikers share this popular destination, so for seclusion, head for the uppermost lake or go on weekdays.

To get there, drive to the base of signed and obvious Lembert Dome, which is situated at the east end of Tuolumne Meadows on Tioga Road (State Route 120). You can also ride the Tuolumne Meadows shuttle to the Lembert Dome parking area. If you are backpacking, you must park along the paved road parallel to Tioga Road. The signed trail begins at the gate after this road turns sharply to the right and heads toward the stables.

Wander through the meadow, gazing behind you to adore Lembert Dome and soon Mount Dana across this spacious and scenic valley. Reach the ramshackle log building at effervescent Soda Springs, a naturally carbonated spring spewing rusty water. Go past the stone building featuring historical exhibits called Parsons Lodge, then traipse past flowery meadows in open lodgepole pine forest. Wade shallow and multi-branched Delaney Creek and follow the trail as it reaches the edge of northernmost Tuolumne Meadows before climbing to the signed Young Lakes Trail at 2.1 miles, where you bear right.

Cross a broad expanse of grass-pocketed, boulder-strewn glaciated sheet granite. Look for open areas to gaze southwest across expansive Tuolumne Meadows to the rising peaks beyond, including rounded

View of Tuolumne Meadows along the trail to Young Lakes

Fairview Dome and the steeple-like spires of the Cathedral Range. Ascend a tree-blanketed slope to a ridge and soon drop into the bouldery and shallow valley housing Dingley Creek. When you reach the creek, leap across its west fork and then climb in a pine forest laced with daisies, senecios, gooseberries, and lupines along with dainty mariposa lily. As you approach the ridge top, peer past breaks in the lodgepole pine forest for glimpses of the entire Cathedral Range, and relish the notion that you'll replay this scene often during the return.

Upon cresting the ridge, a staggered row of peaks appears from the north, including Shepherd Crest, Mount Conness, Sheep Peak, Matterhorn Peak, Finger Peaks, and Tower Peak. Cross a fork of Conness Creek laden with wildflowers and keep left at a trail fork, where a right turn will be your return route later. Commence a snaking traverse northeast in a forest of lodgepole pine and gray-needled mountain hemlock. Gather a grand view of nearby Ragged Peak's northwest face, round the border of a meadow, and then drop to lower Young Lake at 6.5 miles, where campsites are located on the north side.

A bit farther, tiny and circular middle Young Lake features a single campsite and a spur trail that leads to the photogenic crest, a prime picnic and viewing area. From the middle lake, it's a level, open traverse to the more secluded and shapely upper Young Lake, where good campsites exist far enough away from the water.

Retrace your steps about 2 miles to the trail heading to Dog Lake, and commence a short climb that delves into a whitebark pine region. The trail swings around the southwest shoulder of Ragged Peak and descends through a large and gently sloping meadow. Adore the paintbrush, monkeyflower, and lupines that grace the meandering brooks here. Cross the headwaters of Dingley Creek, descend past exfoliating Peak 10,410, and then make a brief climb to the crest of a large and bouldery moraine. Drop to another large meadow where Delaney Creek drifts lazily past sedges and grasses and the views are prime of Mounts Dana and Gibbs. At 0.5 mile farther, reach the trail that heads a couple hundred yards east to Dog Lake (Hike 64). After your visit to this pretty lake, continue downhill past Lembert Dome to the trailhead

66 PACIFIC CREST TRAIL AND JOHN MUIR TRAIL–TUOLUMNE MEADOW TO SILVER LAKE

Distance: 26 miles one way; 52 miles round trip
Hiking time: 3 days one way; 5–6 days round trip
High point: 11,000 feet
Elevation gain: 4100 feet one way
Difficulty: Moderate to strenuous
Season: June through October
Maps: USGS Koip Peak, USGS Mount Ritter, USGS Vogelsang Peak
Nearest campground: Tuolumne Meadow Campground
Information: Ansel Adams Wilderness, Yosemite National Park
See map page 178

Label this the ultimate high-country/buttkicker backpack trip where virtually anywhere you look there's bound to be an awesome and rugged peak or subalpine lake looming. These sections of the Pacific Crest Trail (PCT) and John Muir Trail don't get any more gorgeous than on this route, which escorts you to five large lakes and furnishes inspirational views of a handful of others, including super-large Mono and Grant Lakes.

The course follows the southernmost stretch of the world-famous PCT and John Muir Trail through and then out of Yosemite National Park, so expect steady foot traffic on summer weekends, especially over the first few miles from the trailhead. But toward the headwaters of Lyell Fork of the Tuolumne River and continuing for several miles to Waugh Lake, the route is refreshingly remote, with fantastic photo opportunities unfolding around every bend.

Bear-proof canisters are required immediately south of Donohue Pass; contact Inyo National Forest for exact locations. Canisters are also required above 9600 feet for backpackers in the park, at both middle and upper Lyell base camps.

To get there, drive Tioga Road (State Route 120) to the middle of the park at Tuolumne Meadows. The trailhead is east of the Tuolumne Meadows Visitor Center, store, and campground. One mile east of the Tuolumne

Silver Lake

River Bridge turn south at the entrance to the wilderness center and follow the road for 0.5 mile to the Dog Lake parking area on the left. If a car shuttle or hitchhike is planned, drive to Silver Lake via U.S. Highway 395 south of Lee Vining. Road 158, signed for June Lake, has two accesses west of US 395. Either one goes a little over 7 miles to the signed Rush Creek trailhead, where you park for free.

For the first few miles, the PCT and John Muir Trail stay mostly flat, giving you a long warm-up as the route traces the banks of the lazy Lyell Fork of the Tuolumne River. Pass by a marshy area and reach the twin bridges over Lyell Fork at 0.6 mile. Pause here to admire the pure waters winding toward you, flowing past deep bowls gouged into the granite by the incessant force of silt from spring runoff. The crystal-clear water patterns over the river rocks are further enhanced by the commanding presence of Mammoth Peak to the southeast.

The trail passes through scattered groves of lodgepole pines and over open rock to another trail junction at 1.2 miles, where you stay straight. Continue through alternating forest with meadow and reunite with the river upon rounding a low ridge. A superb view up the graceful canyon is yours, with swirls and pools in the foreground, lined by grasses and meadow flowers. The turquoise water is caused by glacial "flour," which is rock ground finely by the Lyell Glacier above. The rock remains suspended in the current and reflects green light.

Good campsites exist just uphill from a trail sign at 5.6 miles, a scenic area for spending your first night. Continue south, and after 2 miles, meadow and forest begin sloping upward, eased by staggering views to the southwest of Lyell Glacier, stashed beneath the shaded high flanks of 13,114-foot-high Mount Lyell, the tallest peak in the park. Mount Maclure is a westerly neighbor sheltering its own glacier, sitting just a few feet in elevation below Mount Lyell. Both glaciers feed the Tuolumne River.

Trees gradually vanish as you climb away from Lyell base camp, which is popular with climbers preparing to climb Mount Lyell, as well as with bears. (See the information on bears in the "Wilderness Ethics" section in the Introduction.) As the climbing continues, you're more alone with the towering peaks and glaciers. A splendid view originates from the outlet of a little, unnamed lake bordering a flower-dotted meadow. Ascent occurs over exposed granite past gnarled whitebark pines now, and snow patches often linger into late July for the final mile to 11,000-foot-high Donohue Pass at 12 miles.

Welcome descent ensues as the whitebarks increase in number and size. The John Muir Trail snakes around small bogs and big boulders and arrives at the outlet creek for the alpine Marie Lakes after 2.5 miles. For deep peace and great views, take the trail right that climbs for a bit over 1 mile to the largest of the two Marie Lakes.

Pressing on, the John Muir Trail continues its downhill course, showing off final good views of Banner Peak, Mount Ritter, and Mount Davis. Three miles from Donohue Pass, bear left onto signed Rush Creek Trail, where you descend in a lodgepole pine forest for 0.6 mile to the western shore of Waugh Lake. The trail hugs the northern shoreline of this large lake for more than 1 mile, then it follows Rush Creek for about 1 mile as sagebrush becomes more plentiful to a signed trail junction. Go left, pass two circular ponds, and soon reach the western shore of spacious and shapely Gem Lake, a good place to spend your third night.

Rush Creek Trail traces the northern shoreline of Gem Lake, then drops briefly to overlook Agnew Lake. The trail traces above its north shore, then commences a steep plunge for about 1 mile. The tread levels, revealing loving looks at Silver Lake, larger Grant Lake, and even larger Mono Lake, all to the northeast. If a car shuttle or hitchhike is planned, keep walking the final 1.5 miles to the Rush Creek trailhead. Otherwise, this marks a final, glorious view before heading back to Tuolumne Meadows.

67 | IRELAND LAKE AND VOGELSANG LAKE

Distance: 23-mile loop
Hiking time: 2–3 days
High point: 10,735 feet
Elevation gain: 2100 feet
Difficulty: Moderate
Season: July into November
Maps: USGS Tioga Pass, USGS Vogelsang Peak
Nearest campground: Tuolumne Meadows Campground
Information: Yosemite National Park

Sky blue Ireland Lake lies in a huge glacial cirque well above timberline and beneath the imposing visages of black-colored Amelia Earhart and Parsons Peaks, and the lake features a waterfall that flows beneath it. Much smaller, teardrop-shaped Vogelsang Lake reflects the twin peaks of Vogelsang Peak in its partly shallow waters.

This entire journey is about water. The Lyell Fork of the Tuolumne River escorts you for a few miles, then you visit up to half a dozen alpine lakes before capping the excursion with a downhill blitz along the shores of enticing Rafferty Creek for another few miles. It's a popular journey, and you're likely to enjoy the most privacy and intimacy at Ireland Lake or Townsley Lake.

To get there, drive Tioga Road (State Route 120) to the middle of the park at Tuolumne Meadows. The trailhead is east of the Tuolumne Meadows Visitor Center, store, and campground. One mile east of the Tuolumne River Bridge turn south at the entrance to the wilderness center and follow the road for 0.5 mile to the Dog Lake parking area on the left.

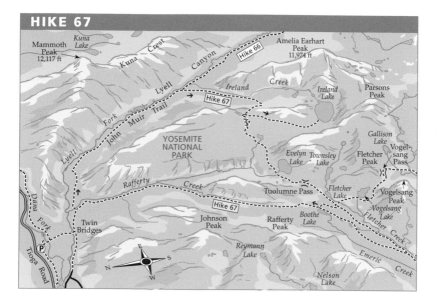

The Pacific Crest Trail and John Muir Trail stay mostly flat over the first few miles, tracing the banks of the lazy Lyell Fork of the Tuolumne River. Skirt a marshy area and reach the twin bridges over Lyell Fork at 0.6 mile. Stop to admire the pure waters winding toward you, flowing past deep bowls gouged into the granite by the incessant force of silt from spring runoff. The clear water patterns over the river rocks are further embellished by the commanding presence of Mammoth Peak to the southeast.

The trail passes through scattered groves of two-needled lodgepole pines and over open rock to another trail junction at 1.2 miles, where you stay straight (a right turn heads up Rafferty Creek, your return route). The John Muir Trail continues alternating forest with meadow and reunites with the river upon rounding a low ridge. A superb view up the graceful canyon is yours, with swirls and pools in the foreground, lined by grasses and meadow flowers. The turquoise water is caused by glacial "flour," which is rock ground finely by the Lyell Glacier above. The rock remains suspended in the current and reflects green light.

Good campsites exist just uphill from a trail sign at 5.6 miles, a scenic area for spending your first night. This is also the junction with Hike 66 to Silver Lake, but your route veers right, leaving the river behind and ascending southwest toward Parsons Peak for nearly 2 miles. Along the way, pass beneath lodgepole pines and alongside gooseberry bushes to a wondrous petite meadow encasing Ireland Creek where a small waterfall flows ahead from Ireland Lake.

The open trail departs the creek for good at 7 miles and reaches the junction with Ireland Lake 1 mile farther. It's a 1.5-mile-long climb to wonderfully desolate and windswept Ireland Lake, nestled beneath both metamorphic and granitic peaks. Back on the trail to Evelyn Lake, climb a trail segment west that contorts along slab after slab of bedrock to a view-filled crest accented by stunted whitebark pines. The Cathedral Range, with Rafferty and Johnson Peaks, spreads from south to north from the west. Pass by an unnamed lake and reach a large rocky bench that holds shapely and shallow Evelyn Lake. Light-colored Kuna Crest is spread behind you, capped by Koip Crest. Dark Parsons and Amelia Earhart Peaks are backed by Mount Lyell, the tallest peak in the park. Mount Conness, third highest peak in the park, displays its glacier to the north.

Reach a long meadow lined with whitebark pines and find Fletcher Lake, which lies at the base of Fletcher Peak. Vogelsang High Sierra Camp at 14.5 miles sits at the other end of Fletcher Lake, and there are exceptional campsites toward the north side of the meadow near the cliff's edge with awesome sightings of Mount Conness and nearby Boothe Lake.

The 1.2-mile-long trail to Vogelsang Lake or the slightly shorter cross-country trip from Fletcher Lake up the inlet creek to Townsley Lake offer deep peace and photogenic opportunities. When it's time to return to Tuolumne Meadows, go north at the signed trail junction at Vogelsang High Sierra Camp (snacks and supplies are sold here) to Tuolumne Pass. Go gently downhill along Rafferty Creek in lodgepole pine forest and enter a large boulder-strewn meadow after 1.5 miles. The stark slopes of Rafferty

Vogelsang Peak in 1942 (photo by R. Anderson)

and Johnson Peaks accompany you from the west. Toward the end, the trail steepens and undergoes several switchbacks to the John Muir Trail, where you head left and soon reunite with Tuolumne Meadows.

68 TUOLUMNE MEADOWS TO MATTERHORN AND RODGERS CANYONS

Distance: 88-mile loop
Hiking time: 8–13 days
High point: 10,400 feet
Elevation gain: 8700 feet
Difficulty: Moderate
Season: June through October
Maps: USGS Matterhorn Peak, USGS Falls Ridge, USGS Ten Lakes, USGS Tioga Pass
Nearest campground: Tuolumne Meadows Campground
Information: Yosemite National Park

Stay virtually undetected deep within four strikingly contrasting high-country canyons while visiting numerous rockbound lakes and exploring several waterfalls, cascades, and meadows. After day one and until the final day, it's possible to go several view-filled hours or even a whole day without being seen. Perhaps the only drawback of this epic journey is the long climb out of scenic Grand Canyon of the Tuolumne River toward the finale. But by then, you'll be mountain fit, and the series of awesome waterfalls along this stretch will be pleasant distractions. This is a busy trailhead, so if the wilderness permit quota is met, add another 10 miles to the trip and come in from Twin Lakes (see Hike 42).

To get there, drive to the base of signed and obvious Lembert Dome, which is situated at the east end of Tuolumne Meadows on Tioga Road (State Route 120). You can also ride the Tuolumne Meadows shuttle to the Lembert Dome parking area. If you are backpacking, you must park along the paved road parallel to Tioga Road. The signed trail begins at the gate after this road turns sharply to the right and heads toward the stables.

Wander through the spacious meadow, and soon reach the ramshackle log building at Soda Springs, a naturally carbonated spring spewing rusty water. Wade shallow Delaney Creek and for the next 2 miles pass over polished granite that was buffed by glacial ice. Little Devils Postpile is an odd volcanic feature to watch for.

Reach a pair of footbridges across the Tuolumne River at 3.5 miles, where the river picks up power and speed and forms a series of cascades all the way to Glen Aulin. The path takes you close enough to breath-taking

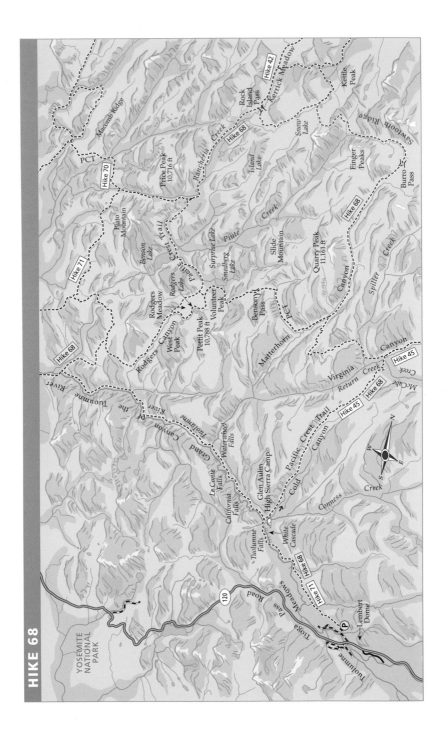

YOSEMITE NATIONAL PARK

120

Tioga Pass Road

Tuolumne Meadows

Lembert Dome

Hike 71

Hike 68

White Cascade

Tuolumne Falls

Glen Aulin High Sierra Camp

California Falls

Le Conte Falls

Waterwheel Falls

Grand Canyon of the Tuolumne River

The Tuolumne River

Comess Creek

Cold Canyon

Pacific Creek Trail

Hike 45

Hike 45

Hike 68

Virginia Canyon

Return Creek

McCabe Creek

Hike 45

Matterhorn Canyon

Benson Pass

PCT

Slide Mountain

Quarry Peak 11,161 ft

Spiller Creek

Canyon

Pinte Creek

Surprise Lake

Smedberg Lake

Volunteer Peak

Pettit Peak 10,788 ft

Rodgers Canyon

West Peak

Rodgers Meadow

Rodgers Lake

Pacific Crest Trail

Benson Lake

Plato Mountain

Hike 71

Hike 68

PCT

Hike 70

Price Peak 10,716 ft

Macomb Ridge

Rancheria Creek

Island Lake

Snow Lake

Hike 68

Rock Island Pass

Kerrick Meadow

Hike 42

Kettle Peak

Sawtooth Ridge

Finger Peaks

Burro Pass

N

W E

S

Sulfur buckwheat and lichens

Tuolumne Falls to feel the cool spray. The trail leads you into deep forest featuring patches of corn lily and fragrant labrador tea shrubs to a junction at Glen Aulin High Sierra Camp with May Lake at 5 miles, where you stay on the Pacific Crest Trail (PCT) by going right.

The peaceful creekside climb up Cold Canyon switches between meadows and open forest to the McCabe Lakes junction (Hike 45) at 12.2 miles. Stay left on the PCT, cross McCabe Creek and Return Creek, and then veer left at another trail junction at 13.2 miles. Drop to cross the creek, then climb steeply up the slopes of Virginia Canyon. Descend briefly, pass a couple of ponds, and then enter the grassy meadow bordering shallow Miller Lake, which is pleasantly warm enough for a summer swim. Campsites exist in the neighboring forest. Cross a shoulder featuring views of the jagged Sawtooth Ridge and Whorl Mountain to the north, then descend steeply into Matterhorn Canyon and eventually enter a meadow at 19 miles where there is good camping. Bear right here and leave the PCT.

Climbing north in the steep and narrow depths of secluded Matterhorn Canyon offers awesome views of Whorl Mountain and Sawtooth Ridge ahead, close-up views of the exfoliating slopes of Quarry Peak hovering high to the west after about 2 miles in, and eventually a commanding view straight on of imposing Matterhorn Peak. Finger Peaks rears to the west. Campsites galore exist along scenic Matterhorn Creek. Climbing abates at 28 miles upon reaching a high point behind Burro Pass in wide open environs. Previously mentioned views of all those fractured granite pillars are closer and clearer here, amid alpine fell fields that support a riot of summer wildflowers, including pussy paws, penstemon, and paintbrush. Drop steeply via rocky switchbacks past lingering snowfield areas and then follow the trail as it hugs slender and swift Piute Creek west past stands of stubby whitebark pines to a meadow. A good campsite exists above, near a small waterfall.

Eventually Slide Mountain and its 1600-foot rock wall takes center stage as climbing resumes. After some switchbacks over rocky terrain with countless views in all directions, the trail swings to a junction at 35 miles, where you swing left and soon reach rock-littered Snow Lake. Consider spending the night here and catching a sunset. Traipse up meadowed terrain to broad Rock Island Pass, where photo opportunities await. Descend 1.5 miles and go left for several miles of intimacy descending gently along Rancheria Creek. It's a mix of lupine-flecked, sandy meadows and intimate lodgepole pine forests to the reunion with the PCT, where you head south on it for 4 miles to Benson Lake, this trip's largest lake. The lake features a broad and sandy beach, angling for brook and rainbow trout, good campsites nearby, and a great view across the lake to brushy domes at the outlet. The next 2 miles climb along the creek that drains Smedberg Lake and feeds Benson Lake.

The PCT swings south away from the creek to a trail junction where you stay left on the PCT for 1.5 miles to rock-encased Smedberg Lake, where tiny islands and a peninsula are featured beneath the daunting vertical flanks of Volunteer Peak to the south. There are good campsites along the lake's north and west shores. Retrace your steps to a trail junction, and leave the PCT, heading south for 1 mile to subalpine Rodgers Lake, which is divided into two bodies by a low granitic isthmus. The larger, eastern section is more open and rocky. The trail winds around the lake where mountain hemlocks and lodgepole pines adorn the northern shore, and where there are good campsites that show off Regulation and West Peaks. Continue south for 1 mile of descent along a cobbly ridge to small and circular Neall Lake, which has good campsites and reflects the sharp crest of West Peak directly above it.

The trail angles west for 1 mile, turns left at a trail junction, and proceeds past lodgepole pines down to long and sedge-filled Rodgers Meadow 2 miles farther. Here Rodgers Canyon Creek snakes lazily at trailside for a good mile. The path then heads near creek cascades and ascends a series of heavily forested steps to its junction with the Grand Canyon of the Tuolumne River and Pate Valley. From here, follow Hike 71 in reverse to the trailhead.

69 | TUOLUMNE MEADOWS, TUOLUMNE RIVER, AND SODA SPRINGS

Distance: 1.8 miles round trip; up to 5 miles round trip
Hiking time: 2–3 hours
High point: 8600 feet
Elevation gain: None
Difficulty: Easy
Season: May into November
Map: USGS Tioga Pass
Nearest campground: Tuolumne Meadows Campground
Information: Yosemite National Park
See map page 182

Photo buffs, families, and anglers find this level stroll rewarding, constantly scenic, and view-filled. Especially busy on summer weekends, this route crosses through 2.5-mile-long Tuolumne Meadows, which is the largest subalpine meadow in the Sierra Nevada. It reaches iron-rich, rust-stained Soda Springs, then lets you wander along the willow-lined banks of a placid and meandering stretch of the Tuolumne River that's good for

Lembert Dome from Tuolumne Meadows

swimming. The ever-changing views of jagged peaks and glacier-smoothed granite domes may inspire you to use a variety of nearby, signed trails to extend your flat hike.

To get there, drive to Tuolumne Meadows Visitor Center on Tioga Road (State Route 120) and park. The trail starts 0.1 mile east of the visitor center.

A wide trail heads north past a few scattered lodgepole pines directly into the sedge-covered meadow. The views ahead to the northeast are of Lembert Dome's northwest face, laced with vertical fractures. Reach a large wooden bridge at 0.5 mile, where it's a good idea to pause and stare southward at several rocky mountains that spike skyward, including Cathedral Peak, Unicorn Peak, the Cockscomb, and Echo Peaks.

Take the path that leads to the left and traces the lazy Tuolumne River and walk to a trail junction a short distance ahead. Note that you can continue straight along the river and through the meadow as part of your return, but for now, turn right and check out Parsons Lodge, which was built entirely from native log and rock by the Sierra Club in 1915. The trail leads east to a grassy knoll where naturally carbonated, effervescent Soda Springs pours its tonic water. From here, the trail heads back to the bridge, where you can walk in either direction on slim paths.

70 TUOLUMNE MEADOWS TO SONORA PASS VIA PACIFIC CREST TRAIL

Distance: 78 miles one way; 53 miles to Dorothy Lake; 45 miles to Tilden Lake
Hiking time: 7–12 days
High point: 10,100 feet
Elevation gain: 12,000 feet
Difficulty: Strenuous
Season: June through October
Maps: USGS Tioga Pass, USGS Falls Ridge, USGS Dunderberg Peak, USGS Matterhorn Peak, USGS Piute Mountain, USGS Tower Peak, USGS Pickel Meadow, USGS Sonora Pass
Nearest campground: Tuolumne Meadows Campground
Information: Yosemite National Park; Stanislaus National Forest; Toiyabe National Forest

For the unforgettable, ultimate journey of a lifetime, plan this one carefully and do it. You can hike for days and see no one on this very photogenic stretch of the Pacific Crest Trail, but you'll be exclaiming in amazement at the endless array of glacial-carved peaks, deep and wild canyons,

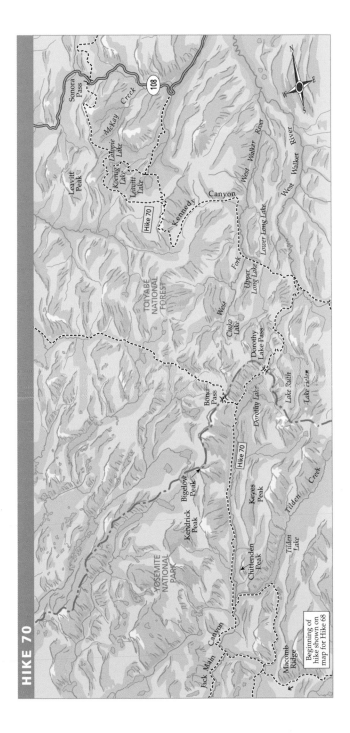

Sonora Pass

108

McKay Creek

Lafonie Lake

Leavitt Peak

Koenig Lake

Leavitt Lake

Hike 70

West Walker River

Kennedy Canyon

West Walker River

West Fork

Lower Long Lake

Upper Long Lake

TOIYABE NATIONAL FOREST

West Fork

Cinko Lake

Dorothy Lake Pass

Bond Pass

Dorothy Lake

Lake Ruth

Lake Gieler

Bigelow Peak

Hike 70

Keyes Peak

Tilden Creek

Kendrick Peak

YOSEMITE NATIONAL PARK

Chittenden Peak

Tilden Lake

Jack Main Canyon

Macomb Ridge

Beginning of hike shown on map for Hike 68

unexplored meadows, abundant wildlife, and precious trout streams. Some of the visual highlights to look for include Seavey Pass, famous Matterhorn Canyon and Matterhorn Peak, Benson Lake with its huge white sand beach, and Dorothy Lake with its incredible views to the north of the Sonora Pass area. This epic endeavor is all about heading up one canyon and down another on butt-kicking climbs featuring breathtaking views that make it all well worth it. See "permits" in the Introduction.

To get there, drive to the base of signed and obvious Lembert Dome, which is situated at the east end of Tuolumne Meadows on Tioga Road (State Route 120). You can also ride the Tuolumne Meadows shuttle to the Lembert Dome parking area. If you are backpacking, you must park along the paved road parallel to Tioga Road.

Two enjoyable routes cover the first 25 miles or so: check Hike 71 which details the wonderfully scenic stretch of the Grand Canyon of the Tuolumne River, then follow the Rodgers Canyon and vicinity description of Hike 68 in reverse past Benson Lake to the junction with Kerrick Canyon; or read Hike 42 to its junction with Matterhorn Canyon 19 miles into your journey. From Matterhorn Canyon's trail junction, stay straight on the Pacific Crest Trail (PCT), climbing along serene Wilson Creek, which you cross several times before it swings west and snakes up to expansive and grassy Benson Pass, featuring stunted whitebark pines. This spot marks the highest elevation of the trip. As with all subalpine and alpine backcountry outings, snow may cover portions of the trail into late July, so

Dorothy Lake in 1941 (photo by R. Anderson)

carefully negotiate these spots to keep on the trail. Gradual descent ensues to the crossing of Smedberg Lake's outlet at a meadow edge. Smedberg Lake (good campsites) nestles at the foot of chunky Volunteer Peak at 25 miles. Depart the lake and follow a trail west to a major junction, where you head right, continuing on the PCT past Benson Lake, along Piute Creek, and past a few tarns to wooded Kerrick Canyon, where you bear left and continue on the PCT at 35 miles.

Proceed down to the junction with the Bear Valley Trail, then switchback way up and then way down steeply into the next valley, hopping Thompson and Stubblefield Creeks in the process. Negotiate another thigh-burning climb followed by a knee-wobbling descent over Macomb Ridge and finally cross Tilden Creek to reach the Tilden Canyon/Wilma Lake junction at 42 miles. You soon reach large and shallow Wilma Lake, a warm lake you can use for taking a much needed bath. Bear right at the junction with Jack Main Canyon Trail, wander dreamily along a flat valley floor, and soon take the trail that heads briefly east to a long and slender finger of clear water called Tilden Lake. There is good camping near the southeast shore, and 11,755-foot-high Tower Peak rises above the far end of this secluded lake.

Back on the PCT, continue north past Chittenden Peak and a small water-fall, then stroll miles of grassy meadows that culminate in Grace Meadow, the largest. The gorgeous view ahead from west to east consists of Bond Pass, Dorothy Lake Pass, and Forsyth Peak. Climb steadily out of the meadow (good campsites), reach a trail junction with nearby Bond Pass and the boundary with Stanislaus National Forest after 1.5 miles, and then continue on the PCT to large, lovely, and exposed Dorothy Lake 1 mile farther.

After some picnicking, swimming, and/or fishing at 9300-foot-high Dorothy Lake, continue on the PCT, soon departing Yosemite National Park and entering Toiyabe National Forest. Pass by rocky Stella Lake, then switchback east down to Lake Harriet (good campsites) at 1 mile past Dorothy Lake. Cross Cascade Lake 0.5 mile farther, stay straight at a trail junction, and then bear left (west) 0.7 mile farther on the original PCT route, which winds 1 mile to Cinko Lake (good campsites). Descend 0.5 mile to the West Fork West Walker River and follow this old route along the river 1.5 miles down to the reunion with the newer route of the PCT. By now, it's more and more obvi-ous that the glacial-cut backcountry you left back in the park is changing to volcanic rock here in Toiyabe National Forest.

Pass among granite and lodgepole pines through Walker Meadow, and eventually veer northwest up a brown-walled, volcanic canyon called Kennedy Canyon. By the time you cross its creek, all reasonable campsites are left behind, and so are all permanent creeks. Unless snowbanks linger on the ridge ahead, purify water and fill your bottles here, some 10 miles away from the Sonora Pass Trailhead. You now switchback northward up a closed jeep road (still the PCT), enjoying ever improving views past stunted whitebark pines of the stark, brown-and-gray volcanic landscape that encases Kennedy Canyon.

Eventually, you stand next to 11,570-foot-high Leavitt Peak, a giant scree slope that beckons to be bagged. It's a safe and short climb up its east face. Armed with sunglasses, windbreaker, and hat, descend Leavitt Peak when you're done with the great views and contour a while along the ridge before making a steady descent for 1 mile and then following a winding course that puts you at the Sonora Pass trailhead after 5 miles.

71 | TUOLUMNE RIVER TO WATERWHEEL FALLS AND PATE VALLEY

Distance: 40 miles round trip; 15 miles round trip
   to Waterwheel Falls
Hiking time: 2–4 days
High point: 8600 feet
Elevation gain: 4200 feet
Difficulty: Moderate to strenuous
Season: June through October
Maps: USGS Falls Ridge, USGS Tamarack Flat, USGS Ten
   Lakes, USGS Tioga Pass
Nearest campground: Tuolumne Meadows Campground
Information: Yosemite National Park

This is the only route that traces the spectacular Grand Canyon of the Tuolumne River, and it's the classic way to reach popular Waterwheel Falls. It's a rugged and rocky ramble in a deep and famous river canyon past five cascades. Unless you time your hike to be there on weekdays or after Labor Day, you'll have a lot of company to Waterwheel Falls, which should be visited before mid-August to see the curving sprays of water that get tossed into the air, thus giving the cascade its name. From the falls to Pate Valley, solitude awaits.

To get there, drive to the base of signed and obvious Lembert Dome, which is situated at the east end of Tuolumne Meadows on Tioga Road (State Route 120). You can also ride the Tuolumne Meadows shuttle to the Lembert Dome parking area. If you are backpacking, you must park along the paved road parallel to Tioga Road. The signed trail begins at the gate after this road turns sharply to the right and heads toward the stables.

Wander through the meadow, gazing behind you to see Lembert Dome and soon Mount Dana across this spacious and scenic valley. Reach the ramshackle log building at Soda Springs, a naturally carbonated spring spewing rusty water. Go past the stone building featuring historical exhibits called Parsons Lodge, then traipse past flowery meadows in open lodgepole pine forest. Wade shallow Delaney Creek and after almost 2 miles of walking in a daydream, you emerge from behind a low ridge to stare at

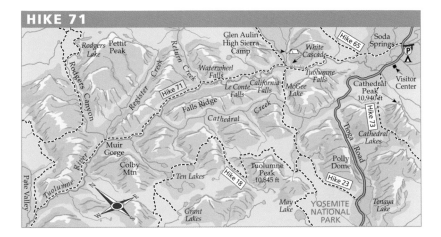

awesome Cathedral Range to the west, fronted by the twisting Tuolumne River. The ensuing 2 miles are filled with photo ops, as the trail passes over granite that was buffed by glacial ice. Watch for Little Devils Postpile on the left, an odd volcanic feature much younger than the surrounding rock.

Reach a pair of footbridges across the Tuolumne River at 3.5 miles, where the river begins picking up power and speed and forms a series of cascades all the way to Glen Aulin. The path takes you close enough to breathtaking Tuolumne Falls to feel the cool spray. As the descent continues, watch for views up Cold Canyon to admire Matterhorn Peak. The trail takes you into deep forest featuring patches of corn lily and fragrant labrador tea shrubs to the junction with May Lake at 5 miles. Some steep switchbacks lead down to White Cascade, which spills over polished gray granite and then topples tumultuously into a deep pool. Glen Aulin High Sierra Camp sits next to it, and it's a good spot to spend night one.

Pressing on, arrive at the brink of cascading California Falls, perched at the base of an ominous rocky cliff. Keep descending in a forest where sugar pines join red firs and lodgepole pines in the dark areas and Jeffrey pines, incense cedars, and Sierra junipers occupy the open spots. Broad Le Conte Falls glides over granite slabs, and then farther on, extensive Waterwheel Falls at 7.5 miles sprays the canyon full of color and light.

Just beyond Return Creek, a prime swimming hole is situated between a pair of low cascades, and swimming holes become a recurrent theme from here all the way to Pate Valley. These dipping spots are cherished on hot days, as you descend to lower and warmer elevations. Evergreen canyon live oaks and incense cedars get more and more common as the elevation drops, joining black oaks. Ground squirrels abound at this approximate 5000 foot elevation, and the lower you go, the more rattlesnakes there are. Commence a climb around the stark and powerful Muir Gorge under shade, then look for a gorgeous scene of the glaciated, plunging Ten Lakes

Tuolumne Meadows and Mount Gibbs

Canyon to the south. The Grand Canyon of the Tuolumne River eventually meets the sprawling Pate Valley at 19.5 miles, where campsites abound. Factor in extra time to climb virtually the whole way back, or turn south to climb 10 miles to White Wolf, if a car shuttle was prearranged there.

72 | ELIZABETH LAKE

Distance: 4.8 miles round trip
Hiking time: 3–5 hours
High point: 9580 feet
Elevation gain: 900 feet
Difficulty: Moderate
Season: July into November
Map: USGS Vogelsang Peak
Nearest campground: Tuolumne Meadows Campground
Information: Yosemite National Park

Perhaps the ultimate way to get up close and personal with the pointed minarets of the ash gray Cathedral Range is via dark gray-blue Elizabeth

Lake. Horn-topped Unicorn Peak stands close guard over this irregularly shaped lake that is popular with families on summertime weekends. The other stark granite cliffs that form an impressive backdrop to sparkling Elizabeth Lake comprise the northerly wall of photogenic Cathedral Range.

To get there, drive to the Tuolumne Meadows Campground, which is about 9 miles northwest of the Tioga Pass entrance station on Tioga Road (State Route 120). Pick up a parking pass and a campground map at the campground kiosk, follow the map through the campground, and turn left between Loops B and C. Park alongside the locked gate near the restrooms where there's a clearly marked trailhead sign.

Proceed with a moderate climb in a peaceful forest of mountain hemlock and lodgepole pine, where you reach bustling Unicorn Creek, which drains from Elizabeth Lake. Enter an open meadow at 1.5 miles, where youthful lodgepole pines have bent and contorted trunks caused from heavy snowpacks. Paintbrush and bistort flowers decorate the meadow, and swirling Unicorn Creek flows through the middle, featuring colorful rocks on its shallow bottom and darting fish. Gaze behind you for an impressive sighting of Ragged Peak and Mount Conness permanently posing above sprawling Tuolumne Meadows. In front of you, the striking wall of Cathedral Range feels closer than it really is.

Reach Elizabeth Lake at 2.3 miles, where shoreside pathways beckon a thorough lake's-edge stroll. Attain classic views of Unicorn Peak from the north and east sides of the lake. Adore this glacier-carved lake basin from

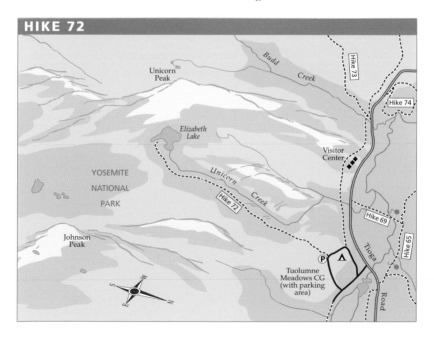

Tuolumne River and Unicorn Peak

above the western shore, where Ragged Peak, North Peak, and Gaylor Peak jut into the distant skyline.

To gather a supreme panorama, pick and choose the easiest and safest route up the east face of Cathedral Range, eventually getting to the base of Unicorn Peak's sheer rock horn. The equally pointed spire of Cathedral Peak to the west is photogenic, as is shallow and open Budd Lake below it. The huge hulk of Johnson Peak protrudes closely from the east.

73 | TUOLUMNE MEADOWS TO YOSEMITE VALLEY VIA JOHN MUIR TRAIL

Distance: 24 miles one way; 8 miles round trip for Cathedral Lakes
Hiking time: 2–4 days
High point: 9800 feet
Elevation gain: 1800 feet
Difficulty: Moderate
Season: July into November
Maps: USGS Tenaya Lake, USGS Half Dome
Nearest campground: Tuolumne Meadows Campground
Information: Yosemite National Park

Roam mostly downhill along a classic stretch of the John Muir Trail that takes you up to the fabulous Cathedral Lakes and then gradually down past miles of meadows and stupendous views. The one-way journey also includes gorgeous Sunrise Creek and the upper reaches of the colorful Merced River.

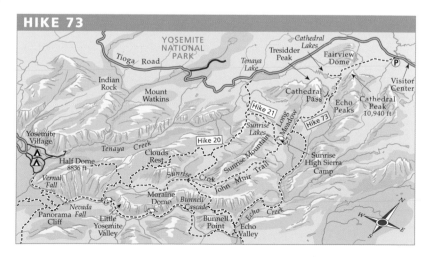

Before you get to your car or the shuttle bus at Happy Isles to take you back to Tuolumne Meadows, you'll wander past Nevada Fall and Vernal Fall, two of Yosemite National Park's most photographed waterfalls. The first 3 miles and the last 3 miles of this trek are typically jammed with hikers, especially on summer weekends. For more privacy, spend the bulk of your time in the middle parts of the journey, or go after Labor Day or on summer weekdays.

To get there, drive to 1.5 miles west of the Tuolumne Meadows Campground entrance on Tioga Road (State Route 120) and park on the side of the highway. You can also ride the Tuolumne Meadows shuttle bus to the Cathedral Lakes trailhead after parking your car at Happy Isles at the east end of Yosemite Valley.

Follow the wide and flat path 0.1 mile to a large signboard with trail information and a map. Stay straight and ascend through a lodgepole pine forest. Enter a flowery meadow after 1 mile, cross several tributaries of Cathedral Creek, and pass through an often mosquito-infested dell just before reaching the trail fork to the Cathedral Lakes at 3.2 miles.

These subalpine lakes are a major highlight of the trip, punctuated by the needlelike spire of Cathedral Peak piercing the sky. This mass of granodiorite looms more than 1000 feet above the lakes. Glacial action has repeatedly battered and chiseled away on the peak's flanks to form a steep-walled monolith that attracts mountain climbers. Descend 0.5 mile to justifiably popular Lower Cathedral Lake and reach its bedrock-lined east shore. Too many folks choose to spend the night here, and bears have raided many a knapsack here as well. But swimming in the shallow, clear waters on a sunny afternoon during a heat spell can be comfortable and refreshing. Hike to the lake's outlet for good views of nearby Polly Dome and Tenaya Peak, with Mount Hoffmann in the distance.

To get to the smaller and even more shallow Upper Cathedral Lake and back to the trail, pick a rocky course southeast for 0.6 mile. From this paradise of a lake, note that Cathedral Peak features a point and a triangular minaret, and the entire mountain reflects in the lake.

The trail now climbs 0.25 mile to broad Cathedral Pass, where Matterhorn Peak looms far to the north and nearby Tresidder Peak and the four crowded Echo Peaks can be viewed clearly. Traverse up the east side of Tresidder Peak on a gentle ascent to this journey's high point, where the Clark Range and surrounding high peaks to the south are striking. The trail now switchbacks down to aptly named Long Meadow, passes a junction with a trail down Echo Creek, and then bends west to near Sunrise Camp at 8.5 miles. Perched on a granite bench, this High Sierra Camp is superb for spending the night and makes an ideal base camp for a 3-mile round-trip day hike to scenic Sunrise Lakes on a trail heading northwest.

The John Muir Trail continues through the south arm of Long Meadow, then commences an ascent up the slopes of Sunrise Mountain. It parallels

Facing page: Mount Watkins (left) and Mirror Lake

the headwaters of Sunrise Creek, then snakes steeply down the rocky canyon. Stay straight at a pair of trail forks, where good camping spots pop up along Sunrise Creek. One mile past the junction, cross Sunrise Creek in a shaded red fir forest and then reach the junction for Clouds Rest (Hike 20) about 1 mile farther. The fork for Half Dome (Hike 1) appears about 0.5 mile farther, and your trail, still the John Muir Trail, switchbacks down through a changing forest featuring stately incense cedars to the floor of Little Yosemite Valley, where camping is directed by rangers stationed, due to the area's popularity.

The polished granite of Liberty Cap takes center stage where Sunrise Creek empties into the Merced River. The John Muir Trail now follows the meandering course of the Merced River, which features several deep swimming holes. Pass a lot of brush and erratic boulders to reach a pair of single falls that plunge dramatically over sheer granite cliffs called Nevada Fall and Vernal Fall (Hike 2). Breathe the mist that sometimes passes in the breeze while you stare at the falls, grayish, dome-shaped Liberty Cap to the nearby north, and Glacier Point to the west. The mostly shaded hike from here on out descends steeply in spots for almost 3 miles to Happy Isles and Yosemite Valley.

74 | POTHOLE DOME AND THE TUOLUMNE RIVER

Distance: 1.5 miles round trip
Hiking time: 1–2 hours
High point: 8800 feet
Elevation gain: 200 feet
Difficulty: Easy
Season: May into November
Map: USGS Tioga Pass
Nearest campground: Tuolumne Meadows Campground
Information: Yosemite National Park

Here's the easiest way to get to know sprawling Tuolumne Meadows and the numerous granite domes that surround it. This short, safe climb up aptly named Pothole Dome allows for a commanding view over the meadows and neighboring peaks. An exceptionally scenic strip of the Tuolumne River awaits nearby, where glacier-smoothed granite slabs invite sun bathing and picnicking.

Because of the hike's comfort, easy trail access, superb views, and splendid photo ops, a lot of folks do this one. For the most privacy, go at the break of dawn or at twilight time, or go on a weekday just before Memorial Day or after Labor Day weekend. This is a must-do quickie for those staying at nearby Tuolumne Meadows Campground, and it can be done in the same day as Dog Lake (Hike 64).

To get there, pull into the turnout at the west end of Tuolumne Meadows on Tioga Road (State Route 120). It's 1.5 miles west of the Tuolumne Meadows Information Center.

The trail begins northwest along a meadow that stays damp usually into late summer. From the meadow tip, the path heads east along the base of Pothole Dome where you commence your ascent of it when you see a safe route. Dur-

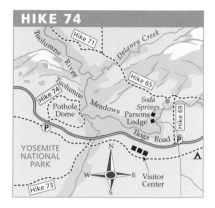

ing the wet season please skirt the meadow and do not walk through wet areas. To see the most potholes, wander over to the south slopes. Potholes are typically noted in streams, where rocks swirl around in a bedrock depression and slowly drill out a hole. This process on Pothole Dome was done by glaciers trapping

Mammoth Peak and Tuolumne River

flowing watercourses. Detecting blocky crystals of potassium feldspar lodged into the polished slabs is easy. Enjoy views of nearby Fairview Dome to the southwest and Daff Dome to the northwest. The centerpiece of Tuolumne Meadows, Lembert Dome (Hike 63), fronts Mount Dana (Hike 60) and Mount Gibbs.

To explore a stretch of rapids and pools on the Tuolumne River, get back to the trail and follow it for 0.25 mile as it crosses a very low divide, passing lodgepole pines visited by mountain chickadees. Look for white-crowned sparrows flitting in the willow bushes along the banks.

Facing page: Carson Peak

ANSEL ADAMS WILDERNESS

75 | SARDINE LAKES AND MONO PASS

Distance: 10 miles round trip; 7 miles round trip
  for Lower Sardine Lake
Hiking time: 6–8 hours or overnight
High point: 10,500 feet
Elevation gain: 3600 feet
Difficulty: Strenuous
Season: July through October
Map: USGS Koip Peak
Nearest campground: Silver Lake Campground
Information: Inyo National Forest, Ansel Adams Wilderness

This is a classic but physically challenging backdoor entry to an eastern edge of Yosemite National Park where visual highlights unfold. Tucked into rugged High Sierra granite, the deep and cold Sardine Lakes are strikingly beautiful, with their clear waters that transform to black on cloudy days. Be sure to find a perch above one of the lakes to stare eastward at the desert that features Mono Lake and Mono Craters. From the shallow and adorable lakelets at historic Mono Pass, an adventurous hiker will be dazzled by a close-up array of Yosemite National Park place names, such as Kuna Peak to the south, Mammoth Peak to the west, and Mount Gibbs to the north.

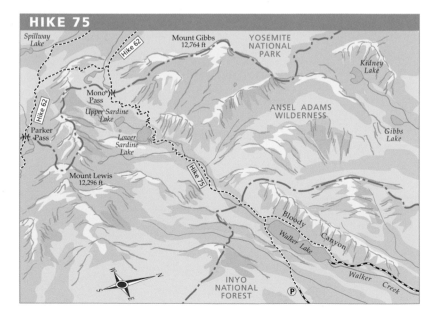

Walker Lake

Expect some solitude with this route, which is agonizingly steep and shadeless in spots heading toward the lakes. This trail up Bloody Canyon used to be steeper long ago, but it still traverses up big rocks and loose stones in the higher parts. Camping is prohibited in the entire Dana Fork drainage.

To get there, drive U.S. Highway 395 north of Mammoth Lakes and take the more northerly of the two June Lake exits. Stay on the paved road for 1.5 miles, then turn west onto the unpaved road signed for Walker Lake. Veer left at the junction immediately afterward, drive 0.4 mile, and then go right for Walker Lake. Follow all signs for Walker Lake, and after 4.3 miles of unpaved roads, park for free at the small parking area near the pit toilet.

Commence climbing right off, in an open forest of Jeffrey pine, Sierra juniper, red fir, and mountain mahogany. Gain a view down on sprawling and scenic Walker Lake after 0.2 mile. Cheery yellow-green meadow strips adorn the northern shore, and these rewarding views of lake and meadow accompany you the entire way down to Walker Lake, which is enjoyed by anglers and swimmers alike. Reach a trail junction at 0.5 mile, where a right turn takes you quickly to lake's edge for a break. The left trail, your route, angles along the hillside past red firs and above willows and quaking aspens for a while.

The rousing chorus of Walker Creek eases your climb along a series of switchbacks, where comfort is afforded by views behind of Walker Lake and Mono Lake. The summer wildflowers that decorate Walker Creek's banks are profuse in spots, and they include scarlet gilia, ranger buttons, monkeyflower, columbine, and nude buckwheat.

The ascent intensifies as the trail snakes up for the final 0.5 mile to Lower Sardine Lake. Reach a small ridge, enjoy level strolling for a bit, cross Walker Creek, and climb some more. A waterfall is overhung by massive rock slabs just below the lip of the lake at 3.5 miles. Lower Sardine Lake, elevation 9890 feet, is crammed into a cranny beneath barren and rocky cliffs.

When fully rested, watered, and fed, begin a sweat-inducing climb for 0.5 mile to smaller, teardrop-shaped Upper Sardine Lake, which you find by heading south at a bench. The final mile-long climb to view-filled, sometimes windy Mono Pass and shallow Summit Lake is gentler. Look for white-crowned sparrows perhaps nesting in the willows in the lake's outlet. Brewer's blackbirds sometimes migrate up to Mono Pass in midsummer.

76 | PARKER LAKE AND UPPER PARKER CREEK

Distance: 7 miles round trip; 4.4 miles round trip
  for Parker Lake
Hiking time: 4–6 hours
High point: 8600 feet
Elevation gain: 900 feet
Difficulty: Moderate
Season: Year-round
Map: USGS Koip Peak
Nearest campground: Silver Lake Campground
Information: Ansel Adams Wilderness

Parker Lake and Parker Creek's remote headwaters occupy a basin carved out steeply beneath the abrupt eastern face of the High Sierra Mountains. The cross-country hike in the canyon above the lake is amazingly wild yet peaceful, in a land where the walls of towering Mount Lewis and Parker Peak are so jaggedly vertical you can't see their tall heads.

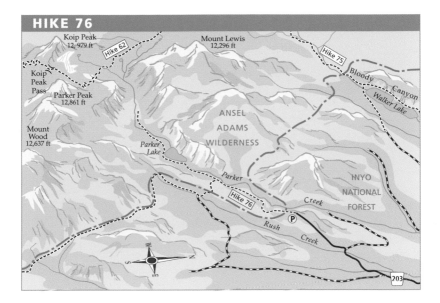

The easy trail that follows a meadow-lined stretch of pretty Parker Creek leading to Parker Lake is obscure enough to get missed by most. It ends at granite-walled Parker Lake, where all the rugged terrain above is unreachable, except for the upper creek clogged with willows and quaking aspens that heads west up the canyon. The swimming in the creek and lake is refreshing, and the fishing is relaxing. Getting to the lake via snowshoes in winter is a delight, although you may have to park on the side of the road well below the trailhead.

To get there, drive U.S. Highway 395 between Lee Vining and Mammoth Lakes and take the more northerly of the two June Lake turnoffs. Drive paved Road 158 for 1.5 miles, turn west onto the unpaved road signed for Parker Lake, and then swing left at the junction immediately following. Follow all signs for the lake for 2.3 miles, then park for free at the small trailhead lot.

Sagebrush, mountain mahogany, mules ears, and sulfur flower accompany you on the sandy trail during the mellow ascent. Jeffrey pines join the overstory along the creek stroll, where improving views of glistening Mono Lake appear to the east. Scattered lodgepole pines and quaking aspens add beauty to Parker Creek as you wander along the edge of a meadow laced with corn lily, larkspur, and yarrow.

Reach a trail junction signed for Silver Lake at 2 miles, and then reach midsize Parker Lake 0.2 mile farther. To the west, a glacial waterfall can be discerned below 13,002-foot-high Kuna Peak, whose top can also be seen. The view of Kuna Peak improves after taking the scant trail around the south side of Parker Lake to its aspen-lined inlet. It's here that 1 mile's

worth of gently sloping, pick-and-choose hiking happens in a fantasy wonderland of summer wildflowers along the banks of Upper Parker Creek's meandering course.

77 | FERN AND YOST LAKES

Distance: 6.8 miles round trip; 3.6 miles round trip
   for Fern Lake only
Hiking time: 4–7 hours
High point: 9100 feet
Elevation gain: 2500 feet
Difficulty: Strenuous
Season: June through October
Maps: USGS Mammoth Mountain, USGS June Lake
Nearest campground: June Lake Campground
Information: Ansel Adams Wilderness

Stashed beneath the imposing east face of Carson Peak, cute and petite Fern Lake is granite-encased, and fishing is often good while swimming is always refreshing. Neighboring Yost Lake, resting invitingly under the rocky slopes of Peak 11,014, adds even more zest and seclusion to an already

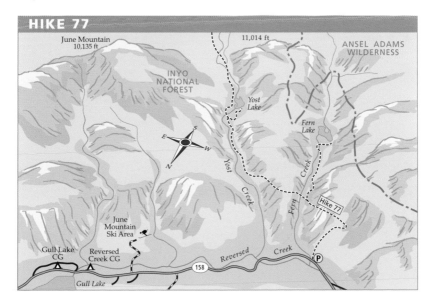

Facing page: Mount Lewis from Grant Lake

Elderberry and Silver Lake

vigorous journey on rugged trails. Typical of high mountain lakes just east of Yosemite National Park, summer wildflower displays and views of towering mountains and steep canyons abound.

To get there, travel U.S. Highway 395 north of Mammoth Lakes and turn west on the more southerly of the two June Lake turnoffs. Go west on paved and scenic Road 158 for 5.3 miles, then turn south at a sign for Yost

Creek Trail. Drive a short distance on unpaved road, stay left at a metal gate, and soon park for free at the small lot at the trailhead.

With hikes that start with strenuous climbing like this one, warming up the muscles and beginning with a slow trudge will save energy and reduce the chance of tired and/or pulled muscles. At first the steep trail is lined with quaking aspens, with shimmering yellow leaves in fall, but these soon give way to lodgepole pines and Jeffrey pines towering over sagebrush, broadleaf lupine, and fragrant mountain pennyroyal.

Pause occasionally to rest and admire nearby, sky blue Silver Lake just to the north. If time and energy permit, you can stroll its photogenic 0.75-mile-long trail starting from the outlet creek and tracing the eastern shore. The trail to Fern Lake keeps climbing, with Sierra junipers augmenting the improving vistas, which soon include June Lake. Orange-flowered Indian paintbrush and yellow-blossomed mules ears adorn the dusty and rocky trail, which in spots traverses a steep slope.

If it's early through midsummer, Fern Creek's little waterfall at 0.8 mile still packs a punch. Reach a trail junction 0.2 mile farther and keep right for Fern Lake, noting that the left turn climbs to Yost Lake, your final destination. Ascend steadily as mountain hemlocks join the open forest, and soon you make the final steep push to reach precious Fern Lake, which is walled by rock on three sides. Carson Peak, at 10,909 feet, is quite bulky to the west.

Retrace your steps 0.8 mile, then bear right for Yost Lake. The open forest and wildflower sprinklings are similar to the Fern Lake Trail, but the climbing is gentler. The final 0.7 mile stays just above the banks of slender Yost Creek with Peak 11,014 in your face. It towers over penguin-shaped Yost Lake, which offers granite slabs for picnicking and tiny beaches for wading.

78 | GLASS CREEK MEADOW AND OBSIDIAN DOME

Distance: 5 miles round trip
Hiking time: 3–5 hours
High point: 8850 feet
Elevation gain: 800 feet
Difficulty: Moderate
Season: May through October
Map: USGS Mammoth Mountain
Nearest campground: Glass Creek Campground
Information: Ansel Adams Wilderness

To the naked eye, obsidian rock looks deceiving. It's indistinctly gray from afar, yet shiny black up close. This journey is mostly about piles and piles

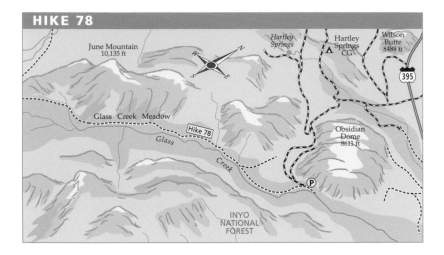

of obsidian, but it also features cascades, views of High Sierra peaks, and a wildflower-dotted meadow.

A favorite with horseback riders, this hike gets overlooked by hikers who opt for more popular rambles in the Mammoth Lakes area. But this is an ideal region for spotting wildlife, such as yellow-bellied marmots scurrying in the obsidian piles or Belding ground squirrels harvesting pine nuts. Look for Cassin's finches and hermit thrushes exiting limbs.

You'll be more comfortable on this hike by wearing sunglasses to reduce the glare reflected from the harsh volcanic landscape and high-top boots to better negotiate the long trail sections of deep sand and pumice chunks.

To get there, turn off U.S. Highway 395 onto signed Obsidian Dome Road, located 3.7 miles south of the more southerly June Lake junction and 0.2 mile north of Deadman Summit. Travel this dirt road 2.8 miles, staying left at the first junction. The road branches into three routes as you near the trailhead. Stay to the right, but don't cross the creek, and soon reach a small lot where you park for free. The path for Glass Creek Meadow takes off from the north side of Glass Creek, where a trail post sits 15 yards from a huge red fir.

Climb gently along slim Glass Creek in a light forest of lodgepole pines, Jeffrey pines, and red firs. At 0.2 mile, carefully cross the willow-lined creek and climb alertly up the obsidian flow. Obsidian rocks of all shapes and sizes are found on this hill, and the higher you climb, the better the views get of June Mountain and the nearby cascades to the west.

Back on the trail, climb to a series of Glass Creek's noisy cascades rushing down the canyon. Monkeyflower and larkspur border the charge 0.3 mile farther, and the grade then mellows through sagebrush, ranger buttons, and sulfur flower. You may lose the indistinct trail, but if you keep

Obsidian Dome in foreground

just up the hillside on the north side of the creek, you'll reach the meadow.

Gain the crest of a low ridge at 1.7 miles, where there are views of Obsidian Dome to the east and expansive Glass Creek Meadow just below to the west. Behind the meadow, towering San Joaquin Ridge punctuates the sky. Rainfall from its east side makes its way to the Owens River and the Los Angeles Aqueduct; precipitation from the west side of the ridge winds up in San Francisco Bay.

Descend into conifer-ringed Glass Creek Meadow, which is moist and green virtually year-round owing to the multitude of small streams that filter in from higher ground. Wildflowers flourish here, including monkeyflower, Brewers lupine, yarrow, yampah, penstemon, and gentian. The backdrop of the distant Mammoth Mountains adds to the ambience.

Back at your car, drive back and park for free at the signed Obsidian Dome area for a mile-long stroll beneath tall Jeffrey pines next to this huge pile of mushroom-shaped obsidian rubble. The black glass obsidian is mixed with rhyolite.

79 | MINARET VISTA TO TWO TEATS VIA SAN JOAQUIN RIDGE

Distance: 9.4 miles round trip; or 4.8 miles round trip for Deadman Pass
Hiking time: 5–8 hours
High point: 11,387 feet
Elevation gain: 2600 feet
Difficulty: Moderate to strenuous
Season: March through October
Map: USGS Mammoth Mountain
Nearest campground: Lake Mary Campground
Information: Ansel Adams Wilderness

Virtually every step of this journey along the curving spine of the San Joaquin Ridge is steeped in breathtaking scenery and laden with summer wildflowers. From the get-go and throughout, the views of Mount Clyde, Mount Ritter, and Banner Peak to the west are superb, and by the time you get on top of Two Teats, a final panorama unfolds that includes Mono Lake to the northeast and prominent Yosemite National Park peaks.

Most folks are satisfied to get well away from the crowds, bag Deadman Pass, and head back with a batch of spectacular photos. You may see an occasional mountain biker or four-wheel driver along the route as well.

Facing page: Laurel Mountain from San Joaquin Ridge

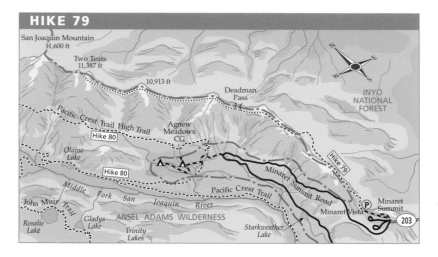

The rough and bumpy dirt road that doubles as a hiking path makes for an ideal snowshoe route in winter. The hike is shadeless and therefore sometimes windy, so bring a lot of water, a windbreaker, sunblock, sunglasses, and a hat.

To get there, turn west on Road 203 at Mammoth Junction from U.S. Highway 395. Drive about 3 miles through the town of Mammoth Lakes, then go right at the sign indicating Devils Postpile. Continue 5.5 miles climbing on a paved road, following signs for Minaret Vista. Park for free in the large lot near the interpretive signs and the restroom, which fronts the unsigned trailhead.

A slim path leads north 100 yards or so, connecting with the old dirt road, where you bear left on it. After a 0.5-mile climb, reach a flat featuring scattered young lodgepole pines. Stroll west on it a few paces for fantastic views of the Minarets, which are mainly Mount Clyde, Mount Ritter, and Banner Peak. Their glaciers are gleaming white in the morning, converting gradually to dull gray by late afternoon.

At 0.8 mile, look behind you for sensational views of Mammoth Mountain, Laurel Mountain, and 12,268-foot-tall Mount Morrison, from west to east. Continue your steady ascent past red firs, whitebark pines, lodgepole pines, and mountain hemlocks over loose and crumbly pumice, remnants of the region's hot volcanic history. The San Joaquin Ridge is part of the Sierra Divide, which is the watershed between east and west. Little precipitation happens here, and therefore drought-tolerant flowers take center stage, including mat lupine, sulfur flower, mountain pennyroyal, nude buckwheat, and mules ears.

Reach a footpath that descends to Deadman Pass at 2.4 miles and soon make your way to the sandy saddle. From here, the San Joaquin ridgeline gets slimmer, and you can gaze north by northwest to scout and plan your cross-country route to Two Teats. As you resume steady climbing, the views are more pronounced to the northwest, where Yosemite National Park's Mount Lyell, Donohue Peak, and Blacktop Peak march from south to north. There are a lot of chances to peer down to the west into the origin of the San Joaquin River as it flows smoothly into Agnew Meadows. When you finally crown Two Teats, note the grayish, native bunchgrasses on these mostly nude, pumice-coated bumps.

80 THOUSAND ISLAND, GARNET, AND EDIZA LAKES

Distance: 18-mile loop
Hiking time: 2–3 days
High point: 9900 feet
Elevation gain: 2100 feet
Difficulty: Moderate
Season: July into November
Maps: USGS Mammoth Mountain, USGS Mount Ritter
Nearest campground: Agnew Meadows Campground
Information: Inyo National Forest, Ansel Adams Wilderness

Snow-gouged Banner Peak rises gloriously over a trio of uniquely shaped, rock-encased lakes. Your mission is to take your sweet time deciding which lake best shows off this 12,945-foot-tall mountain that

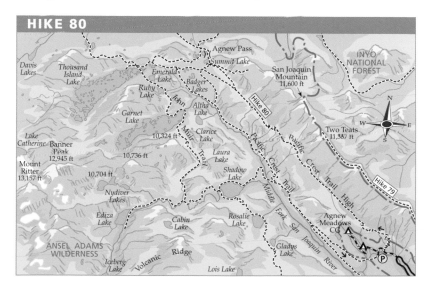

Banner Peak and Mount Ritter

stands guard over the San Joaquin River Canyon in tandem with 13,157-foot-tall Mount Ritter. Capture this drainage in its splendor from above along the Pacific Crest Trail (PCT), which also unveils views of distant Yosemite National Park peaks along with Mount Ritter and Banner Peak. Then take the John Muir Trail to these Shangri-la-like lakes along with at least half a dozen other lakes.

Be sure to call ahead to determine which lakes might be closed to camping either totally, partially, or not at all, because the situation varies. A classic one-way backpack trip can be completed to Silver Lake by combining this hike to Thousand Island Lake, then continuing north (see Hike 66). Fewer folks use these popular trails to these well-known lakes on weekdays and after Labor Day.

To get there, turn off U.S. Highway 395 at Mammoth Lakes Junction and travel Road 203 through the town of Mammoth Lakes. Angle right for Devils Postpile at the road junction after 3.7 miles. Continue about 10 miles, following signs for Agnew Meadows Campground. (Note: Unless you're camping here or in the Devils Postpile area, you must leave your vehicle at the Mammoth Mountain ski resort about 7 miles back, just east of the entrance station. From the resort, you can take the shuttle to the stop at Agnew Meadows Campground, and follow its entry road 0.3 mile to the trailhead.) Walk east on the road that runs by the pack station to find the trailhead signed for the Pacific Crest Trail, which is also called High Trail. This well-graded zigzag climb in a pine and fir forest heads northeast along the lower slopes of the San Joaquin Ridge. The ascent stays steady but gentle by the time the PCT veers in a continuous northwest contour along the midslopes of the San Joaquin Ridge at 1 mile. Get lost in a daydream over the ensuing 4 miles on a route that winds mostly up but sometimes down past scattered stands of pine and through stretches of sagebrush and bitterbrush. Willows and mountain alders adorn the crossings of several tributaries of the San Joaquin River, which you see intermittently below. The contrast is striking: dry brushy slopes are slashed by flowing streams decorated with larkspur, shooting star, tiger lily, corn lily, and monkeyflower thriving high up the slope. Views keep improving of the rocky Ritter Range to the west.

Return to dense forest cover, stay straight at a trail junction, and soon reach a cluster of lakes called Badger Lakes at 6.2 miles. If it's early season, have your mosquito repellent ready here. Wander along the PCT through scattered lodgepole pines and soon the trail follows the outlet of Thousand Island Lake past a trail fork. When you get to this large, mostly open lake, be sure to stroll west to midway along the north shore to capture the most photogenic views of wondrous Banner Peak, at times reflecting majestically over the lake. The aptly named lake features countless tiny rock islands strewn across it—some are so small only two people could fit on them.

From near where the meadowy outlet emerges from the lake, head south on the John Muir Trail and soon stroll by several snowmelt tarns, including Emerald Lake. Wander along the shore of Ruby Lake, cross its outlet which flows into Middle Fork San Joaquin River, and then commence a short climb followed by a brief descent to Garnet Lake at 9.5 miles. This precious and slightly less visited lake is as long but half as wide as Thousand Island Lake, but Mount Ritter joins Banner Peak to tower over it.

The John Muir Trail now climbs 0.5 mile to a small pass, then soon connects with a trail fork at 10.4 miles where you stay right. The trail follows a fork of Shadow Creek, descending in a lodgepole pine forest to a trail junction, where you head right and proceed on a mile-long gradual climb to Ediza Lake. After crossing several small meadows, reach ghost-shaped Ediza Lake and once again check out the visages of Banner Peak and Mount Ritter.

Retrace your steps to the last trail fork, go right, and descend to tree-lined Shadow Lake at 14 miles. Trace the northern shore, watch cascades topple down steep cliffs from the outlet, and then descend via open and rocky switchbacks that are filled with views. Cross the Middle Fork San Joaquin River via a solid footbridge, pass into an aspen grove, make a right at a trail junction, and soon pass by small and shallow Olaine Lake at 16 miles. From here, follow signs southward for Agnew Meadows to your trailhead.

81 | McCloud Lake

Distance: 2 miles round trip
Hiking time: 2–3 hours
High point: 9320 feet
Elevation gain: 300 feet
Difficulty: Easy to moderate
Season: June through October
Map: USGS Crystal Crag
Nearest campground: Lake George Campground
Information: Ansel Adams Wilderness

Hikes like these, that are easy and interesting, bring families closer together. Although swimming isn't allowed at picturesque McCloud Lake, a relaxing stroll around the lake soothes the soul and awakens the senses. To avoid the throngs of fishermen, horseback riders, and hikers, visit this lake on weekdays or after Labor Day weekend. This is a great hike to combine with Hike 82 (TJ Lake and Crystal Lake).

Crystal Crag from Lake George

HIKES 81 & 82

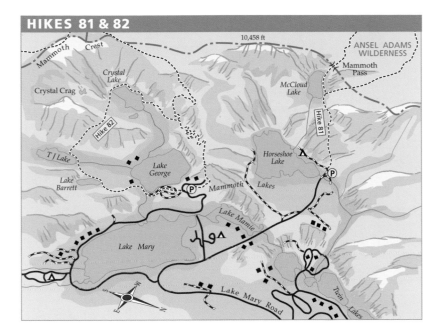

To get there, turn off U.S. Highway 395 at Mammoth Junction and drive Road 203 through the town of Mammoth. Continue straight onto signed Lake Mary Road, drive 5 miles to road's end, and park for free in the large lot next to Horseshoe Lake.

Commence climbing past the sign for Mammoth Pass in a forest that features scattered large and stately specimens of lodgepole pines and mountain hemlocks. The steep grade eases as you bear left at the trail fork for McCloud Lake at 0.2 mile, where western white pines and red firs gradually join the forest. Cliffy Mammoth Crest dominates your view to the south, while to the north, the hogback-shaped south face of Mammoth Mountain looks a bit like the east face of Lassen Peak.

Take another left at a final signed trail junction at 0.7 mile and reach a beach adorning the east shore of McCloud Lake soon after. Gooseberry, willows, and pinemat manzanita form a decorative understory beneath hemlocks and lodgepole pines, bordering the lake's sandy shoreline. A lakeside path leads you to several picnic spots and nice views of Mammoth Crest and Mammoth Mountain. Fishing is permissible on a catch-and-release basis. From granite slabs just off the east shore, gaze southeast at an impressive grouping of large, mostly unnamed mountains. Rook-shaped Peak 10,458 reflects in the clear lake in late afternoon. To extend the hike, follow the path that leads from the northwestern shore of the lake. It ascends 0.4 mile to vistaless Mammoth Pass, the lowest gap between east and west in the entire portion of the central Sierra.

82 | TJ LAKE AND CRYSTAL LAKE

Distance: 7.6-mile loop
Hiking time: 4–6 hours
High point: 10,450 feet
Elevation gain: 1900 feet
Difficulty: Moderate to strenuous
Season: June through October
Map: USGS Crystal Crag
Nearest campground: Lake George Campground
Information: Ansel Adams Wilderness; John Muir Wilderness
See map page 231

Look for ominous Crystal Crag's reflection in four High Sierra lakes and climb ridges that display enchanting views of numerous 12,000-foot-plus peaks, including a few within Yosemite National Park.

Lake Barrett and Crystal Lake feature refreshing afternoon swimming and usually better than average fishing. But these lakes are very crowded during July and August weekends, so plan your journey for other times.

To get there, turn off U.S. Highway 395 at Mammoth Junction and travel Road 203 a couple miles through the town of Mammoth Lakes. Continue straight at the junction on paved Lake Mary Road and drive 3.9 miles before going left onto Road 4S09. Go 0.3 mile and turn right for Lake George. Arrive at the campground 0.3 mile farther and park for free. Hint: To be assured of a parking spot, come on weekdays, early mornings, or after Labor Day.

A wide path traces the eastern shoreline of large and scenic Lake George, featuring a picturesque knob called Crystal Crag that looms above. The trail narrows at 0.2 mile, crosses Lake George's outlet amid alder and willow bushes, and then reaches a junction. Go left for little Lake Barrett and climb steeply on a rocky trail brightened by angelica, fireweed, and cow parsnip in moist spots. Shaggy mountain hemlocks join stalky western white pines, forming a canopy for thorny gooseberry shrubs. At 0.6 mile, keep right at a trail junction for Lake Barrett.

Much larger TJ Lake lies just ahead, after a brief climb and then a descent. There are some scenic campsites with a view over the lake from a ledge on the east side. Stroll the lake to a sloping green garden at the south end where the inlet stream charges in. Two-headed Crystal Crag overhangs the lake, which is lined with labrador tea and red mountain heather. Fishing is good, but swimming is not allowed.

From here, the route to Crystal Lake is via cross-country. Get to TJ Lake's driftwood-clogged outlet, then climb in a dense hemlock and western white pine forest to emerge in a few minutes atop a shelf featuring a

TJ Lake outlet

granite ledge positioned steeply above the lake. Pick and choose your way to a ridge just to the south of Crystal Crag along a granite slope. Veer northwest along a granite slope, amid bushy whitebark pines, angling toward Crystal Lake, which is nestled beneath the protective bulk of Mammoth Crest to the west and Crystal Crag to the east.

Trace the rocky shore of hippopotamus-shaped Crystal Lake to its inlet, where the return trail leads 0.2 mile to a signed junction. Heading right shortens the trip by 1.5 miles. Going left means a hefty climb for a rewarding vista atop Peak 10,458, which caps Mammoth Crest. The trail snakes up the exposed rock amid stubby hemlocks and whitebark pines, and the improving views will lead you on. The views to the east of Mammoth Lakes, including Lake Mary and Lake George, will seem better on the return when you encounter them face first. Mammoth Mountain bulges to the immediate north. When you reach Mammoth Crest, ascend Peak 10,458 for a breathtaking panorama that features the jagged Minarets, Mount Ritter, and Banner Peak to the distant northwest.

Back at the junction to Crystal Lake, stay straight and descend past western white pines and mountain hemlocks shading pinemat manzanita on the return to Lake George.

83 | SHERWIN LAKES AND VALENTINE LAKE

Distance: 12.8 miles round trip or 6 miles round trip for Sherwin Lakes
Hiking time: 7–10 hours or overnight
High point: 9710 feet
Elevation gain: 2200 feet
Difficulty: Moderate to strenuous
Season: June through October
Map: USGS Bloody Mountain
Nearest campground: Sherwin Creek Campground
Information: John Muir Wilderness; Ansel Adams Wilderness

A well-graded trail offering good footing leads into a remote region of John Muir Wilderness, where you visit seven high mountain lakes that look distinctively different from one another. You start in desert scrub, continue in a high and dry region scattered with junipers, and finish in a moister region laced with grasses, lodgepole pines, and mountain hemlocks. You can always swim and picnic at the Sherwin Lakes and then

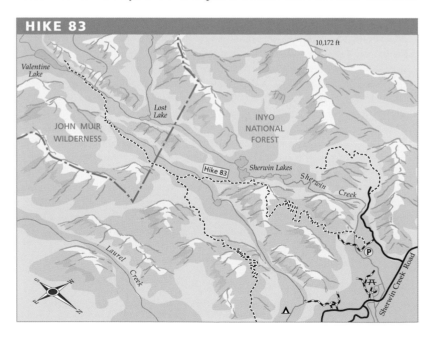

HIKE 83

Mount Morrison from the Sherwin Lakes trailhead

head back. But Valentine Lake, at twice as far, is even more peaceful and arguably more photogenic.

To get there, turn off U.S. Highway 395 at Mammoth Junction and follow Road 203 through the town of Mammoth Lakes. Turn south on Old Mammoth Road, drive 0.8 mile, and turn left onto Sherwin Creek Road, where you lose the pavement after 0.2 mile. After 1.1 miles of dirt and gravel road, go right at the sign for Sherwin Lakes trailhead. Park for free at the signed trailhead 0.4 mile farther near the pit toilets.

Laurel Mountain, at 11,812 feet, dominates to the southeast along with its massive ridge stretching north as you begin in a land of sagebrush, bitterbrush, and mules ears. This low growth is soon replaced by mostly white firs and Jeffrey pines as you reach and cross slim Sherwin Creek at 0.2 mile. A series of switchbacks ensues, intensifying after just less than 1 mile.

The grade abates as you reach a large flat that houses the Sherwin Lakes. The trail heads southwesterly for 0.3 mile, where you veer a bit northwest to reach the first granite-ringed lake at 2.2 miles. Mammoth Mountain, at 11,053 feet, gets noticed beyond the first two lakes to the northwest. After your fill of this pair of lakes, double back to the trail, wind through the conifers, and soon take the spur trail that leads to a second pair of Sherwin Lakes easily four times the size of the first pair.

The dry landscape continues as you hike toward Valentine Lake back on the steadily climbing main trail. The twisted weather-sculpted fat trunks of ancient Sierra junipers get your attention. Cross a small creek 0.4 mile from the junction to the larger Sherwin Lakes, stay straight at a signed trail junction, and soon resume climbing to reach an entry sign for the John Muir Wilderness. A gentle climb beside a quaking aspen-lined stream leads to a moist, wildflower wonderland 1.5 miles from the spur trail to the larger Sherwin Lakes. Linger here to adore the angelica, ranger buttons, and monkeyflower, then resume climbing.

Cross a dinky stream, look down on Lost Lake on the right, and note that mountain hemlocks have joined the forest. Towering, sheer rock cliffs and peaks soon dominate as you slowly leave a medium-dense forest for open country in the rugged and rocky canyon capped by Valentine Lake. Pass a grass-lined pond, stroll along fern-lined Sherwin Creek awhile, and then prepare for a final haul up the ravine. The climb is steep but short, and soon you're marveling at long and sky blue Valentine Lake, which is wrapped by steep, stark mountains on the east, south, and west sides.

84 | CONVICT LAKE AND MILDRED LAKE

Distance: 3 miles round trip for Convict Lake; 10 miles round trip for Mildred Lake
Hiking time: 2–9 hours; or overnight (permit required)
High point: 9760 feet
Elevation gain: 100 feet for Convict Lake; 2200 feet for Mildred Lake
Difficulty: Easy for Convict Lake; strenuous for Mildred Lake
Season: June through October
Map: USGS Convict Lake
Nearest campground: Convict Lake Campground
Information: John Muir Wilderness

It's ironic that a scenic and peaceful place like Convict Lake would be the site of a shoot 'em up bloodbath. But in 1871, 29 prisoners in Carson City, Nevada, shot the warden and escaped to this 7650-foot-high, sky blue lake. When the posse finally caught up with them, this 168-acre lake with a steep, glacial peak on the west, a lush meadow on the east, and a lazy creek was transformed into a bullet-flying spaghetti western featuring death. Mount Morrison, hovering nearly 5000 feet above the lake to the south, was named after posse member Robert Morrison, who died in the shootout. A few prisoners eluded the shoot out, were never caught, and to some they still haunt the area.

The astonishingly contrasting environments of high desert, mature forests, and lake-studded peaks make this an ultimate hike, whether you merely follow the meandering and flat trail around populated Convict Lake or venture up Convict Canyon for a retreat at isolated Mildred Lake. Convict Lake, with a depth of 140 feet, is one of the deepest lakes in the Sierras, and its enticingly open, arid setting is climaxed by rugged and rocky mountains. Ninety-nine percent of the fish in the lake are rainbow trout, and it's heavily stocked. The trail to Mildred Lake is a favorite with horse riders. Both lakes are good for swimming, especially after a hot spell in late summer.

To get there, drive U.S. Highway 395 4.5 miles south of Mammoth

Junction. Turn west at the sign for Convict Lake and travel the paved road 2.3 miles and park for free near the toilets.

Follow the trail in a counterclockwise direction, and promptly savor fantastic views looking west over the lake with Laurel Mountain looming above. The level, gravel path is lined with aspens and willows on the lake side and tobacco brush, sagebrush, bitterbrush, and rabbitbrush on the open, north side. At 0.4 mile, scurry above the trail when you reach the grotesque but photogenic tree snag at lake's edge. Prime pictures await, with Convict Lake and mighty Mount Morrison taking center stage.

Pass a lone Jeffrey pine specimen at 0.8 mile and reach the northwestern edge of the lake 0.4 mile farther at a trail junction. Here, you have three choices: One, you can follow the Convict Lake Trail another 0.3 mile past previously encountered trees and shrubs along with Sierra juniper and mountain mahogany to the inlet stream. A picnic awaits beneath the pure white trunks of quaking aspens, a real bonus when the leaves turn golden in late September. Two, you can retrace your steps from here, or three, you can forge on to encircle the lake. If the south side trail is too overgrown, resort to option number one.

However, if you have enough food, water, and gear, you have one more alternative, and that is to claim the serene shores of crystal clear Mildred Lake. Head right on the trail back at the northwestern edge of the lake and immediately begin a mostly moderate climb that doesn't cease until the lake is reached. As you head up inviting Convict Canyon, the north face of snow-flecked Red Slate Mountain soon appears ahead. A bit higher, the

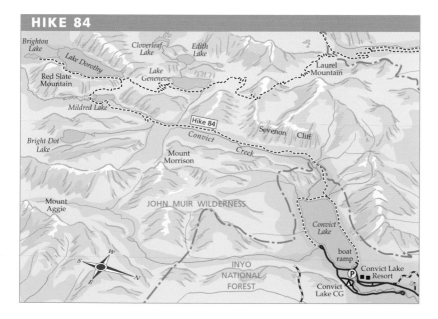

HIKE 84

Convict Lake and Mount Morrison

rugged trail escorts you to views eastward of the sprawling White Mountains, which soon disappear for good as you climb beneath the ominous west-facing flanks of Mount Morrison.

At 2 miles from Convict Lake, the trail stays closer to Convict Creek, offering plenty of chances to cool off in its clear, shallow waters. The streamside scenery is a mix of summer wildflowers, including sulfur buckwheat and angelica, randomly strewn boulders and scree, and grassy meadow splotches. As you pause to catch your breath, gaze behind you to admire Laurel Mountain, which at 400 million years old contains some of the oldest rocks in the Sierras. Limestone gradually changed to gray marble (hence its primary color), and mudstone changed to brown slate (hence its secondary color).

The path gets occasionally indistinct over the final mile-long, steeper ascent, but simply stay just to the west of the creek, and before you know it, nirvana is attained at scintillating Mildred Lake, 3.5 miles from Convict Lake. If you camp, be sure you have a wilderness permit and stay 50 yards or so from the lake. Dorothy Lake is just 1 mile farther up the canyon.

Facing page: Chilnualna Creek cascades

SOUTHWEST CORNER OF YOSEMITE NATIONAL PARK

85 | LEWIS CREEK: RED ROCK FALLS AND CORLIEU FALLS

Distance: 4 miles round trip or longer
Hiking time: 2–3 hours
High point: 4200 feet
Elevation gain: 400 feet
Difficulty: Easy to moderate
Season: Year-round
Map: USGS White Chief Mountain
Nearest campground: Bass Lake Campground
Information: Sierra National Forest, Oakhurst Ranger Station

Breathe the mist of two distinct waterfalls on this shaded and peaceful journey along the wild banks of scenic Lewis Creek. These picturesque waterfalls make for an ideal family excursion and a good alternative to the waterfall hikes within Yosemite National Park that may be crowded.

To get there, travel north from Oakhurst on State Route 41. Some 4 miles north of the Bass Lake turnoff, spot the 4000-foot elevation sign, soon followed by the marker indicating a turnout to allow passing. Park for free in the large gravel turnout just beyond, signed for Lewis Creek. The trail starts just past the green gate, on the east side of the road.

An unpaved road promptly leads to the trail, where you note that the left turn leads 1.5 miles to Red Rock Falls, but you first turn right for the 0.3-mile descent to less popular but equally impressive Corlieu Falls, Madera County's highest waterfall. A few scant side paths lead to this waterfall, which is not visible from the Lewis Creek Trail. If you venture farther downstream, watch for poison oak at trailside. There are a handful of big, smooth boulders to mount at Corlieu Falls, which tumbles into a clear and inviting pool, ideal for dipping in summer.

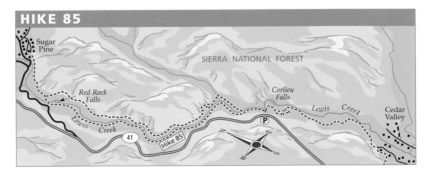

Corlieu Falls

Return to the Lewis Creek Trail after your picnic and head north, retracing your steps for 0.3 mile. After that, the mild climb to Red Rock Falls is shaded and ensconced with a variety of native plants. Large colonies of mountain misery ground cover occupy sunny patches next to large, moss- and lichen-coated granite boulders, a recurrent theme on the hike. The trail, designated in 1982 as part of the National Recreation Trails System, stays enticingly intimate with swift and narrow Lewis Creek, mostly beneath a canopy of incense cedars, canyon live oaks, and occasional but tall white firs. Look for Pacific dogwoods and western azaleas, featuring their fragrant white blooms in mid-spring. If the weather is hot, you'll be tempted to wade in the many clear, cool pools. Cross an inlet creek 1 mile from Corlieu Falls via a small footbridge, where tiger lilies poke from the stream banks. One mile farther, past the above-mentioned plant species as well as occasional sugar pines, ponderosa pines, alders, and wild filberts, veer left at a trail junction and make a brief descent to Red Rock Falls. A major torrent of Lewis Creek spills over a bench of silky smooth, reddish rock, slipping 5 yards to a clear pool.

From here, you can continue 0.5 mile or so upstream. Most of the Lewis Creek Trail follows along the route of the old Madera–Sugar Pine Lumber Company flume that operated until 1931.

86 | MARIPOSA GROVE OF GIANT SEQUOIAS

Distance: Up to 6 miles round trip
Hiking time: 3–4 hours
High point: 6700 feet
Elevation gain: 1000 feet
Difficulty: Moderate
Season: March through December
Map: USGS Mariposa Grove
Nearest campground: Wawona Campground
Information: Yosemite National Park

Feel as small as an ant among some 500 giant and ancient sequoias gracing Yosemite National Park's largest and most popular of three sequoia groves. To seek solitude, go during weekdays after Labor Day and before summer. A maze of trails are well-signed here, so it's easy to tailor your own custom hike, but this route highlights all the sequoias with informative signs, goes the farthest, and flees the crowds the most.

These giant sequoia conifers have an average height of 250 feet, and they're closely related to the taller coast redwoods of northern California.

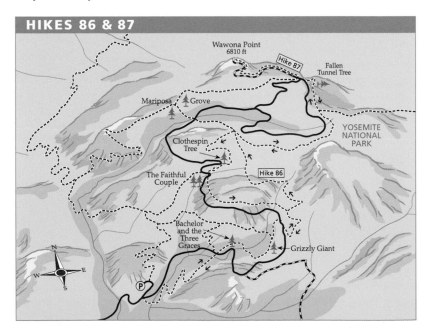

California Tunnel Tree

They have survived snow, lightning, and heavy winds for some 3000 years. Only the bristlecone pines in the nearby White Mountains to the east are older. The sequoias' shallow roots venture only 3 to 6 feet deep. Some of these giant sequoias, which have base diameters of 15 to 20 feet, feature 2-foot-thick bark.

To get there, drive to Yosemite National Park's south entrance station on State Route 41 (Wawona Road). Turn east and drive 2.1 miles to road's end at the Big Trees parking lot, which can be full by midmorning, especially on weekends. During summer and early fall, you can take the shuttle bus that leaves from the Wawona Store, just northwest of the Wawona Hotel. The buses run every 20 minutes. A snack bar, water fountains, restrooms, and a gift shop are all next to where the tram tours begin near the Big Trees parking lot.

Climb gently on a wooden railed pathway to arrive at the Fallen Monarch tree, featuring upturned roots resembling a tangled mess of huge ropes. A brief stroll puts you beneath the Bachelor and Three Graces, and then the notably leaning Grizzly Giant at 0.8 mile, the largest tree in the grove.

The path descends to the California Tunnel Tree. This tunnel was cut in 1895 so stagecoaches could transport tourists through the fat tree. Much of the crowd diminishes just beyond this point, as you now climb steadily and sometimes steeply, past a turnoff for the Clothespin Tree. Go right at the Upper Grove Trail at 1.5 miles and skirt along a hillside beneath a large cluster of unnamed sequoias. Make another right and soon reach the Telescope Tree, which is off the trail to the left at 2.6 miles. Stand inside it and stare skyward past the top of this still living giant.

At the crest of the climb, look for the Fallen Tunnel Tree. It toppled in

1969, due to record winter snows. From here, a trail veers west to reach the Galen Clark Tree and Wawona Point (Hike 87), which can be visited for the investment of a 1.6-mile round trip that returns you to this spot. Look for the nearby sign for the 0.3-mile descent to a small meadow hosting the Grove Museum, which features historical displays, books, and a drinking fountain. Continue downhill, following signs for the nearby Clothespin Tree, which was transformed into an amazing shape by repeated lightning fires. Keep going downhill to a pair of sequoia giants called the Faithful Couple, then follow signs to the trailhead.

87 | WAWONA POINT

Distance: 1.4–5 miles round trip
Hiking time: 1–2 hours
High point: 6810 feet
Elevation gain: 300 feet
Difficulty: Easy to moderate
Season: March through December
Map: USGS Mariposa Grove
Nearest campground: Wawona Campground
Information: Yosemite National Park
See map page 242

Here's a quick and easy way to check out some giant sequoias, get a grand view of the Wawona area and beyond from Wawona Point, and escape most of the large crowds that congregate in the lower reaches of Mariposa Grove. You can combine the entire Mariposa Grove walk (Hike 86) or take the tram to the Fallen Tunnel Tree and stroll west to the Galen Clark sequoia via an old closed road and beyond to Wawona Point. With the tram, you'll get an informative guided tour of the featured sequoias in Mariposa Grove, and you can get out to explore selected sequoias and then take the next tram.

Some of these sequoias have survived snow, lightning, and heavy winds for 3000 years, and they are closely related to the coast redwoods of northern California. There are several more and much larger coast redwood groves than sequoia groves, so it's a more unique experience to stare at these sequoias in Mariposa Grove, Yosemite National Park's largest sequoia grove.

To get there, drive to Yosemite National Park's south entrance station on State Route 41 (Wawona Road). Turn east and drive 2.1 miles to road's end at the Big Trees parking lot, which can be full by midmorning, especially on weekends. During summer and early fall, you can take the shuttle bus that leaves from the Wawona Store, just northwest of the Wawona Hotel. The buses run every 20 minutes. A snack bar, water fountains, restrooms, and a gift shop are all next to where the tram tours begin near the Big Trees parking lot.

After taking the tram or hiking to the Fallen Tunnel Tree, stroll the quiet old road, which like other roads in Mariposa Grove, was once open to park visitors sightseeing in autos. The sequoias rapidly disappear and are replaced by pines as this trail switchbacks up a fairly steep hill the entire 0.6 mile. The viewing site at Wawona Point is paved and marked for a helicopter landing area. There are stone wall railings that keep you secure as you gaze across the Wawona area, peering down on Wawona Meadow some 2600 feet below. To the north, the rocky, curving cliff of Wawona Dome juts above the densely forested, green hills. Buena Vista Peak to the northeast stands nearly 3000 feet taller than where you're standing, and it's capped by the pointed Clark Range beyond.

Pondersosa pine in winter

88 | WAWONA MEADOW

Distance: Up to 4 miles round trip
Hiking time: 2–3 hours
High point: 4200 feet
Elevation gain: 200 feet
Difficulty: Easy
Season: Year-round
Map: USGS Wawona
Nearest campground: Wawona Campground
Information: Yosemite National Park

Here's a serene stroll all about the greenery of a meadow and large conifers. It's also about meandering brooks and wildflowers, including some rare species. Occasionally, you might encounter romantic couples or an equestrian group; otherwise, you're apt to have the hike to yourself. For more solitude, hike along the southwest edge of the tree-encircled meadow via an old, mostly dirt road closed to vehicles. This way, you'll be farther away from Wawona Road and closer to an attractive feeder stream for the nearby South Fork Merced River.

To get there, travel to the tiny hamlet of Wawona on State Route 41 (Wawona Road). Just across from the Wawona Motel, take the road that cuts through the middle of a golf course to a parking lot with pit toilets and a trailhead signed with useful information and photos.

Begin by skirting the south side of the golf course on the old dirt road and soon leave manicured turf behind for the grasses and sedges of Wawona Meadow. Most of the excursion stays in the wind-protected, shaded forest at

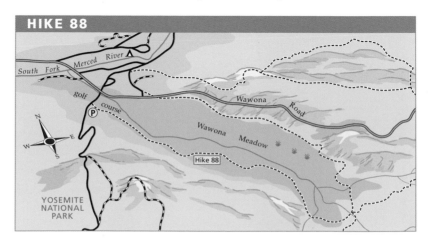

HIKE 88

Wawona Meadow and Wawona Dome

meadow's edge, a border zone teeming with organisms and wildlife called the ecotone. Look for purple finches, blackbirds, warblers, and woodpeckers frolicking in the meadow or low in the trees, or perhaps a great horned owl perched high in the ponderosa pines or incense cedars. In early morning and late afternoon, mule deer congregate in the meadow.

Plenty of spur paths lead directly into the meadow, which is delicate and moist from midwinter into mid-spring. Yellow-flowered buttercups bloom in early spring, three-petaled white star tulips blossom in mid-spring, and the huge-leafed corn lily thrives in clumps and features white flowers in June. Clusters of chokecherry and willow shrubs adorn the stream that swirls along the southwest section of the meadow. Western azalea shrubs flourish amid the conifers at meadow's edge, peaking in early June with fragrant flowers. At trailside in the deepest, darkest parts of the forest, find saprophytes, which are leafless plants that live on the rotting twigs, cones, and needles that form a cushion on the ground. Look for the odd orchids called coral root, crimson-colored snow plants, and the brown spikes known as pinedrops.

This west side of the meadow features an old loading ramp and segments of a time-worn wooden fence, both remnants of when sheep and cattle pastured here long ago. The trail crosses a tributary at 1.5 miles and swerves north at a trail junction and a second brook 0.2 mile farther. Look for pretty clumps of chokecherry here along with patches of monkeyflowers amid tiny rock islands.

Reach a final stream a couple hundred yards farther, where there are arguably the best views across the long meadow of the spring wildflowers. There are also fewer trees here at trailside. Traipse a bit farther to a point where the trail turns briefly away from the meadow. This is a good turnaround point that keeps the hike secluded. This is also a good spot to wander west by southwest out on the meadow to a point where all three tributaries you crossed earlier merge into one to form a feeder stream into the South Fork Merced River. Otherwise, follow the trail northwest for 1.2 miles to the trailhead.

89 | CHILNUALNA FALL

Distance: 8 miles
Hiking time: 5–6 hours
High point: 6000 feet
Elevation gain: 2100 feet
Difficulty: Moderate to strenuous
Season: Year-round
Maps: USGS Wawona, USGS Mariposa Grove
Nearest campground: Wawona Campground
Information: Yosemite National Park

Spectacular Chilnualna Fall is one of the tallest waterfalls outside of Yosemite Valley, tumbling powerfully for hundreds of feet down a narrow, confining chute. The somewhat strenuous ascent starts and ends at swift-flowing Chilnualna Creek, with another meeting with this scenic stream near the midway point. The creek includes a series of cascades and other lesser water-falls, with the most awesome found at the very start and the climax of the journey. Because the hike is located away from the high tourism sections of Yosemite Park and it involves a lot of climbing, few folks do this excursion. That's more solitude for you, especially on hot summer days when you're sweating and watching for rattlesnakes at the lower elevations. The best times to do this hike are in late spring, when the falls are mighty, and early fall, when you can see more gray rock beneath the less potent falls and cascades.

To get there, follow signed Chilnualna Road from Wawona through the tiny hamlet of North Wawona for 2 miles to a signed parking lot on the right at road's end.

The trail commences as a gently ascending dirt road, promptly converting to a footpath that heads briefly up Chilnualna Creek to a 25-foot-tall water-fall. You can scramble cross-country to a few enticing swimming holes just before and after this waterfall. The noisy creek blocks the sound of chirping birds, including warblers, woodpeckers, and colorful western tanagers.

From here, it's steady but moderate climbing most of the way, as you ascend away from the creek, passing the horse trail on the left at 0.5 mile and eventually crossing a manzanita-draped ridge. You then enter a cooler forest of ponderosa pines and incense cedars. Through occasional clear-ings, view Wawona Dome to the east and Wawona Point to the southeast. At 1.5 miles reunite with Chilnualna Creek, your last reliable source for more than 2 miles, unless it's January through April.

Negotiate more than a dozen ascending switchbacks as the trail soon

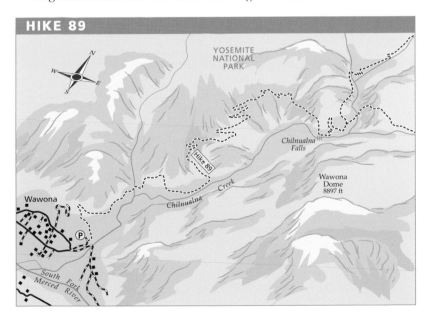

HIKE 89

Chilnualna Creek cascades

enters a shady forest before making a mostly open traverse toward Chilnualna Fall, which you now can see in its entirety. Your trail soon comes to within a few steps from the fall's brink. A few campsites are situated just above, and so is a 20-yard-long cascade frothing in a small gorge. From various vantage points here and at the falls, gaze southwest to take in Wawona Meadow (Hike 88) below, as well as the densely treed Chilnualna Creek canyon you just climbed.

The trail then switchbacks and curves up promptly to the lip of the gorge and a trail fork, where you can continue to the Chilnualna Lakes and Royal Arch Lake (Hike 94).

90 | ALDER CREEK FALL

Distance: 12.8 miles round trip
Hiking time: 6–8 hours or overnight
High point: 5800 feet
Elevation gain: 1800 feet
Difficulty: Moderate
Season: Year-round
Map: USGS Wawona
Nearest campground: Wawona Campground
Information: Yosemite National Park

This is one of those isolated, spiritually cleansing journeys where a soul can peacefully wander amongst tall and ancient trees. Whether you make it all the way to Alder Creek Fall is not so important as spending even a few hours in this remote and seldom-visited portion of the park. After the experience, you'll come out refreshed and with answers to some of your troubles.

Wildflower enthusiasts will want to be here in spring to adore pink lupines and flamboyant mariposa lilies. Late winter through spring is the best time to admire the power of Alder Creek Fall as it topples some 60 feet in a narrow and rocky gorge. If you go only part way, October and November are the ideal months to check out the orange leaves of the big black oaks during their fall leaf color show. February and March are just right for marveling at the pinkish blossoms of the evergreen manzanitas, some reaching tree-sized heights of 20 feet. This lower elevation area is often too hot for summer hiking.

To get there, drive to the village of Wawona, which is 4 miles north of the State Route 41 entrance to Yosemite National Park. Cross the new bridge over the Merced River and go right on Chilnualna Fall Road. Just 0.2 mile up this road, park in the lot on the right signed for Alder Creek trailhead. The ranger station, which has restrooms and water, is just behind the parking lot.

The mostly wide trail ascends gently but steadily along what used to be an old railroad bed. It immediately heads up a ridge that eventually turns into tree-clad Turner Ridge. Many of the ponderosa pines along the first 2.5 miles of the trail, which faces the west, are gigantic, but the black oaks and occasional incense cedars are no slouches either. Look for western fence lizards scurrying on the ground and white-headed woodpeckers knocking on tree trunks in this more exposed region.

Keep right at a trail junction at 2.8 miles, cross a fork of Mosquito Creek 1 mile past the trail fork, and stroll along the trail, which now traverses a

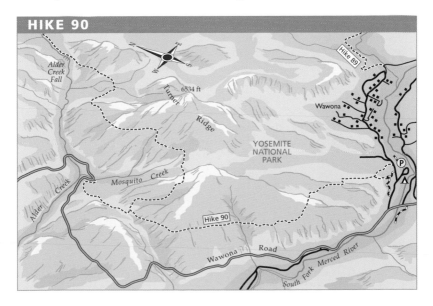

HIKE 90

Tiger lily

north-facing slope. This ecosystem is noticeably shadier, moister, and cooler, with more mosses and ferns at trailside. There's a denser canopy above you, furnished by white firs and occasional sugar pines (with their foot-long cones). In this region, look for scrambling Douglas squirrels and catlike great horned owls, which hunt them. Warblers look for small insects from the outer branches of the conifers.

At 1.2 miles past Mosquito Creek, cross two consecutive feeder streams of Alder Creek. The path soon levels, then widens, revealing a steep segment of the Alder Creek gorge, where the waterfall spills over a cliff. From this vantage point, several petite hanging gardens, springs, and seeps make for a prime picnic spot. There are several camping spots just beyond the fall along Alder Creek, where chokecherry and alder dominate.

Facing page: Jeffrey Pine

91 | BADGER PASS TO GLACIER POINT

Distance: 21 miles round trip
Hiking time: 2–3 days
High point: 7830 feet
Elevation gain: 2200 feet
Difficulty: Strenuous
Season: December through March
Maps: USGS Half Dome, USGS El Capitan
Nearest campground: Bridalveil Creek Campground
Information: Yosemite National Park

Capture the scenic and sprawling Yosemite Valley in a special way that only a few lucky souls get to experience—from atop Glacier Point when it's hooded with snow. The thousands of tourists who drive to this popular vantage point in summer won't feel your cherished solitude and sense of major achievement, nor will they embrace the snowcapped views that you'll encounter. Snowshoe alongside the tracks of the groomed cross-country ski trail on Glacier Point Road or don cross-country skis during clear weather in winter or early spring. You'll gaze 3200 feet down into Yosemite Valley, which is bordered by stark granite, with the graceful Merced River meandering through it. Along the snowy route, you'll see plenty of picturesque, snowcapped sites, such as the nearby Clark Range, which stands above 11,000 feet in elevation.

   To get there, turn northeast onto Glacier Point Road from Wawona Road, drive 5 miles to Badger Pass Ski Area, and follow the blue signs to

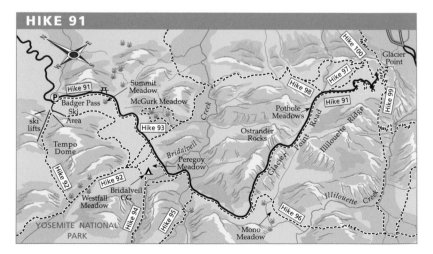

HIKE 91

Nevada Fall from Glacier Point

the upper parking lot, where you'll find the signed Glacier Point trailhead.

Climb the well-traveled, snow-covered road in a red fir forest for 1 mile to the signed Dewey Point Ridge Trail and stay straight. Continue a gentle climb for 0.3 mile past Summit Meadow, then negotiate 1.5 miles worth of mildly twisting, slightly descending trail. Look for initial views of the Clark Range ahead, then stay straight at a signed junction at 2.8 miles. Make a brief ascent away from Peregoy Meadow, descend to and then cross Bridalveil Creek, and then climb moderately to another signed trail junction at 4 miles, where you stay left.

Continue east on the wide swath of the Glacier Point Road, climbing moderately in a light Jeffrey pine forest interspersed with dead timber from the 1987 fire. Stay straight at another signed junction at 4.7 miles, and continue climbing as the route bends north, soon to reveal several clear views of the Clark Range, including Mount Clark, Gray Peak, Red Peak, and Merced Peak, stretching from north to south.

A steady ascent continues until the 7-mile point, where mostly flat terrain over the next 2 miles allows you to enjoy the plethora of views that unfold. Pass Pothole Meadows, then watch for hulking Sentinel Dome. The final mile consists of a twisting descent to Glacier Point, closely following the route of the original wagon road built in 1882. Gain the awesome vista at Washburn Point at 9.6 miles, featuring sweeping views of Mount Starr King and the Clark Range to the southeast, and Half Dome to the northeast as well.

Get set for a whole new scene below when you reach the railing at Glacier Point. Sweeping east to west, gawk at Half Dome, North Dome, Royal Arches, Yosemite Falls, and El Capitan rising abruptly above U-shaped Yosemite Valley.

92 TEMPO DOME AND WESTFALL MEADOW

Distance: 6.4-mile loop
Hiking time: 4–8 hours
High point: 7845 feet
Elevation gain: 1400 feet
Difficulty: Moderate to strenuous
Season: December through March
Map: USGS El Capitan
Nearest campground: Bridalveil Creek Campground
Information: Yosemite National Park

Admire the jagged spikes stretched in a long row that forms snowy Clark Range, framed by regal red firs, and glide through a large and peaceful meadow on this mostly serene and isolated snowshoe and cross-country ski route. Because there are other more popular snowshoe routes in the Badger Pass area, and since this route starts out with a hefty climb followed by a lot of little ups and downs, you're apt to have this trekking treat to yourself.

To get there, turn northeast onto Glacier Point Road from Wawona Road, drive 5 miles to Badger Pass Ski Area, and follow the blue signs to the upper parking lot, where you'll find the signed Glacier Point trailhead. The trailhead begins at the "Eagle" chairlift.

Trudge slowly upward alongside the chairlift, smiling politely whenever someone in a moving chair above you ridicules your hard work. After 0.8 mile and 600 vertical feet of climbing, reach the ridge top and promptly find the signed Merced Crest Ski Trail. Progress along the open crest for 0.2 mile and then make a brief descent followed by a short climb to reach Tempo Dome at 1.3 miles. From intermittent clearings in the forest, check out impressive vistas of the Clark Range to the east and the granitic mountains above Little Yosemite Valley to the southeast, including Half Dome (see Hike 1).

Continue to check out the views as you drop off the back side of Tempo Dome and head back into a light red fir and Jeffrey pine forest. The denser the forest sections, the more you have to watch for the rectangular and yellow markers to stay on your snowy route. After a trio of ups and downs, descend diagonally across the mountainside. Continue down toward the basin south of Westfall Meadow, getting to a signed trail junction at 2.5 miles. Your course curves gently north and promptly enters a small pocket meadow. After a brief stint in light forest, you set snowshoe or cross-country ski tracks in graceful Westfall Meadow at 2.8 miles.

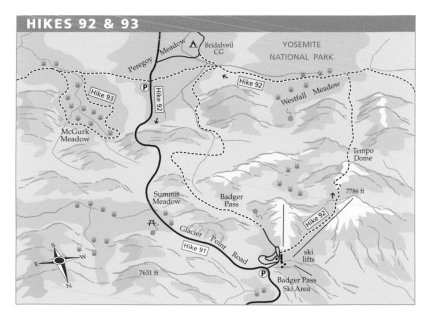

Jeffrey pines in winter

Stroll effortlessly across the expansive, scenic, and isolated meadow. Follow the left branch of clearing into the trees at the end of the meadow at 3.7 miles and climb mildly through forest to the gap. Descend to the north for 0.3 mile into a narrow meadow, then turn left on the snow-covered Old Glacier Point Road. Follow all signs west to Badger Pass over the final 2.1 miles.

93 | McGurk Meadow

Distance: 3 miles round trip
Hiking time: 2 hours
High point: 7200 feet
Elevation gain: 300 feet
Difficulty: Easy
Season: May through November
Maps: USGS El Capitan, USGS Half Dome
Nearest campground: Bridalveil Creek Campground
Information: Yosemite National Park
See map page 257

Among the five meadows within 1.5 miles of Glacier Point Road, McGurk Meadow arguably boasts the earliest summer wildflowers. And unlike Mono Meadow, Summit Meadow, Peregoy Meadow, and Westfall

Corn lily, senecio, and orange paintbrush

Meadow, McGurk Meadow features a lot of opportunities to explore clear and shallow Bridalveil Creek, the same stream that eventually forms legendary Bridalveil Fall in Yosemite Valley to the north. Like all meadows, McGurk Meadow's terrain is delicate, and it's best to place most of your footsteps on the trail or along the tree-lined perimeter. Of the several hikes in this book departing from Glacier Point Road, this one is by far the easiest and is best done prior to and during twilight, after one of the other hikes.

To get there, turn east onto paved Glacier Point Road from the Chinquapin junction on State Route 41. Drive 7.6 miles and watch closely for a trailhead sign, then park in a small clearing about 100 yards beyond. If you reach the turnoff for Bridalveil Creek Campground, you've gone too far, but you can also start from the campground, which adds 1 mile to the hike.

Descend gently in a lodgepole pine forest where several of these two-needled pines are long dead. Yarrow, angelica, and fragrant patches of Brewer's lupine adorn the path in sunny spots. Pass an old log cabin on the left near McGurk Meadow, then reach a footbridge across a tributary of Bridalveil Creek. Linger here to adore the display of yellow-blossomed sneezeweed that attracts butterflies and white-flowered yampah wedged in the cheery green grasses and sedges bordering the creek.

After crossing the bridge, depart the trail headed for Dewey Point (Hike 5) and angle left along the tree line to explore the main body of the meadow. Stay on the established paths as much as possible, and admire the patches of yellow cinquefoil and goldenrod, white corn lily, bluish gentian, and orange paintbrush. For the best wildflower display, come in June through early August.

Dangle your feet in the refreshing tributary of Bridalveil Creek, and notice the schools of fingerlings swimming in the mellow current. Gaze east from the meadow and spy the low, unglaciated summits of Ostrander Rocks. Find a spot to picnic at meadow's edge where it meets the trees, for this is a prime spot for viewing wildlife, especially at dawn or dusk. Watch for browsing mule deer, scurrying lodgepole chipmunks and golden-mantled ground squirrels, squawking Steller's jays, and foraging mountain chickadees.

94 | BRIDALVEIL CREEK TO CHILNUALNA, BUENA VISTA, AND ROYAL ARCH LAKES

Distance: 29-mile partial loop
Hiking time: 2–4 days
High point: 9300 feet
Elevation gain: 2600 feet
Difficulty: Easy to moderate
Season: June through October
Maps: USGS Half Dome, USGS Mariposa Grove
Nearest campground: Bridalveil Creek Campground
Information: Yosemite National Park

Mosey along the lodgepole-lined banks of well-known Bridalveil and Chilnualna Creeks for miles and stroll through green fields awash with wildflowers. Capture inspirational views of jagged and rocky Cathedral Range and visit a scattered cluster of small but pristine subalpine lakes on this moderately popular journey. Brace for swarms of mosquitoes in wet areas during June through mid-July.

To get there, drive to Chinquapin Junction on Wawona Road, and drive northeast on Glacier Point Road. After 9 miles, turn right at signed Bridalveil Creek Campground and continue all the way to the south end of the campground. Watch for the trailhead just as the paved road curves to the left, just beyond two signs.

Begin hiking along pure and clear Bridalveil Creek, rambling through wildflower meadows and serene forests. You eventually cross some dainty streams and climb moderately up a slope under lichen-coated white fir and red fir. Ignore trails that go to the left at 1.4 miles and 2.2 miles—they lead to Ostrander Lake (Hike 95). The trail steepens as the forest cover dwindles to brush and then clears on an exposed ridgetop laced with sulfur buckwheat, lupine, and pink pussy paws. Your route returns down into forest, passes a boggy meadow, and continues south at a trail junction at 4.8 miles. Wander past Turner Meadow, where yard-high corn lilies boast white flowers in June and July.

At 6.2 miles, reach a junction where a right turn leads about 3 miles down to roaring Chilnualna Fall (Hike 89), a worthwhile side trip if time and energy permit. Otherwise, continue straight and at 0.8 mile farther turn left to start the 17-mile-long clockwise loop that leads to nine petite lakes amid glacially sculpted granite.

It's a gentle ascent up the lodgepole-lined bank of Chilnualna Creek, heading east for some 3 miles to a cluster of mainly waist-deep lakes called the Chilnualna Lakes. They make for refreshing swimming, especially during a hot spell in late summer. The lake alongside the trail is so shallow in

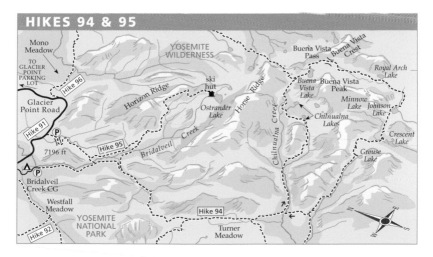

HIKES 94 & 95

spots that it's becoming a meadow. Campsites are available here. Follow the trail closely and climb out of the lake basin (after visiting the other two Chilnualna Lakes) along a slope of rubbly granite that leads to an awesome vista at 12 miles. Half Dome and Mount Starr King to the north are an inspiring sight, while Cathedral Range unfolds before you to the north by northeast. The colorful Clark Range sprawls to the northeast.

Bear right at a trail junction, 0.8 mile from the northernmost lake, and

Bridalveil Creek

promptly reach glistening, talus-surrounded, and bleak Buena Vista Lake, nestled in a glacial cirque on a broad bench perched at the north base of Buena Vista Peak. Because it's the highest lake of the trip and it doesn't get as much sun, it's the coldest lake of this trek. There are a couple of decent camps here. From the lake's outlet, the trail ascends via short switchbacks to 9300-foot-high, mostly viewless Buena Vista Pass. To bag ideal views, make the easy 0.75-mile climb here to 9709-foot-high Buena Vista Peak.

From the pass, descend through a flowery meadow, hike over exfoliating granite slabs, and finally head into a forest before reaching interesting Royal Arch Lake 1.6 miles from the pass. It lies below a broad, granitic arch that frames the lake and features a couple of good campsites. Gigantic granite slabs have popped loose and peeled away from the rock face, and now the rock formation resembles layers of a decayed onion.

Depart the lake and turn right at a trail junction, descending west and soon reaching grassy Johnson Lake, featuring several good campsites at the northwest corner of this lodgepole-ringed lake. Uniquely shaped Crescent Lake awaits about 0.5 mile farther, where you can stroll to its rocky outlet and gaze into the 2800-foot-deep South Fork Merced River Canyon. Leaving the lake, you soon cross a glacial moraine laced with red fir, pass by mediocre Grouse Lake partially concealed by trees, and then head down for 3 miles to a trail fork, where you go right. Rock-hop Chilnualna Creek 0.7 mile farther and reach the trail junction that closes the loop, where you continue straight, retracing your steps to the trailhead.

95 | OSTRANDER LAKE

Distance: 12.8 miles round trip
Hiking time: 8 hours or overnight
High point: 8600 feet
Elevation gain: 1600 feet
Difficulty: Moderate
Season: June into November
Maps: USGS Half Dome, USGS Mariposa Grove
Nearest campground: Bridalveil Creek Campground
Information: Yosemite National Park
See map page 261

Hemmed by naked granite ridges and lined with conifers, grasses, and granite slabs, 25-acre Ostrander Lake invites a stroll around its vase-shaped shoreline. Climb a mere 500 feet in elevation during summer and fall and mount Horse Ridge for inspirational views of Mount Starr King to the north and the entire Clark Range to the east. This is a popular trip, especially on summer weekends, but also during winter and spring weekends

Red fir in winter

when groups snowshoe or cross-country ski to the stone ski hut. For the most privacy, backpack in during autumn or day-hike in starting at dawn.

To get there, drive to the signed Chinquapin junction from Wawona Road, and turn northeast onto paved Glacier Point Road. Travel 9 miles (1.3 miles past the Bridalveil Creek Campground) and park in the turnoff on the right.

It's easy to get lost in a pleasant reverie over the first 3.5 miles, as the trail, a former jeep road, gently climbs through a forest interspersed with small meadows. These open and grassy areas are worth stopping at for a snack and/or drink to admire the purplish fireweed, yellow goldenrod and sneeze-weed, and white yampah flowers that bloom in the summer. Yarrow, paint-brush, and lupines adorn the meadow edges and open areas at trailside.

Ignore two trail junctions on the right at 1.7 miles and 2.5 miles, which head for Bridalveil Creek and its campground. Steady and moderate ascent ensues in a forest rapidly recovering from a 1987 fire. The climb starts in a mixed conifer forest and continues to an exposed slab that furnishes inaugural views of the sprawling, treed Bridalveil Creek basin. Enter a large and scattered stand of Jeffrey pine, and then hike into a forest of white firs, which are soon supplanted by red firs higher up atop the saddle that bisects Horizon Ridge. Open stretches occur next, as the old jeep road snakes up the ridge amid sulfur flower, lupine, and sagebrush. You soon obtain extensive views spanning the Illilouette Creek drainage, where Mount Starr King rules. Half Dome, North Dome, Washington Column, and Royal Arches poke farther north. The jagged pinnacles of the Clark Range reign to the east.

Descend to Ostrander Hut, which was built on a rocky, glacial moraine. Snowshoers and cross-country skiers can stay in it if they've made reservations. Next to the hut, tucked in a bedrock basin, sits typically dark gray Ostrander Lake. Camping is best along the west shore and fishing here is relaxing. Horse Ridge, an example of exfoliating granite, features an obvious overhanging temple to the south.

96 | MONO MEADOW

Distance: 3 miles round trip
Hiking time: 2–3 hours
High point: 7400 feet
Elevation gain: 500 feet
Difficulty: Moderate
Season: May into November
Map: USGS Half Dome
Nearest campground: Bridalveil Creek Campground
Information: Yosemite National Park

Explore peaceful Mono Meadow and dangle your feet in crystal clear and soothing Mono Creek. Be prepared to see wildlife and hike to a viewpoint to savor a vista of Mount Starr King. Because several very popular trail-heads are nearby, you may have the meadow and viewpoint to yourself, especially on weekdays.

To get there, drive northeast on Glacier Point Road from the Chinquapin junction at State Route 41 (Wawona Road). Drive 11 miles to a forested saddle and park in the signed, dirt parking area on the right.

Descend moderately, heading northeast in a dense forest of magnificent red firs, where an occasional porcupine is lodged high in the evergreen boughs and golden-mantled ground squirrels make squeaking noises. Mushrooms often thrive in the rich, shady duff. Reach lodgepole pine-ringed Mono Meadow at 0.5 mile and prepare to get your boots muddied in the sloshy meadow bogs, especially in late spring and early summer. Logs make the numerous crossings of a Mono Creek tributary meandering through the meadow doable. In midsummer, several wildflowers grace the scene, including gentian, goldenrod, and cinquefoil. Watch for the agile lodgepole chipmunk climbing in the lodgepole pines, and the dark-eyed junco foraging at meadow's edge.

From the east end of the meadow, the trail gradually ascends in shady forest to scenic Mono Creek at 1 mile. Carefully choose your way to the

White-flowered corn lily and Mono Creek

water's edge, where cascades have carved out the rock under it. There are tunnels and pits gouged in the polished granite.

Back on the trail, stroll leisurely in open forest for another 0.5 mile to a clearing just before the trail drops steeply down to Illilouette Creek. Admire numerous granite mountain features to the northeast, including Mount Starr King, Half Dome, and Clouds Rest.

97 | SENTINEL DOME AND GLACIER POINT

Distance: 5 miles round trip for Glacier Point; 2.4 miles round trip for Sentinel Dome
Hiking time: 3–5 hours
High point: 8122 feet
Elevation gain: 1000 feet
Difficulty: Moderate
Season: May through October
Map: USGS Half Dome
Nearest campground: Bridalveil Creek Campground
Information: Yosemite National Park

Sentinel Dome features comparable views to that of Half Dome, but it takes only a smidgeon of the time and energy to claim Sentinel Dome. Standing smooth and rounded at elevation 8122 feet, Sentinel Dome is the second highest viewpoint above Yosemite Valley (Half Dome is first). With these attributes, no wonder Sentinel Dome is so popular. Therefore, for more privacy, go on weekdays, especially after Labor Day.

With a prearranged car shuttle, it's a view-filled, varied, 7-mile one-way journey almost all downhill from the Sentinel Dome parking lot (see below) to Yosemite Valley at Happy Isles (see Hike 100). Also note that a prearranged car shuttle can be planned at Glacier Point, making this hike an easy 2.5 miles, mostly downhill.

To get there, from the signed junction along Wawona Road, go east on Glacier Point Road. After 14 miles of paved driving (2.3 miles before Glacier Point parking lot), park on the left at the signed, scenic turnout in a clearing.

At the start, climb moderately, as the trail crosses a stream right off and then alternates with open forest and clearings. Sentinel Dome appears sporadically ahead as the path weaves past pinemat manzanita and huckleberry oak shrubs beneath Jeffrey pines, red firs, western white pines, and lodgepole pines.

An old, partly paved service road temporarily becomes the trail at 0.5 mile, which you follow to the base of the dome at 0.9 mile. By now, you're at the more gradually sloping, northeastern base of the dome, and a safe but steep climb briefly ensues, over solid and massive granite. These eroding, tremendous sheets of rock gradually pop loose like layers of an onion.

The much anticipated panorama is achieved by slowly encircling the dome top, which used to be centered by the statuesque, skeletal outline of a stunted and dead Jeffrey pine that Ansel Adams frequently photographed. This iconic tree recently fell to its side. To the west, Yosemite Valley is trapped by El Capitan's sheer cliff face to its north and the jagged spires of Cathedral Rocks to its south. Watch Yosemite Falls as it free-falls powerfully; farther east Basket Dome and North Dome are notably smooth and rounded. Tenaya Canyon holds the sheer, gray face of Half Dome and polished Clouds Rest. The Alps-like Cathedral Range lies beyond. Continuing clockwise, enjoy an ideal view down on Vernal and Nevada Falls, flanked by Liberty Cap. To the southeast, Mount Clark and Mount Starr King highlight the colorful Clark Range. Snow often lingers atop these mountains as well as the Cathedral Range into July.

When the view savoring is finally done, retrace your steps down Sentinel Dome's base, and follow the obvious trail down to the east if you are continuing to Glacier Point. Within 300 yards, you're in the middle of a deep and dark red-fir forest, where colorful, short snow plant and pinedrops occasionally poke through the duff. These plants are saprophytes, meaning they lack chlorophyll and obtain carbohydrates from forest humus. The peaceful forest accompanies you all the way to Glacier Point at 2.5 miles, where the previously mentioned views to the east are shared by throngs of tourists.

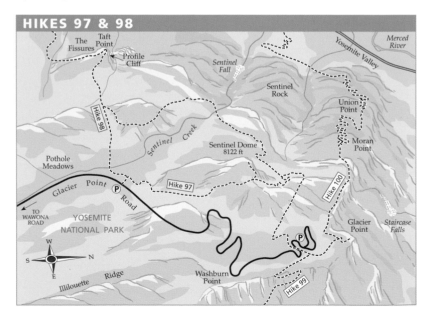

HIKES 97 & 98

Jeffrey pine skeleton on Sentinel Dome (no longer standing)

98 | TAFT POINT AND THE FISSURES

Distance: 2.6 miles round trip
Hiking time: 2–3 hours
High point: 7750 feet
Elevation gain: 300 feet
Difficulty: Easy to moderate
Season: May through October
Map: USGS Half Dome
Nearest campground: Bridalveil Creek Campground
Information: Yosemite National Park
See map page 268

If you want to stare down on as much of gorgeous Yosemite Valley as possible, do it from an exposed, sheer rock overhang called Taft Point. The views of Half Dome and El Capitan are just as jaw-dropping from Taft Point's vertical edge as from Glacier Point, except that more of the Yosemite Valley is seen from Taft Point, minus the troops of tourists that crowd Glacier Point.

The nearby Taft Point fissures, originally knife-blade thin, have gradually eroded into dramatic chasms—as if the cliff top were slowly splitting apart. These narrow, deep cracks in solid granite are 40 feet long, revealing Yosemite Valley more than 3000 feet below. Along the way, tall and handsome conifers tower above, and a stretch of meadow seep sports an abundance of summer wildflowers.

To get there, from the signed junction along Wawona Road, go east on Glacier Point Road. After 14 miles of paved driving (2.3 miles before Glacier Point parking lot), park on the left at the signed, scenic turnout in a clearing.

Pick up the signed trailhead near the information signboard, proceed west, and after about 150 yards admire a trailside pile of glistening grayish white quartz with trace amounts of pink potassium feldspar. You soon cross modest Sentinel Creek while wandering comfortably beneath western white pines, lodgepole pines, red firs, and some extraordinarily tall Jeffrey pines. Pussy paws, mat lupine, and aromatic mountain pennyroyal occasionally decorate trailside; clusters of pinemat manzanita, huckleberry oak, and chinquapin shrubs grow in open areas.

Reach a crest junction with the Pohono Trail and keep following the obvious path signed for Taft Point. Descend to a seeping brook festooned with grasses and wildflowers. Luckily, the trail follows this moist fairy-tale garden for a couple hundred yards, revealing mostly corn lilies (huge leaves and white flowers), but also sprinklings of monkeyflower, bluebells, senecio, green gentian, cow parsnips, and bracken fern.

Descend along dry slopes freckled with Sierra wallflower and sulfur flower buckwheat and soon reach the fissures: five vertical, parallel fractures

Mount Hoffmann from Taft Point

that cut through overhanging Profile Cliff. Young children should be restrained, but if you don't mind a bit of butterfly churning in your stomach, peer cautiously down the precipitous cliffs that plunge to Yosemite Valley.

Head for the rising outcrop called Taft Point that leans out over the valley and thankfully has an iron railing around it. Grayish Three Brothers are located straight across Yosemite Valley, which is a colorful mix of meadows and forest strips. The massive face of El Capitan poses to the west while Yosemite Falls plunges to the east of Three Brothers. Mighty Mount Conness stands powerfully in the distance. Taft Point was named for President William H. Taft, who visited Yosemite Valley in 1909. Go west a way to check out the knifelike edges and needlelike spikes of the Cathedral Spires to the west.

99 | MERCED RIVER TO WASHBURN LAKE AND CLARK RANGE

Distance: 50-mile loop; 25 miles round trip for Merced Lake
Hiking time: 4–6 days
High point: 11,180 feet
Elevation gain: 6500 feet
Difficulty: Moderate to strenuous
Season: July through October
Maps: USGS Half Dome, USGS Merced Peak, USGS Mariposa Grove
Nearest campground: Bridalveil Creek Campground
Information: Yosemite National Park

Get intimate with Nevada Fall, explore the wild, often cascading uppermost stretch of the Merced River, visit half a dozen gorgeous and small lakes, and wander to Yosemite National Park's highest trail section over Red Peak Pass on an epic journey to some of the park's most isolated high backcountry. Much of the Illilouette drainage was charred in 2001 during the Hoover fire, burning out some of the brush and not reaching most of the trees' crowns.

To get there, from the signed Chinquapin junction along Wawona Road, travel northeast on Glacier Point Road for 15.5 miles to its end. The parking lot is usually not full on weekdays. If it's a busy weekend, consider taking the park bus to this very crowded place. If the quota for wilderness permits for this trailhead is full, you'll have to start from the Mono Meadow trailhead a few miles south of here.

The trailhead starts just east of the entrance to Glacier Point, and quickly forks, where you go left for a brief climb. A long descent ensues, past a lot of

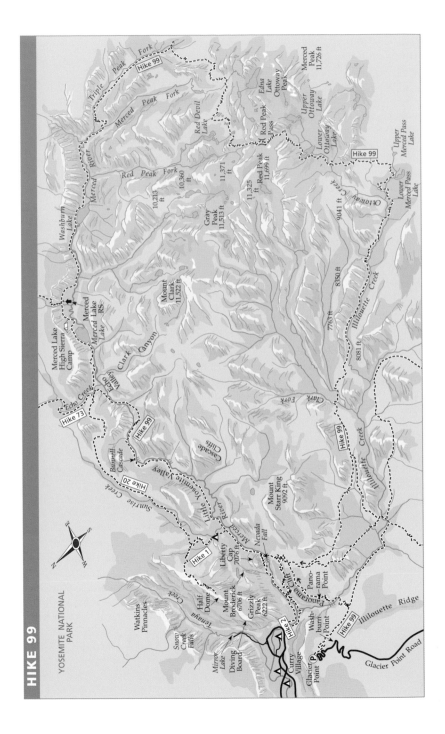

YOSEMITE NATIONAL
PARK

Hike 99

Hike 99

Hike 99

Hike 99

Hike 99

Hike 73

Hike 20

Hike 1

Hike 2

Triple
Peak
Fork

Merced River

Merced Peak Fork

Red Devil
Lake

Edna
Lake

Ottoway
Peak

Merced
Peak
11,726 ft

Upper
Ottoway
Lake

Red Peak
Pass

Lower
Ottoway
Lake

Upper Merced Pass
Lake

Lower
Merced
Pass Lake

Red Peak Fork

Red Peak
11,699 ft

10,360
ft

11,371
ft

11,325
ft

Gray Peak
11,513 ft

9041 ft

Ottoway Creek

10,213
ft

Washburn
Lake

Merced River

Mount Clark
11,522 ft

8350 ft

7763 ft

Illilouette Creek

8081 ft

Merced Lake
High Sierra
Camp

Merced
Lake RS

Merced
Lake

Echo
Valley

Clark Canyon

Clark Fork

Illilouette Creek

Echo Creek

Bunnell
Cascade

Cascade
Cliffs

Sunrise Creek

Little Yosemite Valley

Mount
Starr King
9092 ft

Merced River

Nevada
Fall

Pano-
rama
Point

Watkins
Pinnacles

Half Dome

Liberty
Cap
7076 ft

Mount
Broderick
6706 ft

Grizzly
Peak
6222 ft

Clark

Panorama Cliff

Illilouette Ridge

Snow Creek Falls

Tenaya Creek

Mirror
Lake

Diving
Board

Curry
Village

Glacier
Point

Glacier P.
Point

Wash-
burn
Point

Glacier Point Road

N

S

E

W

black oaks and grand views of Liberty Cap towering over Nevada Fall, Mount Starr King, and Half Dome. Reach a trail junction at 1.7 miles, go left, and soon take a spur trail that promptly leads to a railing and a clear view of slender Illilouette Fall, which topples 370 feet over immense Panorama Cliff. Your trail eventually passes just above the brim of Illilouette Fall, then climbs in forest to a fascinating view of Yosemite Falls, Royal Arches, and North Dome to Half Dome. Contour east past more awesome views, now including Clouds Rest and 594-foot-high Nevada Fall to a trail fork at 4.2 miles. The path to the right will be explored during the return descent. Stay left for now and descend for 1 mile to the John Muir Trail and the brink of robust Nevada Fall. Watch the fall roar over the lip from one of several railings.

Follow the north shore of the rushing Merced River along the obvious and heavily used trail and eventually reach shade, where the river transforms into a peaceful, deep, and dark current. Bear right at 6 miles, leaving the John Muir Trail behind and heading into Little Yosemite Valley, where you spend your first night.

Continue through level and deep forest where two saprophytes, brownish pinedrops and bright red snow plants live on the deep, decaying material in the lush soil. At 7 miles, climb out of the valley and beneath the massive dome of Bunnell Point, where the Merced River flows over the long, dark, and slick slide of impressive Bunnell Cascade. Ascend switchbacks blasted out of the smooth granite, descend to Echo Creek in a valley, and then climb along a rapid stretch of the river a final mile to Merced Lake at 12.5 miles. Reach the campground at the far end of the lake and the High Sierra Camp about 0.5 mile farther. Merced Lake, lined with grass and lodgepole pines, features mellow granite ridges that rise over it.

The 4.5-mile journey to Washburn Lake leaves much of the lingering crowds behind. The trail's interesting plant features start with aspens along the river, soon followed by a stretch of lodgepole pines, which then give way to junipers, white firs, and Jeffrey pines as a gentle ascent ensues. Next comes a drier stretch, evidenced by bracken fern, chinquapin, huckleberry oak, and sagebrush shrubs. Pass a couple of tempting swimming holes before reaching bedrock-dammed Washburn Lake, a deep, partially tree-lined lake with a good campsite upstream on the left side of the trail.

The trail escorts you upcanyon, deep into the more secluded, higher reaches of the Merced River and its many tributaries. Pass numerous cascades and climb to rewarding views of Mount Florence to the northnortheast and pyramid-shaped Merced Peak, which holds a large region of snow on its flanks sometimes into September. Climb across glaciated slabs and through a thinning lodgepole pine forest to a riverside junction 7 miles from Washburn Lake.

Bear right (west) and begin a long climb, eventually crossing several weathered granitic benches. The higher you get, the better the views of the peaks that guard the upper reaches of the river, including Merced Peak, Red Peak, and Gray Peak that form the Clark Range. The whitebark pines and mountain hemlocks here are sparse and stubby, making for superb foreground matter for your photos. Reach a second crest at a broad saddle that holds a gorgeous lakelet, an ideal place for a sleepover. Climb to a spacious bench and enter metamorphic rock country for a while. During the thin-air climb, more and more summer wildflowers appear, along with a handful of scenic tarns on the way to Red Peak Pass, which is typically snowbound into midsummer. The breathtaking views here from this mid-

Red Peak (photo by R. Anderson)

point of the Clark Range include Matterhorn Peak far to the north and Mount Lyell and Mount Maclure joining Mount Florence to the northeast. The sawtooth Ritter Range juts to the east.

Descend to Lower Ottoway Lake, an ideal spot for camping, past open country sporting paintbrush, columbine, monkeyflower, phlox, yarrow, and cinquefoil. Roam up and down over glaciated backcountry for 1.8 miles past Lower Ottoway Lake to cross Illilouette Creek, then to Upper Merced Pass Lake, featuring quality campsites. Your trail descends northwest past numerous creeklets, and in a few spots you'll need to pay close attention to not lose the trail. Cross the crests of a handful of moraines to a stream where several campsites exist for a final night, about 7 miles from the trailhead. A 1.3-mile-long traverse ensues past handsome Jeffrey pine and white fir specimens to a junction, where you make a left and follow signs from here on out to Glacier Point.

100 | GLACIER POINT TO YOSEMITE VALLEY

Distance: 4.6 miles one way (with bus trip) or 9.2 miles round trip
Hiking time: 2–4 hours
High point: 7200 feet
Elevation gain: 100 feet as described; 3200 feet round trip
Difficulty: Easy as described; strenuous round trip
Season: May through November
Map: USGS Half Dome
Nearest campground: Bridalveil Creek Campground
Information: Yosemite National Park

Here's an ideal way to enjoy populated Glacier Point, one of the nation's most spectacular lookouts, and take an all-downhill hike that gets you closer to many of the fantastic sights you admire from Glacier Point. Starting the hike from Yosemite Valley can end in disappointment when you emerge all tired, sweaty, and dusty only to have everything you've earned seemingly stripped away when you see the throngs of tourists in cars eating ice cream at Glacier Point. But by starting from Glacier Point, you get an enriching and remote experience much closer to what John Muir encountered there more than a century ago. The downhill journey faces most of the major place-names seen from Glacier Point, only you're now closer to them and the perspectives keep changing, presenting you with fresh views. You wind up catching one eye-popping natural wonder after another the whole 4.6 miles. To make it work, take a shuttle bus from Yosemite Valley to Glacier Point, or arrange a car shuttle down in Yosemite Valley.

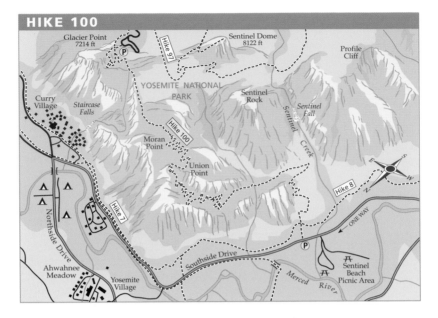

One way to avoid the crowds at Glacier Point is to climb this trail from the valley when the 4-Mile Trail opens in early spring, which is a few weeks before Glacier Point Road does. (Bring enough water.) Or, consider hiking just the first mile up the trail from the valley floor to the dry creek crossing in the fall, while the maples are turning color.

To get there, from the signed junction along Wawona Road, go east on Glacier Point Road. After 16.3 miles of paved driving, park in the spacious lot at road's end just beyond the restrooms, drinking fountains, and snack bar. To get to Yosemite Valley, follow signs and drive east from State Routes 120 or 140 into Yosemite Valley. Continue east on one-way Southside Drive to the parking area on both sides of the road just past the Sentinel Beach/Yellow Pine picnic areas. Follow the bike path across Swinging Bridge, go right, and stroll about 50 yards to the signed trailhead. If you drive to Glacier Point and plan to take the bus back up after hiking down, check the bus schedule closely, make a reservation, and don't miss the bus.

Feel like an ant and join the crowds atop Glacier Point, featuring a prime view of Vernal and Nevada Falls to the east. Then, from behind the snack bar, your trail takes off in deep shade furnished by white firs and sugar pines. You eventually come out of the trees for views eastward of unglaciated Glacier Point's pair of overhanging rocks capping a vertical wall. Drop into a cool gully and then reach a descending ridge, where the eye-catching views switch from the north of Royal Arches and North Dome to the north and west of Yosemite Falls, El Capitan, and Sentinel Rock.

After 1.3 miles, switchbacks commence through extensive clusters of chaparral, including greenleaf manzanita, huckleberry oak, and chinquapin. Here on this exposed slope section is where you'll be glad you're not wheezing up it from the valley floor on a hot summer afternoon. After a dozen or so switchbacks, white firs return, along with Douglas firs and canyon live oaks, and soon after the trail straightens, incense cedars and black oaks (orange leaves in autumn) join the overstory.

Leidig Meadow appears intermittently below via small clearings. You come even with Yosemite Falls on the left, and eventually cross a creeklet lined with thimbleberry and mariposa lilies, and shaded by bay laurels, oaks, and bigleaf maples. More and more mossy boulders come into play on the now asphalt trail that leads to an informative signboard at 4.6 miles (the trailhead in Yosemite Valley).

Yosemite Valley, North Dome, and Basket Dome

APPENDIX A:
AGENCY INFORMATION

Ansel Adams Wilderness   619-647-6525
Hoover Wilderness   760-932-7070
Inyo National Forest in Lee Vining
   760-873-2408; *www.r5.fs.fed.us/inyo/index.htm*
Inyo National Forest in Mammoth Lakes
   760-924-5500; *www.r5.fs.fed.us/inyo/index.htm*
John Muir Wilderness   619-934-2505
Mono Lake Scenic Area   760-647-3044
Mono Lake Tufa State Reserve   760-647-6331
Road Conditions
   800-427-7623; *www.dot.ca.gov/hq/roadinfo/*
Sierra National Forest in Mariposa
   209-966-3638; *www.r5.fs.fed.us/sierra/*
Sierra National Forest in Oakhurst
   559-658-7588; *www.r5.fs.fed.us/sierra/*
Stanislaus National Forest in Groveland
   209-962-7825; *www.r5.fs.fed.us/stanislaus/*
Stanislaus National Forest-Summit Ranger District
   209-965-3434; *www.r5.fs.fed.us/stanislaus/*
Toiyabe National Forest in Bridgeport
   760-932-7070; *www.fs.fed.us/htnf/h-trec.htm*
Yosemite Association
   209-379-2646; *www.yosemite.org/*
Yosemite National Park
   209-372-0200; *www.nps.gov/yose/*

PERMITS

Inyo National Forest
   619-647-6525
Toiyabe National Forest
   619-932-7070
Wilderness Reservations
   209-372-0740
Yosemite National Park
   209-372-0200

For more information on purchasing a National Parks Pass, visit *www.nationalparks.org*

TRAIL INDEX

KEY TO SYMBOLS

R = rock features
BP = backpack trip option

W = water features
V = spectacular views

F = flowers
LC = less crowded

SS = snowshoe hike possibility
C = good hike for children

YOSEMITE VALLEY

1. Half Dome and the John Muir Trail	R V BP
2. Happy Isles to Vernal Fall and Nevada Fall	R W V
3. Mirror Lake and Tenaya Creek	R W V C SS
4. Bridalveil Fall and Lower Yosemite Fall	R W C SS
5. Inspiration Point, Stanford Point, and Dewey Point	R V SS BP LC
6. Yosemite Falls and Eagle Peak	R W V BP
7. Yosemite Falls and Royal Arches	R W V C
8. Yosemite Valley: El Capitan and Bridalveil Fall	R W V SS SS
9. South Fork Merced River to Hite Cove	R W LC F

TIOGA ROAD: TAMARACK CREEK EAST TO TENAYA LAKE

10. Tamarack Creek and Cascade Creek	W BP LC
11. Tamarack Flat to El Capitan	R V BP

12. Harden Lake		C			BP		
13. Lukens Lake		C			BP		
14. Yosemite Creek to Yosemite Valley via Tioga Road	R		W	V	BP		
15. Porcupine Flat to North Dome	V				BP	LC	
16. Mount Hoffmann Meadow		C				LC	F
17. May Lake and Mount Hoffmann	R			V		LC	F
18. Old Tioga Road to Ten Lakes Basin	R			V	BP		
19. Tenaya Lake to Snow Creek and Mirror Lake	R		W	V	BP	LC	
20. Tenaya Lake to Clouds Rest	R			V	BP		
21. Tenaya Lake to Sunrise Lakes	R		W	V	BP		
22. Tenaya Lake	R		W	V	C		F
23. Murphy Creek to Polly Dome Lakes	R	C			BP	LC	

CRANE FLAT AND HETCH HETCHY RESERVOIR

24. Crane Flat Lookout	V	C		SS		LC	
25. Tuolumne Grove and Hodgdon Meadow				SS	BP	LC	
26. Merced Grove		C		SS			
27. Tuolumne River to Preston Falls	R		W		BP	LC	
28. Smith Peak via Cottonwood Meadow	R			V	BP	LC	F
29. Tuolumne River and Poopenaut Valley	R		W			LC	
30. Wapama Falls and Rancheria Falls	R		W	V	C		
31. Hetch Hetchy to Lake Vernon and Tiltill Valley	R		W	V	BP		
32. Kibbie Ridge and Miguel Meadow via Lake Eleanor	V				BP		
33. Cherry Lake to Kibbie Lake					BP		

EMIGRANT AND HOOVER WILDERNESS AREAS

	R	W	V	C	SS	BP	LC	F
34. Pinecrest Lake	R	W	V	C				F
35. Kennedy Meadow to Relief Reservoir		W	V			BP		
36. Saint Marys Pass to Sonora Peak	R		V			BP	LC	F
37. Sonora Pass and Pacific Crest Trail	R		V			BP	LC	F
38. Sardine Meadow to Sardine Falls		W		C		BP	LC	F
39. Leavitt Lake		W		C		BP	LC	
40. Leavitt Meadow and West Walker River	R	W	V			BP		
41. Pickel Meadow				C	SS		LC	
42. Barney Lake, Peeler Lake, and Kerrick Meadow	R		V			BP	LC	
43. Twin Lakes		W	V	C	SS		LC	
44. Hoover, Green, and West Lakes	R	W	V			BP	LC	F
45. Virginia Lakes to Summit Lake and Miller Lake		W	V			BP	LC	F
46. Virginia Lakes		W	V	C	SS		LC	
47. Lundy Canyon to 20 Lakes Basin	R	W	V			BP	LC	F
48. Lundy Lake to Oneida Lake		W	V		SS	BP	LC	F
49. Black Point	R	W	V	C				
50. North Mono Lake Beach	R	W	V	C				
51. Burgers Animal Sanctuary			V	C	SS		LC	
52. Mono Lake Tufa Castles and Navy Beach	R	W	V	C				

TIOGA ROAD: SADDLEBAG LAKE WEST TO TUOLUMNE MEADOWS

	R	W	V	C	SS	BP	LC	F
53. Ellery Lake	R	W	V	C				
54. Gardisky Lake and Tioga Peak	R	W	V			BP	LC	
55. Saddlebag Lake to Shamrock Lake	R	W	V			BP		F

56.	Mine Creek to Fantail and Spuller Lakes	R	W	V	C	BP	LC	F
57.	Tioga Lake	R	W	V	C		LC	
58.	Glacier Canyon to Dana Lake	R		V		BP	LC	
59.	Gaylor Lakes and Gaylor Peak	R	W	V	C	BP	LC	
60.	Mount Dana	R		V				F
61.	Dana Meadows to Spillway Lake and Mono Pass			V		BP		F
62.	Dana Meadows, Parker Peak, and Silver Lake	R	W	V		BP		F
63.	Lembert Dome	R		V				
64.	Dog Lake		W	V	C			
65.	Young Lakes		W	V		BP	LC	F
66.	Pacific Crest Trail and John Muir Trail–Tuolumne Meadow to Silver Lake	R	W	V		BP		F
67.	Ireland Lake and Vogelsang Lake	R	W	V		BP		F
68.	Tuolumne Meadows to Matterhorn and Rodgers Canyons		W	V		BP		F
69.	Tuolumne Meadows, Tuolumne River, and Soda Springs		W	V	C			F
70.	Tuolumne Meadows to Sonora Pass via Pacific Crest Trail	R	W	V		BP	LC	F
71.	Tuolumne River to Waterwheel Falls and Pate Valley	R	W	V		BP		
72.	Elizabeth Lake	R	W	V	C	BP		
73.	Tuolumne Meadows to Yosemite Valley via John Muir Trail	R		V		BP		
74.	Pothole Dome and the Tuolumne River	R	W	V	C			

ANSEL ADAMS WILDERNESS

75.	Sardine Lakes and Mono Pass		W	V		BP	LC	F
76.	Parker Lake and Upper Parker Creek	R	W	V		BP	LC	F
77.	Fern and Yost Lakes		W			BP	LC	F
78.	Glass Creek Meadow and Obsidian Dome	R		V	C	BP	LC	F
79.	Minaret Vista to Two Teats via San Joaquin Ridge	R		V	C	SS	LC	F

#	Trail	R	W	V	C	SS	BP	LC	F
80.	Thousand Island, Garnet, and Ediza Lakes	R	W	V			BP		F
81.	McCloud Lake		W	V	C				
82.	TJ Lake and Crystal Lake	R	W	V	C		BP		
83.	Sherwin Lakes and Valentine Lake		W	V			BP	LC	
84.	Convict Lake and Mildred Lake	R	W	V	C		BP		F

SOUTHWEST CORNER OF YOSEMITE NATIONAL PARK

#	Trail	R	W	V	C	SS	BP	LC	F
85.	Lewis Creek: Red Rock Falls and Corlieu Falls		W					LC	
86.	Mariposa Grove of Giant Sequoias				C				
87.	Wawona Point			V	C				
88.	Wawona Meadow			V	C			LC	F
89.	Chilnualna Fall	R	W				BP	LC	
90.	Alder Creek Fall		W				BP	LC	F

GLACIER POINT ROAD

#	Trail	R	W	V	C	SS	BP	LC	F
91.	Badger Pass to Glacier Point			V		SS	BP		
92.	Tempo Dome and Westfall Meadow			V		SS		LC	
93.	McGurk Meadow		W		C				F
94.	Bridalveil Creek to Chilnualna, Buena Vista, and Royal Arch Lakes		W	V			BP		F
95.	Ostrander Lake		W			SS	BP		
96.	Mono Meadow			V	C				F
97.	Sentinel Dome and Glacier Point	R		V	C				
98.	Taft Point and The Fissures	R		V					F
99.	Merced River to Washburn Lake and Clark Range	R	W	V			BP		F
100.	Glacier Point to Yosemite Valley	R		V					

INDEX

ABOUT THE AUTHOR

Marc J. Soares is a landscape consultant and teaches plant and yoga classes for Shasta College Community Education. He is a professional outdoor photographer and naturalist who writes columns for the Redding Record Searchlight newspaper. He also plays guitar and sings in a local classic rock band.

Marc has written five other hiking guidebooks: *100 Hikes in the San Francisco Bay Area* (The Mountaineers Books, 2001); *100 Classic Hikes in Northern California* (The Mountaineers Books, third edition, 2007, co-written with John R. Soares); *75 Year-Round Hikes in Northern California: The Ultimate Guide for Fall, Winter, and Spring Hikes* (The Mountaineers Books, 2000); *Snowshoe Routes in Northern California* (The Mountaineers Books, 2001); and *Best Coast Hikes of Northern California: A Guide to the Top Trails from Big Sur to the Oregon Border* (Sierra Club, 1998).

Author Marc Soares with his wife, Patricia (Photo by Camille Soares Brown)

THE MOUNTAINEERS, founded in 1906, is a nonprofit outdoor activity and conservation organization, whose mission is "to explore, study, preserve, and enjoy the natural beauty of the outdoors . . . . " Based in Seattle, Washington, it is now one of the largest such organizations in the United States, with seven branches throughout Washington State.

The Mountaineers sponsors both classes and year-round outdoor activities in the Pacific Northwest, which include hiking, mountain climbing, ski-touring, snowshoeing, bicycling, camping, kayaking and canoeing, nature study, sailing, and adventure travel. The organization's conservation division supports environmental causes through educational activities, sponsoring legislation, and presenting informational programs. All its activities are led by skilled, experienced volunteers, who are dedicated to promoting safe and responsible enjoyment and preservation of the outdoors.

If you would like to participate in these organized outdoor activities or programs, consider a membership in The Mountaineers. For information and an application, write or call The Mountaineers, 7700 Sand Point Way NE, Seattle, WA 98115; 206-521-6001; info@mountaineers.org.

The Mountaineers Books, an active, nonprofit publishing program of the organization, produces guidebooks, instructional texts, historical works, natural history guides, and works on environmental conservation. All books produced by The Mountaineers Books fulfill the organization's mission.

Send or call for our catalog of more than 600 outdoor titles:

 The Mountaineers Books
1001 SW Klickitat Way, Suite 201
Seattle, WA 98134
800-553-4453
mbooks@mountaineersbooks.org
www.mountaineersbooks.org

 The Mountaineers Books is proud to be a corporate sponsor of Leave No Trace, whose mission is to promote and inspire responsible outdoor recreation through education, research, and partnerships. The Leave No Trace program is focused specifically on human-powered (nonmotorized) recreation.

Leave No Trace strives to educate visitors about the nature of their recreational impacts, as well as offer techniques to prevent and minimize such impacts. Leave No Trace is best understood as an educational and ethical program, not as a set of rules and regulations.

For more information, visit *www.LNT.org*, or call 800-332-4100.